The **FLYING KANGAROO**

Jim Eames is author of *The Country Undertaker*, *Six Feet Under or Up in Smoke* and *Taking to the Skies*. As one of Australia's first aviation writers, and former press secretary to the Minister for Aviation and former Director of Public Affairs for Qantas, he is a man who has lived and breathed aviation. He also tells a great yarn.

The FLYING KANGAROO

GREAT UNTOLD STORIES OF *QANTAS*...THE HEROIC, THE HILARIOUS AND THE SOMETIMES JUST PLAIN STRANGE

JIM EAMES

ALLEN&UNWIN
SYDNEY · MELBOURNE · AUCKLAND · LONDON

First published in 2015

Allen & Unwin
83 Alexander Street
Crows Nest NSW 2065
Australia
Phone: (61 2) 8425 0100
Email: info@allenandunwin.com
Web: www.allenandunwin.com

Cataloguing-in-Publication details are available
from the National Library of Australia
www.trove.nla.gov.au

ISBN 978 1 76011 355 1

Set in 12/17 pt Adobe Caslon by Midland Typesetters, Australia
Printed and bound in Australia by Griffin Press

10 9 8 7 6 5

The paper in this book is FSC® certified.
FSC® promotes environmentally responsible,
socially beneficial and economically viable
management of the world's forests.

CONTENTS

FOREWORD

The Flying Kangaroo is a wonderful collection of stories about Australians, a century of aviation and one of the world's oldest, most iconic and successful airlines.

Unlike most other aviation history books, *The Flying Kangaroo* is written from the inside. A former Qantas communications director, Jim Eames brings together the key stories from battle hardened politicians, leaders, engineers, pilots and the support teams. I flew with many of the extraordinary pilots whose stories follow.

These are stories of passion, pain and glory, stories of risk and resilience. They explore how a company started by a grazier and two WWI pilots in 1920 grew to become an Australian icon. They document technological changes in aircraft engineering, from cloth and wood to metal to composites. From pistons to turbines, biplanes to supersonic jets. From flying low level through New Guinea's dangerous valleys, and up to 45,000 feet on international routes—higher than the reach of today's modern jets. They explore how airlines flew remote routes over unfriendly and hostile areas, opening communications and changing the world back then as much as the internet has changed our lives today.

Jim's stories start in the early barnstorming years when the costs, risks and rewards of flight were high. Accidents were common as a result of building aircraft that went faster, bigger and higher. The airline industry advanced like no other.

The Flying Kangaroo documents how Qantas grew to meet its obligations as a national asset. Aircraft and lives were lost as the airline flew on the front line during WWII and, again, they faced similar dangers when the airline flew as 'Skippy Squadron' in support of Australian troops in Vietnam. You will empathise with the tales of Australians being rescued internationally by the 'Red Tail' anytime and anywhere from wars, revolutions or weather disasters.

Reading *The Flying Kangaroo* deepened my respect for flight, for Qantas and for the Australian spirit. It is really a view into the larrikin Australian attitude—to follow a passion, challenge the status quo, take calculated risks and excel. These hundred stories barely scrape the surface to expose the depth of Qantas culture with the creativity, dedication and teamwork that is needed to get the job done.

Stories abound of the wide range of aircraft that have carried passengers since the first powered flight. From Paul McGinness's and Hudson Fysh's first Avro 504K to the Catalina's Double Sunrise flight, the DC-3, DC-4, Constellation, Comet, Concorde, 707, 747 up to the A330—it's all there.

Finally, the funny anecdotes of flight put an end to the rumours about dead cats, dogs, monkeys, horses, elephants, politicians, princess smuggling, gold, vegemite, Four'n Twenty pies, water skiing to work and streaking women.

Everyone who has ever flown will enjoy *The Flying Kangaroo*. These stories of Australia and Qantas need to be told. Australia's culture evolved from our ancestors' determination, courage, grit and inventiveness. This is a study of corporate resilience of one of the world's most iconic airlines in a fascinating industry. It reflects my pride for the airline that crushed borders, levelled politics and connected the world. The spirits of these Australians and this company must be acknowledged and honoured, and I hope that they continue.

Captain Richard Champion de Crespigny—Pilot in Command of Qantas Flight QF32 that suffered a catastrophic engine explosion in Singapore on 4 November 2010. Author of the multi-award winning book QF32.

INTRODUCTION

As the distant shape of the big Qantas Boeing 747-400 *City of Canberra* lined up for its final landing at Illawarra regional airport near Wollongong early in March 2015, the contrast could not have been more striking.

Twenty-six years earlier, this then brand-new addition to the Qantas fleet had created a world record on its delivery flight from London to Sydney in 20 hours, 9 minutes and 5 seconds. This last flight from Mascot airport, Sydney, to its final resting place had taken 15 minutes.

Many among the thousands watching at the airport perimeter as the Boeing approached were probably unaware of another significant difference. This Boeing and its sister-400s in the Qantas fleet had flown millions of kilometres to and from the world's major airports with their sophisticated landing systems and navigation aids. Illawarra, as a regional airport, had a short runway, no instrument landing system nor even an air traffic control tower, so the landing had to be flown fully hands-on by the pilot, a quality of airmanship now slipping away in today's fully automated airline era.

They made it look easy as the Boeing touched down right on the button—at the very threshold of the runway, prompting one former Qantas 747-400 captain who was watching to mutter: 'Not bad, lads. Not bad.'

There were other aspects that would be noted by old Qantas veterans among the crowd, not least the sparkling condition of the aircraft itself. It still looked brand new, as if it had rolled off the Boeing assembly line in Seattle that morning, yet further testimony to the airline's renowned reputation for the maintenance of its aircraft.

To them, the *City of Canberra*'s 26 years of service may have passed quickly but it also said so much about the Qantas they used to know—an airline that had instilled a feeling of pride among Australians for almost a century.

***

It is difficult to find another Australian enterprise so embedded in the Australian psyche as Qantas.

Even during its formative days in the early 1920s, the air operation being developed by its founders Hudson Fysh and Paul McGinness with its first chairman Fergus McMaster, captured the imagination of a nation that was already developing an aviation reputation of its own.

Indeed Fysh and McGinness's inspiration for the very formation of the company came out of their role in bashing across the outback between Brisbane and Darwin in a long-suffering Ford to select suitable landing fields for the 1919 England to Australia Air Race.

Australian brothers Ross and Keith Smith won the race and collected Prime Minister Billy Hughes's £10,000 prize money, but in the end it would be the formation of Fysh and McGinness's Queensland and Northern Territory Aerial Services that would be the most enduring legacy.

In the years that followed, Australian fliers would stamp a lasting footprint not only on Australia itself but across the world, becoming the first to cross all the world's major oceans with the exception of the Atlantic. But for engine failure in 1919, Harry Hawker would have achieved that as well.

The story of those early years of Qantas, its formation at Long-reach and Winton in Queensland and the fulfilment of its founders' dream of providing an air service for isolated outback communities, is a compelling tale of a small band of dedicated airmen and engineers overcoming the massive challenges of an unforgiving terrain, primitive aircraft with temperamental engines and one of the harshest environments in the world.

When its ambitions outgrew Longreach, it was a confident new airline which moved first to Brisbane in 1930 then eventually to Sydney to establish a base that exists to this day.

Many of the years in between have been well documented, by Hudson Fysh himself in his three major works—*Qantas Rising* (1965), *Qantas at War* (1968) and *Wings to the World* (1970); and in more recent times by historian John Gunn's excellent trilogy— *The Defeat of Distance* (1985), *Challenging Horizons* (1987) and *High Corridors* (1988), all three providing a detailed account of the airline through to the 1970s. Another seminal work, although largely unknown even by the majority of those who worked for the airline, is E. Bennett-Bremner's *Front-Line Airline* (1944), written while a wartime Qantas was still in the air. Interspersed have been a range of excellent works covering such aspects as Qantas engineering, flight operations and cabin crew.

While all the foregoing publications have made an invaluable and lasting contribution to our knowledge of the airline, and take pride of place on the bookshelves of those with a particular interest in aviation, much of their content has been beyond the reach of many Australians who have watched with pride the progress of their national carrier.

As one with a long involvement in the aviation industry, both on the civil administration side, in politics and more latterly many years with Qantas itself, what I feel has been missing is perhaps the story of the more human side of the airline so many Australians have admired over the years.

I hope what follows will serve as a reminder that Qantas is more than just exciting new aeroplanes, stylish cabin crew uniforms or a plethora of exotic destinations and fare types. Behind all that are the people who have made it what it is, from those who service the aeroplanes, clean the cabins and provide the meals, to others who have seen the sharp end of the political challenges and, not least, those who face the dangers that come with operating in an environment that sceptics years ago suggested should be left strictly to the birds.

So this is not meant to be another chronological history of the airline. Achieving this with complete thoroughness today is an impossible task. Despite aviation's relatively short life span since the Wright brothers, all the early pioneers have gone and few of those who served the airline with such distinction during the six years of World War II are still with us today.

It was during the years of World War II and immediately after that we saw the merging of both aeroplanes and people to create an entity that would forge an enviable reputation among the world's airlines for safety and operational excellence.

Getting to this point hasn't all been an easy cruise at altitude and there have been numerous examples of severe turbulence along the way. How Qantas has handled these and other challenges is a story worth telling, along with many of the things Qantas insiders didn't say too much about at the time. Simply, they learnt from their experiences, continued flying, and got on with it. And while superior airmanship and dedication to engineering integrity have been the airline's signature, luck too has played a part. In some cases unimaginable disasters have been only metres away.

Qantas's story is one of overcoming adversity, an often innovative approach to problems, a struggle to maintain profitability in an increasingly competitive world, and of strong-minded, determined personalities dealing with the normal internal conflicts of any large organisation. Above all, it is the story of an airline constantly struggling to maintain its role as Australia's international carrier from the post-war years through the jet era from the Boeing 707 to the jumbo and finally into the politics of a privately owned airline.

Because this is not meant to be a history of the Australian flag carrier but rather a series of its achievements and, occasionally its failings, some of those involved particularly at the most senior level, like Cedric Turner, Bert Ritchie and Keith Hamilton, will come in and out at various parts of the story, largely because their influence was significant not only as managing directors or chief executives but across many other aspects of the airline's progress from the days of Hudson Fysh through to the jumbo jet era. It is a story too of the airline I knew well, which took a baby boomer generation to the world and home again and therefore with only passing references to its more recent history.

But above all it's a story told by and about some of the people who achieved it all and brought a uniquely Australian image to the oldest airline in the English-speaking world.

IT'S A CULTURE THING

1
WE'RE OFF TO POLISH THE ENGINES

Chicago, May 1979: Immediately after take-off, an American DC-10 crashes catastrophically when the left engine separates from the wing. All 258 people, passengers and thirteen crew, on board are killed.

Within days America's Federal Aviation Administration grounds all DC-10s around the world, calling for an inspection of the engine-to-wing mounts. Investigators working on the crashed aircraft find that poor maintenance standards had led to damage in the left engine mounts, causing the engine to break free and take critical controls with it.

With one of Continental Airlines' DC-10s grounded in Sydney, Qantas engineer Peter Thomas and two colleagues were assigned to set about removing fairings and cover plates to gain access to the suspect wing area. After completing the inspection to the FAA's requirements, rather than signing off, Thomas's team decided to go one step further.

Removing further panels they found heavy corrosion of the pylon's inner surfaces, something that would not have been found if they'd merely done the job they were required to do. And since corrosion is an unforgiving 'ailment' in a highly stressed aircraft, after informing Continental and the FAA of their discovery, they set off for Melbourne to inspect another DC-10 operated by Malaysian Airline System. There they repeated the process but in this case gave the DC-10 a clean bill of health.

Ron Yates, the only chief executive in the history of Qantas with an engineering background, always believed the airline benefited from a natural Australian tendency to take things a step further, particularly when it came to engineering and maintenance. At every opportunity, Yates cited the example of the disastrous Chicago crash, and he always delighted in describing the initiative of Thomas and his team as 'Oh well, while we're here . . .'

***

'Culture' can be one of those nebulous terms with a variety of meanings. Dictionaries have it covering everything from the production of bacteria to intellectual development. It's equally as broad in the aviation industry, and can mean everything from the way an airline answers calls in its sales offices around the world to its in-flight service. In flight operations, engineering and maintenance, it can go further than just getting an aircraft to depart and arrive on time—culture can relate directly to the serious business of safety.

Hudson Fysh, Scottie Allan, Russell Tapp—the men from its very earliest days—and others created a template for what was to become one of the safest airlines in the world, but it was a template that demanded rigid operational standards and no cutting of corners when it came to costs relating to maintenance and safety.

This careful attitude was there from the beginning, although aviation itself was a new frontier, full of risk-takers not too bothered by petty rules and regulations. For example, in the first years of Qantas's operations, airports did not necessarily have runways as we know them today. Pilots were expected to observe the direction of the wind from windsocks, and then take off into the wind, as trying to raise an aircraft against a cross-wind or a tail wind could be extremely dangerous. On 30 April 1937, within months of the airline launching its first international service from Darwin to Singapore, a reporter from Brisbane's *Courier Mail* documented the culture of the company. 'A week ago I flew from Brisbane to Darwin in the Royal Mail liner *Canberra* (a Qantas DH-86),' wrote the scribe.

> Taking off from one of the stopping places there was just enough wind to lift the windsock from its pole. A machine belonging to another company left the ground first and the pilot, glancing at the lifeless indicator, took off across wind. Perhaps he did it in perfect safety but when the Qantas plane followed, the pilot religiously taxied across the full length of the aerodrome and, in strict accordance with the company's principle of safety first before all things, rose dead into the faint breeze.

In 1938, just a year later, the airline moved its head office from Brisbane to Sydney. It was a momentous move for an airline less than twenty years from its birth in Western Queensland and which had only just launched its flying boat service to Singapore to link with Imperial Airways. Although he led an airline with less than 300 staff, General Manager Fysh used the occasion to pen a note to 'the Executive and Seniors of Qantas Empire Airways'.

> The shift to Sydney implies a great deal, and where a new environment will be encountered, demanding a much spruced up organisation, and where each one will be judged on his merits anew.

Till the organisation shakes down we must concentrate on essentials, but from the start if a watchword of 'nothing but the best' is taken and followed through in every function, however small, we will have nothing to fear; at the same time unwarranted expenditure must be strenuously avoided. If we fail in this then criticism and censorship must result.

It is our duty to carry on the old standards which have been so successful in the past. The history of Qantas shows that integrity has been one of the dominant factors in the success which has been enjoyed. That, and taking things seriously, and never being satisfied with second best.

Twice in subsequent years, Fysh distributed that note again, first in 1948, though now as merely a foreword to a booklet entitled *Ethics and Other Things—A Souvenir of Qantas Service*, to be issued to every Qantas employee after the airline had come through the war and was establishing its peacetime role as an entirely Australian-owned company 'operating east and west from Sydney to London and north and south from Sydney to Japan'. Jack Dawson, who joined in 1949, can still point to his personal copy with the comment, 'In those days you knew just about everyone else in the airline.'

By the time the booklet was reissued for the third time, in 1955, Qantas had more than 5000 staff, owned a fleet of aircraft valued at over £8 million and had made an unbroken annual profit on operations for 32 years. Fysh now used the occasion to express how proud he was of Qantas's good name and its efficiency with 'our clients and public opinion and the authorities with whom we deal,' but added a warning: 'This is excellent but we must realise that the further we go and the bigger we get the more difficult it becomes to keep up the old standards.'

The booklet itself is a remarkable document for its time and says much about how Fysh saw the key to the airline's future. Heavy on ethics and integrity, it covers more than twenty headings, from grade of service: ('Good and faithful'), advertising: ('Must be Honest'), staff relations: ('Duty towards the company and Duty towards the employee'), loyalty: ('must be deserved') and so on, through Diplomacy, Character, Vision, Initiative and Enterprise, and even a section headed 'Bribery', which he notes 'is not British and not Australian, and is despicable'.

In true Fysh fashion, 'Expenses' also feature, with the challenge to reconcile 'moderate expenses' with the principle of 'nothing but the best'.

Fysh was fortunate in being surrounded by people who would take all such issues seriously, while applying their own high standards in their respective fields. Arthur Baird, who set the criteria for Qantas engineering in the 1920s, was still renowned, years later, for greeting young apprentices with the question: 'Do you know what you're doing, son?' His oft-repeated query would become a catchphrase among those who worked at Qantas's Sydney Jet Base in Mascot, now named in his honour. To Baird, who had experienced those early days of aviation when things went wrong regularly, near enough was never good enough, and generations of Qantas engineers would embrace his philosophy.

David Forsyth, who would eventually occupy senior executive positions in Qantas, was quick to recognise Baird's legacy immediately he joined the company as an engineering cadet in 1970. 'There were these larger-than-life tradesmen who had been with the company for such a long time,' Forsyth recalls. 'They would give you a go and never think of telling you to go sit in the corner.

'They had come from an era where they had to build their own aeroplanes and develop an attitude of self-sufficiency because they were so far away from the people who made the aeroplanes and built the engines. It was a requirement then not only to fix something but to think things through, because in those days things went wrong.'

Forsyth says this requirement to 'fix it ourselves' remained long after the wood, wire and fabric era of aeroplanes. Even in the early Boeing 747 days of the 1970s, the airline was experiencing engine problems because of the effects of altitude on fuel on its extremely long-range flights. 'We had to remedy much of it ourselves with special wiring, special sensors, even special instruments in the cockpit to record the data so that we could see what was happening.'

Forsyth, now retired after 40 years in the industry, admits things don't go wrong as much today. 'In those days if one of our engines lasted on the wing for eight or nine months without having to be taken off, you had a party. These days it's seven or eight years. In fact I think they have one engine on a Boeing 737 that's been there since new—ten years.'

Alan Terrell and his crew were having breakfast at the start of a rest day in Bermuda while flying Prime Minister Gough Whitlam around the world in a Qantas Boeing 707 in the 1970s when his flight engineer Bruce Lawrence and ground engineer Henry Knight came into the dining room carrying a can of Brasso and some rags.

When Terrell asked Lawrence what they were up to, the flight engineer replied: 'We're off out to polish the engine cowlings up a bit.'

Former captain Roger Carmichael is another who can cite the Qantas standards of times gone by, offering one example during a transit of his 747 at Bangkok.

Walking across the tarmac to pre-flight his aircraft, Carmichael was approached by a Boeing representative accompanied by two Thai Airways management people. The Boeing man asked if he could go aboard and show them the flight deck maintenance logbook that records, among other items, the permissible defects the aircraft is carrying that are yet to be fixed. The Boeing man 'wanted to show them how an aircraft should be maintained.'

'Since I hadn't been aboard the aircraft myself to look at what had been entered in the book, we were all going in cold,' recalls Carmichael. 'In the event the logbook was completely clean with no defects listed and the Boeing rep was very happy, the Qantas engineering reputation remained intact and the Thais were very impressed.'

Such circumstances, of course, meant no expense was spared when it came to safety, and from a maintenance and flight operations viewpoint, neither were there any arguments about it. While at various times up into the 1970s and 1980s there might be considerable financial or marketing influence on the direction of the airline, safety was non-negotiable and money for flight operations or engineering was never a problem when justified by safety.

No one, not even the airline's owner—which by then was the Australian government—or, for that matter, the justice system was prepared to stand up against the flight operations division when it suggested something was unsafe. After all, says Carmichael, the only way to prove otherwise was to run the risk of a serious accident and not even a financial supremo was willing to take a razor to the operations budget under such a threat.

For many years, even within its own crewing administrative responsibilities, such a situation provided flight operations management with absolute authority. For instance, if management decided a second or first officer lacked the ability to attain a higher level and would remain at that level for the rest of his career, the edict was final and not even a court would question the right of a training captain or flight operations management to make that decision.

This flight operations culture had been the beneficiary of a massive amount of experience with the pilots who came out of the war, not only through their impact on its training regime, but in general line flying on Qantas routes as well. They were men who had known what it was to fly by the seat of their pants, learnt lessons and had their share of 'frights' along the way as they acquired the highest levels of airmanship. Some applied their skills as training captains; others passed their experience on to first and second officers as they flew the line.

Some pilots were highly decorated individuals. Merv Shipard, Distinguished Flying Cross and Bar, scored an incredible thirteen confirmed 'kills' as a night fighter pilot on Beaufighters in the UK, the Middle East and Malta, joined Qantas in 1957 and flew Constellations, Electras and 707s before being appointed flight simulator instructor in the late 1970s. Shipard was tutoring another pilot on a 707 out of Tullamarine one night when a boost activator broke from its mounting on the wing and the aircraft rolled through 140 degrees. Despite a pitch-black night, at a dangerously low altitude with no visual references and doubtless using his extensive night-flying experience, Shipard took control and recovered the aircraft.

Keith Thiele won a DFC and a DSO serving in RAF Bomber Command and, because he wanted to transfer to fighters, had the rare distinction of declining an offer from Guy Gibson VC to join his famous 617 Lancaster Squadron for the Dam Buster raids. It was as well he did; his replacement for the Dams raid was killed.

Promoted to squadron leader, Thistle was shot down over Holland, became a prisoner of war but escaped on a bicycle and made his way to Allied troops advancing across Europe. After joining Qantas he flew the inaugural 707 flight from Brisbane to Singapore before retiring in the 1960s.

R.F. 'Torchy' Uren DFC was a flight commander with No. 30 Beaufighter Squadron in New Guinea, famed for its key role in the Battle of the Bismarck Sea, when Australian and US aircraft turned back a large convoy carrying thousands of Japanese planning an assault on Lae. Uren received wide exposure in news footage of the battle, shot by Australian cameraman Damien Parer, who crouched behind him in the cockpit. Short of stature and something of a prickly character, Uren would later fly Qantas Catalinas on the secret Double Sunrise route through Japanese territory between Perth and Colombo in 1944. This effort allowed Australia to maintain an air link with the UK. Uren would eventually rise to senior pilot management positions in the company.

'Bunny' Lee, who would eventually be renowned for telling a small cartel of training captains at Avalon what he thought of them, had the rare distinction of having his rear gunner shoot down a night fighter which attacked them as they bombed Berlin with 106 Squadron RAF in early 1944, only to then have his Lancaster 'coned' by a score of searchlights as German anti-aircraft fire smashed into his aircraft. He managed to break free by violently corkscrewing the aircraft back into the darkness, went on to bomb Berlin and arrived back at base in England with dozens of holes through the Lancaster.

Such men were the tip of the post-war iceberg as far as Qantas was concerned and one of their most decorated, former Wing Commander Alan Wharton, would go on to head the airline's operations division as Director of Flight Operations. Wharton won his DSO, DFC and Bar and was Mentioned in Despatches while serving with Bomber Command in Europe and the Middle East.

With those responsible for training reporting to him, Wharton led the airline through the various recruiting changes necessary as the airline entered the jet age, first with the 707 and eventually the 747, taking it through the peaks and troughs of the notoriously cyclical airline industry. In between the ups and downs, Qantas established its own cadet pilot scheme in the mid-1960s where young pilots were trained on single- and twin-engine aircraft, then moved on to command experience in general aviation for two years before joining the airline.

Qantas files back into the 1970s reveal Wharton discussing a future in which pilots would be trained specifically with airline flying in mind, due to some extent to the fact that the skills learnt while gaining hours flying for others didn't relate to airline practice. Wharton, known for his dry wit, put it more bluntly: it was so they didn't pick up any bad habits.

The ideas espoused by Wharton and others in the 1970s would come to fruition with the introduction of multi-crew licences, whereby pilots are specifically trained to fly as part of a crew on regular public transport aircraft, meaning they can only use this licence on multi-crew operations.

At the same time, technological advances such as sophisticated simulators have helped ease the economic pressures of increasing competition in the airline industry by reducing the costly in-aircraft training of years gone by. Such a brave new world, which means pilots get very little solo flight time and no seat-of-the-pants experience, has not always been easy for some in what is traditionally a very conservative industry. Veterans like Roger Carmichael suggest the process may be painful and may add to unpalatable statistics from time to time, but they acknowledge the inevitability of it all both in economic and practical terms.

As for the 'old' culture: 'Whatever is said, either for or against, for the times it speaks for itself—Alan Wharton's people did it right.'

But, as the early 1990s arrived, some believed that there was another factor influencing cultural change—privatisation.

Its precursors were government decisions first to deregulate the Australian domestic aviation industry, approve the sale of Australian Airlines to Qantas, then the sale of a 25 per cent share in Qantas to British Airways, all destined to be the first steps towards the privatisation of Qantas in 1995. While many in the company who had watched Qantas struggle with limited government financial support in a highly capital intensive industry—where one Boeing 747 came at a cost in excess of $200 million—could see benefits in being cut free of the restrictive government oversight, they were wary of other consequences.

Former engineering executive David Forsyth, for one, marks privatisation as the change point. 'I considered Qantas to be an ethical company. If things weren't right and management found out about it they did something about it. That changed in the mid-1990s,' Forsyth says.

Many attribute the cultural change at Qantas to the switch to an environment where the share price became the priority and management positions began to be filled by newcomers at salary levels unheard of in the pre-privatisation era. For many it was certainly not destined to be a long-term career. One former senior executive delights in telling the story of how, when he questioned his successor as to how he saw his future with the company, he was met with the response: 'Five years maybe. I'll make a quid and get out.'

'Such a comment would have been almost unheard of in the Qantas of earlier years but the world had changed and unfortunately some of the old culture was changing with it,' the executive says sadly. 'And as for the name "Arthur Baird" on the entrance to the Mascot Jet Base: I doubt there'd be all that many who'd know who he was.'

Be that as it may, there's little doubt that many in the company appreciate the operational and engineering cultural building blocks that have created the Qantas they know today.

THE IMPORTANCE OF
THE RIGHT CHOICE

2
THE PREGNANT PUP

Airlines run the gauntlet of success or failure on the choice they make in aircraft to fly their flag in a ruthless, competitive environment, where the margins often come down to fuel efficiency and reliability for on-time performance. But while men like Shipard, Thistle, Uren, Lee and Wharton created an unmistakable identity for Qantas, the aeroplane choices themselves, from the early biplanes to the jets, also played a role in creating that identity. The planes as well as the people who maintained and flew them had their own personality traits; some could be cranky and hard to handle, even hard to please, while others would forever win the hearts of those who had anything to do with them.

The Qantas we know today has inherited a worldwide reputation, even among other airlines, as an industry leader when it came to aircraft choice. Other international airlines were known to closely follow Qantas's choices before making their own decision, a situation much to the benefit of companies like Boeing.

But it was not always that way and there are still a few out there who remember times when the right aircraft choice meant a different set of challenges, from putting at risk our ties to the Empire, to terse telegraphic exchanges between prime ministers at opposite ends of the earth. Such things as fuel efficiency and interior decor weren't even on the radar!

No one could foresee, in 1939, the massive strides in aviation that would be made over the next six years of war.

Prior to the war, developing airlines like Qantas had few choices beyond aircraft that were already available. As Qantas developed its inland services and then took its first steps overseas, expanding its reach as far as Singapore (in conjunction with the UK's Imperial Airways), the use of aircraft like the de Havilland DH-86 biplane were largely the result of what Fysh and his colleagues considered to be the most suitable for the role, combined with a large degree of influence by its imperial partner. In historical terms, buying British pretty well came with the territory. Again, later in the 1930s when it came time to upgrade in an era where the flying boat reigned supreme, the obvious answer for Qantas, so links with the old country were maintained, had to be the Short Empire flying boat, skipping its way up Australia's eastern coastline, across to Darwin Harbour, and through the then Dutch East Indies (Indonesian) ports to Singapore.

But by 1945, not only were fighter aircraft on the cusp of entering the jet age but bombers were also carrying loads unheard of in the early days of the war. Some of these engine and airframe advances had spun off into transport aircraft like the Douglas DC-4 and others that would form the basis for the peacetime civil aviation regime that was to follow.

There were two other significant developments that would have a major influence on Qantas after the war. The first was the phenomenal development of land-based airfields under the demands of the war, where countries like England and Australia came to resemble massive aircraft carriers, used as launch pads for assaults against the enemy in campaigns in Europe and the Pacific. This proliferation of airfields would mark the death knell of the large commercial flying boat within several years of the war's end. The second development was the unassailable advantage the United States had in terms of aircraft production capacity, and sheer numbers of aircraft and equipment, over its traditional aviation rival the UK, which was struggling to regain its former aviation prestige while being crippled by war debt.

In Australia's case, perhaps it was inevitable that a shattering of an important aspect of its traditional alliance with its UK partner would need to occur if Qantas was to ensure its future as a major international airline. Indeed, the decision that Fysh's team had to make about aircraft purchases, when viewed in the context of traditional ties, would result in a prolonged, often bitter struggle that would reach the highest levels of both the Australian and UK governments.

Both had much to lose—Qantas risked being forced into a position which would rob it of its competitiveness against a United States seeking civil air supremacy via airlines like Pan American; while the British battled to rebuild their former aviation status with a viable industry. In British eyes, this was not simply a choice of aircraft but a threat to one of the cornerstones of the old Empire itself.

As for the aircraft themselves, two contenders were in question—one American, the Lockheed Constellation 749 already flying, and the other British, the Avro Tudor 11, still under development. From the point of view of Fysh and his senior people, there was never any doubt about which aircraft to choose. Fysh himself had flown on the prototype of the Constellation while visiting the United States towards the end of the war and was immediately convinced it was the way of the future for his airline. In many respects, the Constellation was destined to become one of the classic aircraft of its generation; its sleek, arching fuselage design and distinctive three tails brought with it the next step in long-range air transport services.

As for the British, their arguments were based on the traditional association of Qantas and the British airline BOAC overcoming the drawbacks of an aircraft that wasn't yet beyond the development stage. The Tudor 11, a descendant of the famous Avro Lancaster bomber, might have promised 60 seats but its design was regarded by Qantas as 'uncompetitive, already obsolete and uncertain in performance', about as unforgiving a description of a new aircraft as one could imagine.

But beyond the actual aircraft themselves, the real battleground developed between the British and Australian governments, already complicated by the fact that part of the Australian government aircraft industry was gearing up to produce the Tudor 11.

Regarding the Australia–UK route on which any new aircraft would be operated, something had to be done relatively quickly as the two aircraft flying it had varying degrees of obsolescence. Passengers who could afford the airfares of those days either had the choice of the more leisurely five-and-a-half-day journey from Sydney to London on a Hythe flying boat or cut the journey to 67 hours jammed in sideways-facing seats in the primitive interior of an Avro Lancastrian, little more than a civil version of the wartime Lancaster bomber. Perhaps the most telling description of the latter came from one C.G. Grey, editor of the UK's *Aeroplane and Aviation* magazine in a letter to Fysh:

When you have time to write, do tell me who is responsible for that absurd sideways seating in the Lancastrian. I asked Avros about it and they said BOAC insisted on it. Then I asked BOAC and they swear they had nothing to do with it and it must have been a freak of MAP's [the Ministry of Aircraft Production].

Anyhow, the picture of nine V.I.P.s sitting solemnly in a row, as if on a bench in the House of Commons, all staring out of one side of the machine and not able to see anything on the other side is ludicrous.

Describing the steward's pantry as 'a crime against humanity,' Grey went on, 'Even if you select your stewards for their littleness, you could have difficulty getting them small enough to squeeze between the refrigerator and the electric cooker so as to get into the crew's quarters.'

Grey didn't even bother to mention the inconvenience of the aircraft's wing spar that passed through the centre of the fuselage, requiring passengers and crew to clamber over it while moving through the cabin. Given that such a significant purchasing decision affecting relations with the UK would require Australian government approval, and although there is no record of Fysh doing so, adding Grey's description to his submission to the government for a quick decision might have had some value.

So the battle raged, with Fysh and his Qantas team arguing with the BOAC chairman Lord Knollys and his people of the dire commercial consequences for both sides. But Qantas refused to give ground.

Finally, after a flurry of telegraphic exchanges, in September 1946, a nervous Fysh found himself sitting outside Prime Minister Ben Chifley's office in Melbourne while Chifley and the Minister for Air and Civil Aviation Arthur Drakeford met within.

Finally ushered into the 'presence', Fysh found Chifley puffing on his pipe, waving him to sit down and running his hand over a telegram on his desk.

'You see this? This is an urgent telegram from Clem Attlee, Prime Minister of England, begging us not to go on with the Constellations you want.'

There was a pause, doubtless an agonising one for Fysh, before Chifley's face broke into a smile and uttered the words Fysh was anxious to hear: 'Well, anyhow, I have decided. We'll give it a go.'

Even with the passage of time since that fateful meeting, Fysh's description of Qantas's decision to purchase the Constellation 749 as 'one of the most momentous decisions in the history of what was then known as Qantas Empire Airways,' remains largely true today. For some students of aviation history it remains an echo of an earlier, although largely much more dire, statement by Chifley's predecessor John Curtin in the dark days of March 1942 as an isolated Australia, beyond any British help, faced the threat of the Japanese. Curtin's plea 'We look to America . . .' ushered in a new alliance that remains to this day.

Qantas too, in aviation terms, had 'looked to America' and an aircraft relationship that would last decades into the future.

As for the Tudor, few were ever built. Two crashed with loss of life while operating with British South American Airways in 1948 and 1949, the only airline ever to use them. Ironically, the UK's own airline BOAC, itself employed the Lockheed Constellation on the Atlantic route.

The introduction of the Constellation marked the emergence of an engineering and operational ethos in Qantas that built on the company's already highly respected reputation. This was not to be an aircraft you bought off the shelf. Because of the Constellation's sophistication and the sheer size of the investment in aircraft and spares, Qantas now entered the era of the technical representative: having a man as a direct, on-site link between the manufacturer and the airline. It would be largely this situation upon which Qantas's future engineering reputation would be built, and contribute markedly to the way other airlines would use Qantas's aircraft choices as a guide towards choosing their own.

The technical representative and his team would be there through the subsequent purchase of the larger, longer range Lockheed 1049 Constellation, at the airline's entry into the jet age with the Boeing 707 and on to the Boeing 747. They needed to have an intimate knowledge of the areas for which they were responsible, whether it be the engines, the landing gear or the interior configuration. Unlike the American airlines on Lockheed's order books, Qantas would have to be pretty well self-sufficient, as they were taking their Constellations to their own engineering base on the far side of the world.

But as more 749s and its successor the 1049 were added to the fleet and the airline began to stretch its wings to new routes, problems developed—problems not commonly known today but that presented a massive operational and economic challenge at the time.

It was all to do with the engines. The Constellation might have earned Fysh's own description as a wonderful aeroplane but the Wright Cyclone engines that powered it proved to be little short of a disaster, to the point where it became obvious Lockheed had basically produced a beautiful aeroplane that had got ahead of engine technology. (Decades later Boeing would confront a similar dilemma with the Pratt & Whitney engines on its first 747s but in that latter case Qantas's depth of expertise in aircraft assessment would enable it to skip through it unscathed.)

Within weeks of the first Constellation services along the Kangaroo Route to London in 1948, the Wright Cyclones presented problems. Mechanical delays began to stretch the scheduled 55 hours of flying time to interminable lengths.

Qantas engineers had initially factored in a requirement for eight spare engines to be positioned at strategic points along the 19,000 kilometre route but soon had to lift that 100 per cent to sixteen engines, along with spare parts. Some were relatively minor faults causing frequent shutting down of engines, and others were so catastrophic that cylinders exploded out through the engine cowling! While under normal circumstances the engines would be removed every 800 hours for scheduled overhaul, at one point Qantas found that just over half of the engines were being removed before that. As engine failure followed engine failure, the airline partly remedied the problem by converting one of its Lancastrians, using its bomb bay as an engine carrier via a special, hinged fairing that enabled the spare engine to be loaded and unloaded quickly. The protruding fairing underneath quickly resulted in the aircraft becoming known as 'Yates's Pregnant Pup' after Ron Yates, the Qantas engineer who designed the concept and who was destined to become a chief executive of the company. For a time the Pregnant Pup chased the Constellations up the Kangaroo Route with spare engines but, unfortunately, the addition of the fairing caused dangerous instability in the Lancastrian and it was soon abandoned.

Much to Qantas's dismay, the engine problem continued, compounded by the fact that the engine's manufacturer, Curtiss-Wright, refused to provide field support for the engines, leaving

Qantas to manage for itself. That decision had a significant long-term impact on Curtiss-Wright. When Qantas was looking at a gas turbine engine for its entry into the jet age with the Boeing 707, senior engineers like Ron Yates would not even consider them an option. 'Whatever happened we would never fly another aircraft that was powered by a Wright engine,' Yates later confessed—a decision he considered might have had something to do with Wright eventually ceasing to build aircraft engines.

Over the years the unreliability of the Constellation's engines became something of a running joke within the company. Old hands occasionally referred to the aircraft as the 'best three-engine aircraft the company ever operated', while historian Bruce Leonard, author of several excellent histories on Qantas engineering, recalls once hearing a Qantas engineer watching a Constellation make an approach to land at Darwin remark, 'Now there's an unusual sight.' When asked to explain the engineer offered: 'All four engines are still operating.' Even the ground-breaking achievement of Qantas's first around-the-world service with Super Constellations in 1958 was often referred to as 'Around the World in Eighty Delays'.

Poor engine performance aside, Fysh was correct in describing choosing the Constellation as the right decision to take his airline into the relatively comfortable age of pressurised aircraft.

NOT EVERY CHOICE WAS PERFECT

The Constellation, the 707 and the advent of the jumbo cemented Qantas's reputation for exceptional aircraft choices, but there have been some exceptions along the way. One of these was relatively minor; the other remains something of a mystery even today among old Qantas hands.

Between the late 1940s and the early 1960s, Qantas operated services in Papua New Guinea with an assortment of aircraft. There were few roads. Catalina flying boats handled the isolated island communities on the coast and those on lakes in the country's interior, DC-3s carried out the passenger and freight tasks between major centres, and the several single-engine de Havilland Canada Beavers scurried backwards and forwards between the smaller mountain airstrips.

When the four Beavers needed replacing in 1958, the company chose de Havilland's Beaver successor, known as the Otter. Beyond its floats to allow it to operate as an amphibian to service communities and mining research establishments up rivers, the Otter's outward appearance closely resembled that of the Beaver but, as it would turn out, that's where the similarity ended.

Alan Terrell, who flew every type of aircraft Qantas operated in Papua New Guinea, harboured a particular dread of the Otters and decades later, after rising to become the airline's Director of Flight Operations, he still shook his head when he spoke of flying them. 'I can't understand anyone having bought it in the first place because it was built for Canadian winter operations and certainly not for hot clime flying of New Guinea.'

In the short four months he flew the Otter amphibian based in Port Moresby, Terrell lodged twelve incident reports describing problems with the aircraft, including a full-engine fire. He found the aircraft hopelessly underpowered and, while the Beaver weighed 2.4 tonnes and had a 450 horsepower engine, the Otter's 600 horsepower engine had to propel an aircraft twice the Beaver's weight.

Added to that, de Havilland had fitted a stall warning device to alert the pilot when the speed was get getting dangerously slow, but because the aircraft was flying close to stalling most of the time, the stall warning light never went out.

'Finally we found it so distracting we just disconnected it.'

In later years, as he rose through the airline's executive ranks, Terrell made several attempts to find out who in the company was responsible for the Otter's purchase in the first place. 'I was never able to find out because whoever did it would probably never admit it!'

3
THE NADI 'BUMP'

At the start it was reminiscent of wartime dogfights—but this time it was two former allies who were pitting their flying machines against each other, with shades of empire battles past. In the end it was Qantas's entry into the jet age with the Boeing 707 that firmly established the Australian airline's pre-eminence when it came to aircraft choice.

On one side, the British put forward the de Havilland Comet 2, successor to an earlier version whose reputation, after initial promise, had suffered a series of fatal blows. The Comet would eventually become the flagship of BOAC and other airlines, but by the mid-1950s the choice for Qantas came down to the jet offerings of Boeing's 707 and Douglas Aircraft's DC-8. Given Boeing's history since, with aircraft like the 747, 767 and the 737, it's hard to imagine now that 'going Boeing' in those days was something of a risk as, while the company had made a name for itself with military aircraft, its track record in civil airliners had rested on the double-deck Boeing Stratocruiser, which had been far from a resounding success.

But soon the Boeing 707 began to cement its place among the minds of those in Qantas who were to make the final assessment. Captain Bert Ritchie, a future general manager who was leading the team, probably set the tone after flying the prototype aeroplane. 'I was starry-eyed about it. I wouldn't talk about anything else.' There was one serious problem to overcome—how the version Boeing was producing could fit the key Qantas route to the United States. The American airline giants lining up on Boeing's order books with far more dollars in their pockets were pressing Boeing to stretch the original version to better suit their domestic and intercontinental requirements. In one stroke, that redesign completely destroyed the passenger–range issue facing Qantas on the Pacific route.

The problem itself went down in Qantas folklore as the 'Nadi bump', a very specific aviation phenomenon that related to the critical sector between Nadi (in Fiji) and Honolulu (in Hawaii), a long over-water distance that, because of the relatively short 2100 metre runway at Nadi, made operating the larger, heavier aircraft out of the question. What Qantas wanted was a shorter version, still with good payload and range but with more powerful engines to get airborne out of Nadi.

While Douglas was reluctant to alter its DC-8 from the version more appealing to the US market, in a decision that cemented a relationship that continued for decades to come, Boeing agreed to produce a special version by taking 3 metres out of the 707's fuselage and equipping the Qantas aircraft with a more powerful military version of the Pratt & Whitney engines to give it acceptable payload and range capabilities that Qantas needed out of Nadi. Thus Qantas became the first non-US airline to operate the Boeing 707.

Qantas finally ordered more than thirty 707s before moving on to the Boeing 747—the company's first jumbo jet. With this second Boeing aircraft, once again the company's technical and operational judgement in waiting for the longer-range version, proved an astute decision. Qantas was able to watch as recurring engine problems with the first 747 created nightmares for Boeing, the engine manufacturers and the earliest airline operators. In fact, while Qantas had been among the first to show interest when the 747 was still a 'paper aeroplane', even before a prototype had been built, the Australian airline's first jumbo was number 147 off the Seattle assembly line and such was the input of Qantas's team of representatives that aircraft 747-B Number 147 incorporated around 300 changes to the original specification for the 747, all designed to ensure the aircraft suited the way Qantas wanted to operate it. With a project cost of more than $160 million for its first four aircraft, the airline had to be sure it had things right.

Even Boeing's Joe Sutter, the 'father' of the 747 design, later described as 'courageous' the decision of a relatively small airline like Qantas to launch the 747 in its part of the world. 'They knew what they wanted and were not shy about asking for it. We paid a lot of attention to Qantas.'

Qantas's innovations, such as a lower lobe galley to allow food preparation below floor level, meant the airline was able to fit fifteen more seats in the main cabin, improving the economics of the aircraft, while an extended upper deck increased its passenger appeal. Stepping cautiously into the jumbo era allowed the company to avoid the early engine problems and at the same time introduce a version of the aircraft more suited to its route structure.

There is little doubt that Qantas's attention to aircraft evaluation and the importance of economics left Qantas with few peers in the jet age. At the outset, of course, the main advantage of the Boeing 707 was its ability to, in one massive stride, cut international flight times in half. In those early 707 days, fuel prices didn't matter so much, low-cost charter operators were well into the future and the relatively high fares limited travel to those who could afford it. That began to change with the combination of the arrival of the Boeing 747 and its massive leap in aircraft capacity— and the fuel crisis of the early 1970s.

Barry Phair, a long-time Qantas executive with a close association with fleet assessment and aircraft fleet planning, recalls how Qantas had well-developed systems looking at route profitability as far back as 1974, a decade before most other airlines. The aim was to achieve the lowest possible break-even seat factor, that magic figure that defines the proportion of seats on board the aircraft that have to be sold for the airline to make a profit.

Working out the break-even seat factor is a complex calculation, particularly when ordering a new aircraft, as it involves assessments of revenue from passengers and freight on different route requirements, route operating costs, and the expenses for training the required aircrew and cabin crew to operate the aircraft, as well as the engineering infrastructure and tooling to service and maintain it. All come with high costs and correspondingly high risks in a marginal industry. Phair still talks with pride when, as a senior finance executive during the airline's all-747 fleet era, he saw that break-even figure drop as low as 55 per cent in 1983–84, an achievement airlines of today could only dream about. (In an era where today's airline has international and domestic entities both split by Jetstar, it would be difficult to ascertain a break-even load factor for the traditional Qantas international arm, although somewhere around 70 to 80 per cent would probably be a reasonable guess.)

There was one aircraft that would never carry the Qantas livery, but which was the subject of years of intense study, much of it going on behind the scenes and out of public view.

DISPELLING THE QANTAS BOEING 777 'MYTH'

Whenever the question of recent aircraft choices is raised among former Qantas people these days it is almost certain the Boeing 777 will be up for discussion. Everyone from pilots through to engineers and assorted ground staff will point out what a wonderful aeroplane it is, while claiming Qantas made a serious error in *not* adding it to the airline's fleet.

The evidence, they will say, is there for all to see. While Qantas has continued to fly its large, and now ageing, Boeing 747s across the Pacific, airlines like Virgin, Cathay Pacific and others operate newer, smaller, twin-engine 777s that, particularly in Virgin's case, provide intense competition flying across the Pacific to the west coast of the United States.

It's not an easy argument to debunk but a closer look reveals a different story. It's all about the long lead times, often running into more than a decade, that aircraft manufacturers and their customer airline must deal with when it comes to ordering a new aeroplane.

Those like former Qantas chief executive John Ward and the manager of fleet planning, Barry Phair, confirm that, when Boeing offered the first 777 for delivery to the airlines in the early 1990s, it had no chance of fulfilling the Qantas requirement. The first of the 777s offered for delivery in 1995 was a 777-200 version that was only capable of crossing the

United States, to be followed by an extended-range version that could cross the Atlantic but was still far short of the Qantas requirement to cross the Pacific. Even then, says Ward, it was more of a replacement for the Boeing 767 than a backup for the airline's 747 fleet.

Ward recalls Boeing's response when Qantas indicated it was looking for something with much longer range. 'They basically pointed out they understood where we were coming from but there weren't many like us at the time.'

By the time Boeing was offering the long-distance version of the 777, the airline was already looking at new technology like the Airbus A-380 and the Boeing 787 Dreamliner. 'Unfortunately the original belief has become folklore and it's a little hard to topple with the passage of time,' Ward adds.

When the supersonic Concorde burst on the scene in the 1960s it brought with it the impressive expectations of an industry once again on the edge of a quantum leap into the future.

Although well tested for years by the military, supersonic flight was a new frontier for commercial aviation. The ability to shatter the sound barrier had to overcome some serious economic handicaps, not the least its arrival at the same time as the 747 was opening up a whole new, low-cost, mass travel market.

To ensure its competitive position while it tested the aircraft's economics, Qantas had taken out options on six Concordes in March 1964 and by the time the two Concorde prototypes—one British and one French—had their first flights in 1969, and with the introduction of its first 747-B only two years away, the airline's technical development department had its hands full.

Technical development's advanced projects section had taken responsibility for the ongoing evaluation of the Concorde and its suitability for Qantas's services and would monitor its progress as the aircraft moved through to the production stage. Indeed, Concorde would become the most thoroughly tested commercial aircraft in history, logging 4000 hours flying before entering airline service in 1976.

Bill Bourke, then an engineer in technical development, recalls the countless route studies carried out to assist the airline's economic analysis of its potential to Qantas, as well as keeping a close watch on how other airlines were positioning themselves for possible Concorde introduction. For instance, Bourke says part of Qantas's options deal very much depended on whether Pan Am took up its own options on the aircraft, thus making the production of the aircraft a viable proposition for the manufacturer, something that was not to take place.

Meanwhile, those like Alan Terrell who might be responsible for actually flying the aircraft were also closely involved. Terrell admitted years later that he couldn't contain his excitement when, one afternoon in 1971, his immediate boss, Qantas's deputy general manager Phil Howson, suggested he catch a Qantas service that night for the UK to evaluate the Concorde.

Terrell often conceded how fortunate he had been to fulfil every pilot's dream due to the fact that he was in the right place at the right time. Normally, such an assignment would have fallen to either of two other senior development pilots, Captains Fred Fox and Laurie Clark, but both were in Seattle on 747 development work. Not that Fred Fox would have been all that miffed, as he had beaten Terrell to the supersonic punch by some years. As a further sign of Qantas's determination to keep abreast of the latest technology, as the world was approaching the supersonic transport era in 1963, Fox and another senior captain, Bill Edwards, spent several hours flying a Royal Air Force Avro Vulcan bomber at Filton in the UK to assess its flying characteristics.

Terrell's Concorde experience at the British Aircraft Corporation's (BAC) Bristol complex would have its frustrations. The first of his two evaluation flights went off without a hitch and he took some pride in entering the Concorde as a new type in his logbook as he waited for a Pan American pilot to take his turn the following day. Much to the dismay of BAC's test pilot Brian Trubshaw, the Pan Am pilot, while executing a steep turn, heaved back on the control column, seriously overstressing the machine. Trubshaw immediately took over and straightened the aeroplane, at the same time leaving the Pan Am chap in no doubt about his anger: 'Get out of my bloody cockpit. I never want to see you again.'

The end result was that it was six months before the aircraft could fly again and Terrell could return for his second flight.

Australia had its first look at the Concorde in mid-1972 when it flew into Sydney and Melbourne. It caused traffic jams around the two airports and, while it was a visit designed to show off its paces, one of the main tasks was to assess the impact of the sonic boom as the aeroplane crossed the Australian mainland.

The site chosen for sonic boom recording by Australia's Department of Civil Aviation (DCA) was remote Hamilton Downs station, 80 kilometres north from Alice Springs, where sophisticated noise measurement devices would register the boom effect.

For those there that day, it would turn out to be something of an anti-climax, as hours of waiting in the hot sun finally resulted in the appearance of a sliver of silver metal ahead of a thin vapour trail, which began slashing the sky from the south and streaked overhead, to be followed by a sharp double report as the sonic boom hit. A Channel 9 television crew on site appeared a little disappointed in the resultant footage, although one of the DCA people noticed two crows sitting on a nearby fence momentarily jump slightly, then quickly resume their perches.

Australia's vast expanse of open space might be a benign environment, but the sonic boom was to become a problem for Concorde as key en-route countries like Malaysia and India ruled out supersonic flights over their territory. The United States also banned the Concorde initially, even though Boeing was working on its own supersonic project. Although the American bans would eventually be lifted to allow operations into New York and Washington, increasing controversy surrounding aircraft noise greatly restricted the aircraft's commercial application.

From Qantas's viewpoint, it was more a question of simple economics. Bill Bourke and others continued to be involved in studies to develop possible supersonic corridors across Australia, but Concorde would never make it into the Qantas fleet due to a combination of factors. Although it had the capability to greatly reduce flight times between Australia and the UK, the reality was altogether different, with the aircraft's high-speed fuel requirements severely limiting the number of passengers it could carry on the long stage lengths it was required to cover. One Qantas executive was heard to describe its usage on the Sydney–London route as 'little more than a series of puddle jumps' as it landed to refuel. 'By the time it went subsonic over land and made a couple of extra fuel stops, it was not much quicker than a Boeing 747 on the Kangaroo Route to London and didn't have the range for the Pacific, all due to an appalling thirst for fuel.'

Such a restriction, along with the advent of the 1970s fuel crisis and increasing concerns about airport noise, finally put paid to Concorde's economics on any route beyond the nonstop flight across the Atlantic or between Europe, the Middle East and South America in British Airways and Air France colours. Even then, in an all-first-class configuration, it struggled to make a profit, largely filling the role of a spectacular flagship. Concorde ended its days as a remarkable technical achievement but one that had the misfortune to be in the right place at the wrong time.

Once again, Qantas's rigorous application of its technical and economic forces had come up with the right answer as far as a new aircraft type was concerned. But there are still some who wonder where those 'economic forces' might have been when it came to the airline's purchase of the shortened, long-range special performance version of the Boeing 747, the B747SP, in the early 1980s.

There was always a belief among some in Qantas that the Boeing company actually had the Australian airline in mind when it decided to build the 747SP. Around 14 metres shorter than the standard B747 and carrying almost a hundred fewer passengers, the SP certainly appeared an ideal fit for the airline with the longest route stage lengths in the world, with its ability to fly further than the 747 versions then operating. But the record shows that the two Boeing customers originally pressing for its construction were Pan Am and Iran Air, both seeking a high-capacity aircraft for nonstop operations between New York and the Middle East, with Pan Am also looking towards its services from New York to Tokyo.

Boeing certainly had Qantas in mind as a prospective customer, but by the time the specials were rolling off the assembly line at Seattle, Qantas wasn't on the order books.

Attitudes in Qantas changed when Pan Am decided to use its version of the SP on the Pacific route between Sydney and the

US west coast, where the availability of nonstop flights had considerable passenger appeal. Honolulu may have had its tropical delights but for passengers who wanted to cross the Pacific quickly, stopping there for fuel wasn't one of them.

Obviously, Qantas had to closely watch its US competitor but the fact was that even with the added range of the SP, a nonstop flight was only achievable eastbound due to the prevailing winds that forced a scheduled stop at Auckland on the westbound leg.

Ironically, it would be Wellington in New Zealand that would turn out to be the major catalyst for a change of heart by the Australian airline, and mark the only time for decades when Qantas would not carry out a detailed economic study before the introduction of a new aircraft type.

The New Zealand capital, known as the 'windy city', had severe airport limitations due to a runway of less than 1800 metres, with water at both ends, and had reached a point where neither Air New Zealand nor Qantas could service it adequately with their larger aircraft. In fact, ten years had passed since Qantas had operated there with its own aircraft, the propeller-driven Lockheed Electra. Now operating an all-747 fleet, to keep its Australia to Wellington services open, the airline had been forced to charter an Air New Zealand DC-8—an expensive compromise adding little to the Australian airline's bottom line. But now Air New Zealand had decided to sell its DC-8s and replace them with the DC-10, so Qantas's options were closing fast.

The historically competitive nature of the relationship between Qantas and Air New Zealand made being the only one of the two airlines to service New Zealand's own capital city from Australia a marketing opportunity Qantas's then general manager Keith

Hamilton couldn't resist. The Qantas publicity machine at the time helped spread the belief that the airline had considered aircraft like the three-engine Lockheed L-1011, but Hamilton made no secret of the fact that Qantas would never operate a three-engine aircraft. 'Not under my watch,' he told Barry Phair. 'It's either a two or a four,'—and, although Boeing had its two-engine Boeing 767 in the planning, it was still some years away.

Meanwhile, Terrell and his people out at the Qantas Jet Base were quietly developing their own theories. When Terrell first told his boss their SP performance calculations for Wellington made it a possibility, Hamilton, who had obviously already broached the subject with Boeing in Seattle, disagreed: 'They think it can't be done.'

But Terrell's chief performance engineer, Wal Stack, and his team had been working on an SP version fitted with more powerful Rolls Royce engines.

'Well, you'd better get up to Seattle and talk to them,' ordered Hamilton.

Once Terrell and the Boeing people had agreed, things began to happen quickly and Barry Phair and his numbers men waited for the go-ahead to develop the customary, detailed economic case for the aircraft. The call never came. Hamilton and Terrell's team had made the decision on aircraft performance grounds.

Several weeks later engineering executive Bob Walker, who had close links with Boeing, remembers his phone ringing. Keith Hamilton was calling from Seattle. He'd been offered the SP at a cheap price. Walker was on the flight to the United States that night, under orders from Hamilton to 'sort it out'.

'He realised Air New Zealand were at a disadvantage and the opportunity was too good to pass up. I think we probably bought it for the wrong reasons but it turned out all right in the end,' says Walker.

There's little doubt Hamilton had achieved an attractive deal, as news reports at the time indicate Boeing had found itself involved in a political squeeze between Iran and the United States and the two SPs Iran had ordered had been cancelled. Few in Qantas would ever be privy to the actual cost of the two SPs Qantas acquired, as they came as part of a 'package' deal with Boeing for three other standard 747s at a total cost of $320 million.

Now Wal Stack and his team had to make sure the aircraft worked not only on paper but enough to convince sceptical aviation authorities to make changes to the normal operating procedures for such a large aircraft operating into Wellington. And there was another factor involved.

Wellington is not known as the 'windy city' for nothing and it has an airport renowned for vicious cross-winds, making the landing approach an interesting experience for airline pilots. Stack's team devised a set of non-standard touchdown markings for the threshold of Wellington's runway that would give SP pilots something to aim at. If the aircraft was not 'wheels on' at the right speed within those markings, a go-around was necessary.

After some early reluctance from the traditionally conservative International Civil Aviation Organisation and the New Zealand authorities, Stack fed the unique requirements into the training schedule for Qantas's flight simulators at the Mascot Jet Base so that all crews rostered to operate there were familiar with them by the time the first of the two SPs arrived in early 1981.

While markings were being painted and simulators programmed, to boost the aircraft's profile, Qantas took the SP on a four-day promotional tour along Australia's eastern seaboard, flying dignitaries, travel and tourism representatives and media on joy-flights out of Brisbane, the Gold Coast, Townsville and Cairns. The company heralded the exercise as an outstanding success, although someone hadn't fully taken into account the use of the aircraft for the first time at Cairns and the Gold Coast airports, with the result that each time the SP took off on a promotional flight its outboard engines blew away the runway lights!

Then, on 31 January 1981, a 747SP was on its way to Wellington, the first for a decade to bear the Qantas colours on a regular service, and New Zealand's third-biggest city's population turned out en masse to greet it.

The only person not all that happy about it was the local airport manager, who watched as the SP came to a stop with only half the runway used, and later jokingly complained to a member of the crew: 'Now look what you've done. I've been trying to get this runway extended for years!'

But as another experienced Qantas captain, Cliff Viertal, would admit, despite the markers, Wellington remained an airport where absolute concentration was needed and one that certainly had its moments. Viertal was in command one day and, alerted that legendary American fighter ace and the first man to exceed the speed of sound, General Chuck Yeager, was a passenger, invited him up to the cockpit for the landing. Viertal noticed Yeager became very quiet as the plane descended through about 1500 feet and the airport came into view, then asked: 'You're not going to land on that, are you?'

A modest Viertal claims he 'lucked out' that day, landed right on target and was taxiing the aircraft well before the end of the runway.

As Yeager left the cockpit, he patted Viertal on the shoulder: 'I wouldn't have believed it.' This from a pilot who had assisted

Boeing in the high-altitude certification for the SP at La Paz in Bolivia.

'The procedure worked very well. The pilots readily accepted the need to divert if the reported conditions were out of limits and operated without incident for many years but it did need special procedures, plus Qantas training and discipline,' Viertal explained.

During its service with Qantas, the SP crossed the Pacific nonstop numerous times and covered many of the other routes beyond Wellington. The aircraft 'bought for the wrong reasons' as Bob Walker put it, would be a favourite among aircrew with its powerful engines and large control surfaces making it an exciting aircraft to fly. That, combined with its lighter weight, made it something of a sports car version of its big brother, and as one former pilot commented years later: 'It was a matter of hanging on and going for the ride.'

The SP could also, under certain conditions, fly higher than its bigger brothers, at times reaching 45,000 feet, well above the normal cruising altitude of similar aircraft. Any Qantas pilot, flying at such an altitude, would normally have good reason for thinking he was alone at that height. That was until, after confirming his altitude one afternoon to air traffic control, one SP captain was surprised to hear another pilot call in from thousands of feet above him. He was relieved to hear it was a Lockheed U-2, the renowned American spy plane.

With the arrival of the long range Boeing 747-400 into the Qantas fleet in 1989, an aircraft well capable of flying nonstop across the Pacific with a far greater passenger load, the SP's appeal had diminished, although it would be the catalyst for one of the most bitter and long-running disputes in the airline's troubled industrial history.

In the years to come, the airline's giant Airbus A-380s gradually superseded the 747-400 with a capability of not only flying nonstop between Sydney and Los Angeles, but capable of reaching from halfway across the United States from Dallas to Australia.

EVER-PRESENT DANGER

4
TAIM BILONG BALUS

Almost half a century has passed, and it's probably safe to assume there would be few in the Qantas of today who even realise how deeply important Papua New Guinea (PNG) was in the more recent history of their airline. But, for anyone who has ever flown widely in PNG, particularly in its post-war developmental years and into the 1950s and 1960s, there remains a certain cachet to the experience.

Long acknowledged as one of the world's most difficult and dangerous flying environments, split by a cordillera of mountains, PNG's terrain offers a striking contrast to Australia's relatively open skies and benign weather, with peaks twice the height of Mount Kosciusko, often covered by cloud, forming barriers to its rich, highland valleys.

PNG's infrastructure had been shattered by the brutal campaigns of World War II, and the country had the added disadvantage of having a topography within which those productive highland regions existed without any road access at all. Such was the ruggedness of its terrain that there were numerous examples of tribes on one side of a mountain never having any contact with tribes living on the other side. Thus, opening up the country post-war could only be achieved one way—by air, or by the 'balus' as the aeroplane was known in pidgin.

Maps and charts were often primitive, forcing pilots to fly visually or risk death against a mountainside hidden in cloud. Qantas veteran Hughie Birch recalls reaching for his charts one morning to check the altitude of a ridgeline he was approaching only to find it described simply as: 'Very high.' Such drawbacks provided a unique training ground for Qantas pilots, many of whom went on to hold senior aircrew and management positions within the airline in the Boeing 707 and 747 eras.

The weather dictated the flying. If it was good, you enjoyed yourself, and if it was bad, you earned your money, as it wasn't the place to be courageous. Over the years, PNG has been notorious for claiming the lives of many light aircraft pilots who had vast experience flying the country but, entering one cloud too many, would nevertheless die there. 'Gap' flying was the order of the day, which involved flying parallel to a range when approaching one of the gaps that would let you through to the valley on the other side, although it should be noted that valley itself may be 5000 feet above sea level. Once at the gap, you would peer through to see if it was clear enough on the other side to fly through. If not, you turned away.

Qantas had taken its first steps into the 'Territory' as it was known, with the takeover of Carpenter Airways in 1945 but its role increased dramatically as the Australian government took on the task of opening up the country after the war. By the early 1950s, the airline had a fleet of fourteen aircraft operating there, including DH-84 Dragons, DC-3s, two Catalina flying boats, single-engine de Havilland Beavers and Otters and three-engine de Havilland Drovers.

The majority of the scheduled passenger and freight services would fall to the DC-3s and even these operated under a dispensation from the Department of Civil Aviation, as many of the primitive highland airstrips they were required to operate from were not up to what would be classified as 'normal' by Australian standards. Thus, in some instances, the performance of the DC-3, should an engine fail on take-off, would be marginal to say the least.

While pilots worried about clouds, mountains and their aircraft's performance at high altitudes, their passengers could expect few comforts. Forward-facing seats were something of a luxury, the normal being wartime metal or webbing seats that folded down from the side of the cabin—and back up to the wall to allow for the aircraft's freight role. They soon became known as 'hard-arse' seats and certainly lived up to their name in the bumpy flying conditions!

With no such thing as air conditioning, aircraft became ovens sitting under the scorching tropical sun waiting for passengers to board, even more so once the door was shut and the pilots went through their pre-take-off procedures.

By the time the aircraft was taxiing towards the end of the runway, passengers would be sweating profusely and, only after the aircraft reached a cruising altitude, would the temperature become tolerable. Then, if the weather required a climb to an even higher altitude, the interior of the cabin would drop to near freezing. In-flight catering came in cardboard boxes, usually a sandwich and some fruit, and a trip down to the rear toilet often meant navigating around sacks of potatoes or a trussed live piglet.

Lae on the Huon Gulf became the operational and maintenance base for Qantas, but Australian authorities had chosen

Madang, on the Territory's north shore, as the primary hub for transferring freight to and from main Highland towns such as Goroka and Mount Hagen, taking in everything from construction materials, vehicles and household goods, and bringing the Highlands' produce out to markets on the coast. Such was the demand, and the fact that the flying had to be done before the clouds built up over the mountains towards late morning and early afternoon, Madang at times became busier than some of Australia's main city airports as aircraft landed, loaded up and took off again.

In the frenzy that was Madang, pilots competed with each other for the fun of it. Alan Terrell remembers another captain, Roger Wilson, returning one day to boast he had done six trips that day from Madang to Goroka in the Eastern Highlands.

The next day Terrell did seven.

'Then the day after that the bugger came back and said he's just done eight. They used to call him Mr Hurry-Up because of his habit of standing over the natives as they loaded to make sure they were going as fast as they could because once the gaps in the mountains closed you couldn't fly any more anyhow.'

Achieving the most number of trips was not the only competition dreamt up by the pilots. The airstrip at Madang was comprised of soft bitumen and each time an aircraft landed it left a mark. As Alan Terrell explains: 'The idea was to make sure, on landing, you left a mark on top of the previous mark and if you ever went in and noticed a mark off the centre you would point out such "evidence" in the crew room with the question: "Who was that?"

'We'd always find out because the First Officer would always dob him in!'

But the dangers were always there, not all due to the mountains and the weather. Terrell remembers coming back to Madang from Goroka one afternoon and parking the aircraft and heading off to the hotel for the night. During the evening, the traffic officer at the airport decided to load the next day's cargo—heavy steel sheets measuring 2 metres by 3 metres and about 15 centimetres thick—so that the aircraft could get away without delay next morning.

The next morning's traffic officer, not realising the aircraft was already fully loaded, put more of the sheets on board.

Terrell's co-pilot that day was Larry Blackman, a TAA captain who was training on DC-3s. As they took off, Terrell knew immediately that something was terribly wrong.

'This thing isn't going anywhere,' said Terrell, as the DC-3 on full power was struggling to gain any altitude at all.

Gingerly they turned the DC-3 around some trees at the end of the airfield and, still on maximum take-off power, literally staggered back around the airfield to land again, to be met by a very apologetic traffic officer.

'He was as white as a sheet as he could see us trying to turn around not far above the ground and realised what was wrong. As we switched the engines off I remember saying to Larry: "I don't know about you, but I'm going back to the pub to have a drink."'

Loading mishaps aside, crews also battled with grassed inland airfields that could quickly turn to mud in the rainy season, often requiring the use of leftover wartime Marsden matting to avoid bogging.

Unable to fly in cloud and with high ground often on the fringe of coastal areas, pilots were challenged even by flights between coastal centres. No testimony to the skill required of Qantas pilots can be better expressed than by Gordon Power, who flew as a first officer with Qantas captain Mal Shannon on a DC-3 flight to Baimuru, 180 nautical miles (about 330 kilometres) west of Port Moresby in the Gulf of Papua.

Power was in awe of the ability of pilots like Shannon to find their way around visually, demonstrated in the hour-and-a-quarter flight that day. With overcast conditions below 100 feet above sea level, they were obliged to remain visual for the entire flight as there were no ground aids to assist them to find Bairmuru.

> The accepted procedure was for the first officer to open his side window so that he could visually check the height of the aircraft above the ocean and to ensure that the aircraft did not descend below 50 feet—into the water.
>
> Shannon, hunched over the instruments, flew on a compass heading for an hour in this atrocious weather before we started to pass over mangrove swamps. Visibility forward of the aircraft was minimal, in heavy rain. Mal somehow made a few very slight heading alterations as we passed over some swamps and mangroves.
>
> Personally, I had no idea where we were. Suddenly, while still at barely 50 to 100 feet, the Marsden matting strip at Baimuru passed directly underneath us. To me it was a masterpiece of navigation under appalling conditions and to this day I have no idea how he found it as there were no navigation aids and GPS had not been invented.

One can only wonder at the level of concentration Shannon would have had to apply, flying on instruments, so close to the water for such a protracted length of time in a DC-3 being tossed about by the weather!

Despite the occasional use of Marsden matting, bogged aircraft were commonplace, often requiring some innovative techniques to dislodge them.

Roger Wilson's DC-3, just loaded with 44-gallon drums of fuel, sank to the axles one day at Mount Hagen while taxiing for take-off. After around fifty local villagers had been gathered to unload the drums, they were then assembled under the aircraft in an attempt to lift it by hand. It wouldn't budge.

More villagers arrived and soon all were singing, laughing and dancing as they applied additional manpower to the task. Suddenly, the aircraft broke loose, an event which only increased their excitement and they began running along the airstrip, virtually carrying the DC-3, screaming with delight. They had carried it for some metres before Wilson regained control of his aircraft.

Given the mountains, the weather and dodgy airstrips, Qantas would come through its Papua New Guinea phase with few serious accidents. Although lives were still lost. The worst accident was at Lae in July 1951, when a de Havilland Drover crashed into the sea off the Markham River, killing the pilot and six passengers.

In September the same year Fred Barlogie died when his DH-84, carrying a load of timber, crashed into a ridgeline covered in heavy fog near the eastern end of Karanka airstrip. Suspicions were later raised that the aircraft had been overloaded by the contractor but, as much of the timber had been removed by the time crash investigators arrived, no proof could be obtained.

Among the less serious incidents were a DC-3 that had its undercarriage torn off when it turned into a ditch after landing at Wau in the late 1950s and several DH-84s that ended in trees after flying into rising terrain.

Perhaps in typical Papua New Guinea style for those days, accidents like these often had 'back stories,' sometimes serious, other times humorous, which added to their drama. John Simler was flying the DC-3 when it crashed at Wau, a notoriously steep airstrip with only one direction for take-offs and landings and a runway so steep the throttles had to be opened after landing to taxi to the parking area at the top of the strip.

Simler landed fine but suddenly the aircraft began to aquaplane on the waterlogged strip, veering off towards the primitive passenger terminal. Concerned he would take out the building and anyone in it, Simler attempted to ground loop the aeroplane by turning it sharply to the left but in the middle of the turn the water on the airfield took charge and the DC-3 slid sideways into a ditch.

No one was injured but getting the DC-3 back to Lae for repairs presented a range of typical New Guinea challenges. Since it couldn't be flown out it had to be taken apart and carried, piece by piece, by road, back to Lae for repair. Some of the hairpin bends on the 140 kilometre road were so sharp the fuselage had to be manoeuvred by hand by the team of villagers assisting the recovery.

Not that crashing an aeroplane dimmed a pilot's light-hearted telling of the incident. One of the ever-present dangers was to be able to make the right decision when you came to a fork in the valley you were flying down.

Ross Crabb chose the wrong fork one day and ran into a dead end. Unable to climb out, he was forced to crash his DH-84 into the trees. Telling the story later, he claimed the crash itself had been the least of his concerns. Unhurt he struggled out of the cockpit and began to climb down through the trees to the jungle floor, only to find that every time he shook a branch a batch of the tinned food he had been carrying came crashing down on top of him.

Gordon Power vividly remembers an experience while trying to fly from Mount Hagen to Madang via valleys alongside Papua New Guinea's highest mountain, Mount Wilhelm, which rose to 14,793 feet.

This particular day they were flying at about 6000 feet through a valley towards Mount Wilhelm when they came to a fork in the valley. Circling while they decided which valley might take them through to Madang on the coast, Power remembers clearly seeing native villages above them on either side of the valley.

As they continued to search the valley sides for an opening, to their dismay they suddenly realised that clouds had now moved into the valley behind them. They were trapped and, with the knowledge that Mount Wilhelm was somewhere towering above them, they put on maximum power and climbed in a tight circle through the cloud, eventually breaking out at 12,000 feet, right alongside Wilhelm itself.

'It was a most frightening experience,' Power recalls.

***

Those operating the Catalina flying boats faced their own challenges as they linked isolated coastal and inland lake communities that otherwise would have been impossible to serve.

Flying boat flying was a demanding art as you had to carefully 'read' the wave patterns for take-offs and landings, and unfriendly open seas often called for a high degree of airmanship, something that became even more critical when called upon in an emergency.

Qantas Captains Fred Fox and Ian Ralfe figured in a dramatic 1952 rescue of a Department of Civil Aviation crew when one of the propeller blades on their de Havilland Drover broke off, partly severing the foot of the pilot, Clarrie Hibbert. The Drover's other two engines then failed, leaving Hibbert unable to control the aircraft. Tom Drury, one of the two other DCA officers on board, managed to ditch the aircraft in the Bismarck Sea off Madang.

After a searching DC-3 located the crew in their dinghy, Fox and Ralfe set out from Port Moresby, forced to climb to 14,000 feet to clear the cloud-covered Owen Stanley Range. Fox landed the Catalina alongside the dinghy and flew the injured Hibbert and his companions back to Port Moresby Hospital.

The next day they were off on another emergency mission, this time after a massive cyclone ripped through the Woodlark Islands to the south-east of the mainland. Unable to land there with their cargo of timber, Fox made contact with a government trading vessel off Woodlark and landed beside it, transhipping their cargo while bobbing around in the open sea.

While such dramatic events usually passed unremarked, some did attract wider attention. Several years later Qantas captain Marsh Burgess won a medal for landing in a swell up to 5 metres high to rescue round-the-world yachtsman Danny Weil after his yacht ran onto a reef in the Gulf of Papua.

Beyond their normal scheduled activities, the Catalina crews filled a variety of roles, from locating government patrols engaged on survey work to identifying newly discovered native villages in the more remote parts of the country. Occasionally they flew in the long arm of the law.

Author Jim Sinclair, in his excellent *Balus: The aeroplane in Papua New Guinea* tells of the Catalinas carrying Supreme Court judges on their circuits, often carrying out such functions during a short stopover. Villagers would bring out double-hulled canoes, occasionally with tables and starched white napery, and His Honour would conduct the business of law in the shade of the aircraft wing.

Airdrops were commonplace—delivering everything from flour and rice to fresh meat, tinned fruit and torch batteries. Flight engineer Keith Gordon was in Catalinas that dropped eggs, and the essential bottles of beer, into jungle clearings, assuming that, if the eggs broke, at least they could be scraped up and scrambled. Fowls also made their way by air drops to outstations via various techniques to ensure they didn't open their wings at too high a speed. Fred Fox's crew wrapped them in overlapping pages of newspaper that slowed the 'package' down and disintegrated low to the ground so the bird could use its wings for the last few metres or so to earth. Keith Gordon stuffed them head first in sick bags and by the time they had kicked their way out they were low enough to fly.

Although the Qantas Catalinas had earned a remarkable wartime record for reliability, as the years went by they began to show their age, often testing the ingenuity of their flight and ground engineers.

Holes punched in the worn Catalina hulls, either by debris or human error, were a common problem. Flight engineer Tom Mitchell always carried extra pencils in his tool kit. He'd screw a pencil down the hole in the aircraft's hull and break it off. That would get them home, where a new rivet would be inserted. Keith Gordon had his own remedy. He always carried packets of Wrigleys chewing gum to fill any holes in the leaking hull. At times, such running repairs required the native cabin crew member to dive over the side of the Catalina to find the offending hole. Most villagers relished the task, to the relief of the flight engineers.

Flight engineers filled a variety of roles and were often the unsung heroes of Catalina missions. Sitting at their station in the cabane, or structure that joined the fuselage to the wing above and behind the pilots, they not only monitored engine performance in flight but acted as mechanics as well.

Gordon remembers one afternoon when an out-of-control native canoe punched a large hole in one of his Catalina's floats while it was moored off Kikori in the Gulf of Papua, west of Port Moresby. While they had a group of local villagers stand on the opposite wing to keep the damaged float out of the water, Gordon patched the hole using a sheet of aluminium alloy fabric heavily coated with dope and they flew for another three days before they returned to Port Moresby for repairs.

Pilots flying Catalinas also had their moments of discomfort as the cockpits leaked profusely during rain squalls, prompting one captain's suggestion to his first officer: 'I think the only way we're going to stay dry is if we turn this damn thing upside down.'

Ground servicing too had its shortcomings. Beaching a Catalina for overhaul at Lae meant up to forty villagers dragging the aircraft up out of the open sea and onto an airfield that was well above the waterline. Relaunching required manoeuvring the Cat down a steep incline onto the road to the launch site. On at least one occasion, an aircraft broke away and crashed through nearby scrub, fortunately suffering only superficial damage.

By the late 1950s, the Catalinas were reaching their operational use-by date as delays mounted and maintenance became more difficult. Flight engineer Colin Lock records how Qantas Operations finally told the airline's Board:

These Catalinas bought second-hand have been in continuous service with the company since 1946 and are now obsolete. Being subject to rapid corrosion, they are very expensive to keep in repair. A conservative estimate of the cost of repairs in addition to normal maintenance to keep the aircraft going in 1958 is fifty thousand pounds per aircraft and they will be immobilised for at least two months each to do the necessary work.

With spare parts often difficult to procure, the airline's engineering department felt they could not be kept going much beyond the end of 1957. But they did make it through the first half of 1958 and, although by now based back in Australia, it fell to Keith Gordon to act as flight engineer on the last Qantas Catalina flight in PNG. Gordon's experience gives some indication of the work ethic of those days.

Arriving for duty at Sydney Operations one afternoon, Gordon was told there was a flight engineer shortage and he needed to fly to Port Moresby that night to crew a Catalina from Port Moresby to Lae the next day.

After an all-night flight, he landed at Port Moresby early the following morning to be briefed that they needed to leave as soon as possible as the open sea at Lae was flat and ideal for a landing. They were soon airborne and flew the one-and-a-half-hour trip to Lae, arriving just in time for Gordon to get back on the same DC-4 he had come up from Australia on that morning, now about to depart Lae on its return to Sydney.

'I think it was a 40-hour tour of duty. Not much out of the ordinary for me at that age.'

Lae, on Huon Gulf, was to be the final resting place for the Catalinas. Each was stripped of engines, propellers, instruments and anything else of lasting value and the remainder sold for scrap, one of them bringing the sum total of £80.

Even though their crews had been drenched by their leaking cockpits and at times accidentally pushed fingers through their ageing hulls, a small group of them watched sadly as the Catalinas were chopped up.

Two years later Qantas too flew out of New Guinea skies as the airline's routes and ground infrastructure were handed over to Trans-Australia Airlines, who, along with Ansett Mandated Airlines, would continue domestic operations until the eventual establishment of the country's own national carrier Air Niugini in 1973.

By then many of the Catalinas' former captains, first officers and other New Guinea 'old hands' would be applying their hard-won experience to the airline's international routes.

5
'SKIPPY SQUADRON'

For the thousands lining Sydney's George Street for the Anzac Day march in 2003, it was the first time they'd seen a group of men marching behind a bright red banner announcing, 'Skippy Squadron'. Although there was no mention of the word 'Qantas', the flying kangaroo in the centre quickly identified who they were.

Some among the marchers wore medals that showed they had served in World War II and other conflicts, including as diggers in the Vietnam War, but they were now marching for the first time under their own 'company' colours.

'Skippy Squadron', named after the well-known television marsupial of the 1960s, might have been part of a war still fresh in the memory of those watching the march that day, but the 'squadron' itself was in fact in the genes of an airline that had a long and impressive history of war service, often heroic, but just as often, largely unrecognised. Books by the airline's founder Hudson Fysh and others have chronicled Qantas's participation in World

War II but much of that involvement remains largely unknown to the general public.

In fact the war would cost the airline nearly all of its flagship Empire flying boats, either through enemy action or wartime accidents. Qantas captain Bill Crowther's Empire flying boat might have been the last civilian aircraft to leave Singapore as the Japanese approached the city early in the morning of 4 February 1942, but in the weeks preceding Singapore's fall, Crowther and other crews of the large, vulnerable four-engine flying boats had been playing a cat-and-mouse game with the Japanese as they kept the ever-fragile air route to Australia open.

Not only was there the constant danger from Japanese fighters and reconnaissance aircraft patrolling the skies, but, warned of imminent Japanese air attacks on Singapore itself, they would be forced to divert to remote landing sites to wait for a radio message from Singapore telling them that the attack was over. One such frequently used site would become known as 'Thomas's funk hole', named after one of the captains who had spotted a secluded river estuary on an island where the narrow waters and high jungle-covered sides provided temporary safe haven until Singapore gave the 'all clear'.

With Singapore's fall and the subsequent retreat down through the Netherlands East Indies archipelago, it fell to the Empire flying boat crews to shuttle military personnel into the islands and bring civilians back to the safety of Australia. It was here that the mystery of what happened to flying boat *Circe* had its origins, at Tjilatjap, Java, on 28 February 1942 when, with four crew and sixteen passengers, it left for the relative safety of Broome. Two flying boats left Tjilatjap that morning and, as the crew of *Corinthian* climbed away, they saw *Circe* taxiing for take-off. *Circe* never arrived in Broome but what happened to the twenty aboard would remain unanswered for more than 70 years.

While researching the history of the Qantas flying boats in 2014, Melbourne air traffic controller and historian Phil Vabre found interesting Japanese records. These revealed that a Japanese bomber commanded by Flight Petty Officer First Class Sadayoshi Yamamoto, operating out of Bali, had sighted a four-engine flying boat at a position that matched Vabre's calculations of where *Circe* would have been on the morning of 28 February 1942. Yamamoto had shot *Circe* down. There is little doubt it would have been *Circe* as the only other flying boat in the area was *Corinthian*, which had probably escaped a similar fate by only a few minutes.

Circe's loss and the fate of another Empire boat shot down off Koepang, Timor a few months earlier, along with two more destroyed during an air attack on Broome in March, under-line the dangers the unarmed boats faced in those early days of the war. And as the war quickly began to close Australia off from its north, other examples of loss and exceptional courage would be added to the Qantas wartime story, including the daring rescue of civilians from Mount Hagen in the New Guinea Highlands.

It is impossible to tell the whole story of the Qantas Mount Hagen rescue without describing the part played by a Catholic priest, Father John Glover. Glover, born in Albury, New South Wales, was a flying missionary in New Guinea at the outbreak of the war in the Pacific and had already helped to evacuate people from Wau to Port Moresby in his two-seater Spartan aeroplane. When this became too dangerous, he flew the Spartan to Kainantu, up the Markham Valley inland from Lae, where he hid the aircraft in the jungle at the Seventh Day Adventist Mission.

With the fall of Rabaul in early 1942, as civilians and military personnel fled the island of New Britain and the northern shores of New Guinea in advance of the Japanese, Glover set out on a nine-day trek overland from Kainantu to reach Sek Island off the northern New Guinea coast where he knew the Catholic Mission had a four-seater Moth he could add to his 'fleet'.

At Sek, Glover and his Hungarian-born engineer, Karl Nagy, constructed a raft out of empty fuel drums and floated the Moth 25 kilometres along the coast to Madang where, in between frequent Japanese air attacks, they worked to get it airworthy and then flew it back to Kainantu.

There they hammered a spare fuel tank out of sheets of galvanised iron to achieve Glover's grand plan: to give the Moth sufficient range to reach Thursday Island, which he would use as a base for the rescue of those now gathering at Mount Hagen.

In between working on the modifications for the Moth, Glover used the Spartan in an attempt to fly several ill civilians to Mount Hagen, only to find the Spartan wasn't powerful enough to clear the mountains in between. Forced to turn back, he crashed while attempting to land. Although no one was hurt, the Spartan was now out of action. Turning to the Moth, Glover reached Mount Hagen on his second attempt. While those still at Kainantu started walking towards Hagen to join those already there, Glover and Nagy set off for Thursday Island and Cairns with the aim of alerting authorities to the predicament of those gathering at Mount Hagen.

They managed to make it to Papua's south coast until a combination of poor weather and lack of fuel forced them to land on a beach west of Daru. With the help of friendly villagers in a canoe, then a lugger to Thursday Island, Glover continued on, finally reaching Melbourne where he pleaded for help. Qantas was alerted and within days Orme Denny and his team were underway.

Denny had an impeccable background for the job. Joining the Royal Australian Air Force (RAAF) after service in World War I, he had flown with Qantas in its pioneering days in Queensland before moving to New Guinea with Guinea Airways. He rejoined Qantas in 1938 and was still flying in New Guinea when the Japanese invaded.

Denny decided to use Horn Island, at the very tip of Cape York, as their base of operations. Two DH-86 aircraft were fitted with the long-range fuel tanks they would need to climb through the gaps in the 12,000-foot range surrounding Mount Hagen. There would be no intermediate stops and they would need to be constantly alert for the Japanese aircraft that now controlled the skies over New Guinea.

The first two aircraft, one of them with John Glover on board, made it through on 13 May 1942 to a rousing welcome from the by-now 80 people anxiously waiting at Mount Hagen to be flown to safety. Among them was a group of eighteen who had made their way roughly 1600 kilometres across New Britain, across the Bismarck Sea by launch to Madang, then trekked through the Ramu and Wahgi valleys and into the Hagen highlands.

Denny calculated six or seven could be lifted by each aircraft per flight and began shuttle flights but incessant rain soon began to take its toll on the grassy Mount Hagen airstrip. The softening ground began to make take-offs and landings extremely hazardous. Using his New Guinea know-how, Denny quickly came up with the solution.

Marshalling the hundreds of local villagers who were gathering each day at the airfield to watch the activities, he organised a customary New Guinea 'sing sing' and soon around 2000 natives were enthusiastically dancing and stamping their feet, forming the surface into a firm landing ground.

The flights took three hours each way, at times requiring a climb to 16,000 feet to ensure they cleared the mountains.

In all, the DH-86s made eighteen flights between Horn Island and Mount Hagen, evacuating 78 people. It was mostly seat-of-the-pants flying: at one stage Mount Hagen offered to supply weather reports but Denny's New Guinea flying background told him they could not be relied on due to the tendency of the weather to change rapidly over the route. Neither, for obvious reasons, did he want Mount Hagen on the radio any more than necessary.

After it was all over Denny received the following telegram from the Department of Civil Aviation: 'Congratulations to you and all members of your party on successful conclusion [of] your important and dangerous task. That it should have been completed without hitch demonstrates sound organization and high courage and ability of all personnel concerned.'

It was a sentiment that could just as easily be applied to most of the airline's role in war-torn Papua New Guinea but an achievement on an even greater scale was soon to follow 5000 kilometres away on the Indian Ocean. Known as the Double Sunrise service, Qantas Catalina flying boats operating in secret through enemy airspace would keep the vital air route between Perth and Colombo, and therefore Australia and the United Kingdom, open during the most difficult period of the war.

Flying only senior military personnel and diplomats, the nonstop flights would create their own records, at times exceeding 30 hours in the air and, in doing so, passengers and crew would see the sun rise twice on the journey. Operating in radio silence, crews navigated by taking star shots at night, switching on their radio for the briefest of moments to hear a scheduled weather report from their destination. Although unarmed, the fate of their crews and passengers would have been the same as those of any RAAF aircraft that might have been intercepted by enemy aircraft. Despite their vital role in keeping the air link open and the determined efforts of their leader Hudson Fysh, Qantas staff would receive no official recognition from the Australian government after the war.

With the end of hostilities Qantas began to rebuild but it wasn't long before it would find itself involved in other wars. The first was in Korea between 1950 and 1953. Qantas planes and crews carried troop reinforcements to Iwakuni air base in Japan and flew wounded Australian soldiers on the final stage of their journey home to Australia. First the wounded would be flown from South Korea to Japan in RAAF DC-3 transports. There they were transferred at Iwakuni to stretcher-equipped Qantas DC-4s, with army medical staff on board, for the remainder of their journey, with Darwin their first Australian landfall.

Charles Spiteri, a cabin crew member in those days, admits one of the flights from Darwin to Sydney almost cost him his job. The final leg was a night flight out of Darwin timed to reach Sydney at around 7 a.m. Spiteri remembers one of the young soldiers on a stretcher, who had a series of plastic tubes and drips attached, asking him for a cold beer.

'If I can get you a beer, how are you going to drink it?' was Spiteri's surprised reaction.

'Don't you worry about that, mate. You get me the beer and I'll do the rest.'

Those were the days of 26-ounce (740 ml) bottles and when Spiteri passed it over he watched as the soldier removed the plastic tube from his drip, placed it in the bottle, thanked Spiteri and asked him for his address.

'Unfortunately when we got to Sydney the nurse' on board smelled the beer on his breath and asked him where he got it. He wouldn't tell them who gave it to him but I admitted it was me,' Spiteri recalls. When the report of the incident reached Qantas management Spiteri was disciplined and told if it happened again he would lose his job.

Two months later a new fishing rod was delivered to Spiteri's home with a note of thanks from the soldier, later to become a bank manager in Victoria. He and Spiteri remained in contact for some years after the war.

Qantas DC-4s would also airlift RAAF and army person-nel to Penang during the Malayan Emergency in the 1950s when Commonwealth forces were engaged in guerrilla warfare with the Malayan Communist Party. Then came Konfrontasi, the undeclared war that broke out in Borneo in 1963 as a result of Indonesia's objec-tion to the creation of the Federation of Malaysian States.

One of Qantas's most lucrative engineering contracts at that time was for the overhaul of the engines used on Indonesian airline Garuda's Lockheed Electra aircraft, a contract that included deliv-ering the engines back to Jakarta on completion of the work. Before the conflict, Qantas DC-3s were used to return the engines via a traditional route from Darwin, through Timor and Bali to Jakarta and returning the same way. Qantas off-duty pilots with DC-3 endorsements could volunteer for the flights, although former captain John Fulton describes accommodation at places like Bali in those days as 'hardly exotic'.

'The hotel in Bali was pretty well just bricks and mortar so we would take our own soap, toilet paper and bread and take a boiler off the aircraft to fire up some chicken,' says Fulton.

Later engine delivery flights were made with DC-4s but by now Konfrontasi had broken out, leading to an anomaly where while the Australian government-owned Qantas was delivering engines to Indonesia, soldiers from its Special Air Service (SAS) regiment were engaged in guerrilla warfare against Indonesian soldiers in the jungles of Borneo. Indonesia meanwhile had closed much of its airspace to other traffic, with a direct route through Timor and Bali no longer available.

Norm Field explains: 'That meant we had to fly due north from Darwin around Timor, then left-hand down north of Java almost into Borneo then back into Jakarta. You had to closely watch where you were in the airspace because their navigation aids were primitive and the extra distance meant you had to keep an eye on the fuel usage.'

Konfrontasi also had its moments even for the mainline Qantas 707 services operating on the Kangaroo Route between Australia and the UK. Restrictions on airspace meant that, on the climb out of Singapore, aircraft had to avoid flying over Indonesian territory by using a so-called 'safe zone' to the south-east that took them well clear of the Indonesian flight information region. Alan Terrell recalled a night departure out of Singapore: 'We had flight planned to pass about twenty miles [32 km] clear of the boundary and had just reached 6000 feet when we suddenly saw tracer coming up off to one side. My first reaction was—"Shit, we haven't made a mistake have we?" and did a quick check to make sure we were where we were supposed to be.' To Terrell's relief a quick check of his charts revealed that his Boeing 707 was in fact in airspace that was 'safe'.

Unsettling though the experience may have been it would be Vietnam that would mark Qantas's re-entry into another genuine, and far more dangerous, war.

***

Within weeks of Prime Minister Menzies' April 1965 announcement of Australia's commitment of a battalion of troops to Vietnam, it was obvious the scale of the uplift of troops and equipment would be beyond the ability of Australia's armed forces themselves. Not that it came as a surprise that Qantas would be called on, as the airline's uplift capacity was a nationally accepted strategic element in such situations. But the Vietnam involvement would be on a much grander scale than anything preceding it, would need significant pre-planning and a heavy commitment of the airline's fleet of Boeing 707s, and, as it turned out, would last for seven years.

The first Qantas advance guard to leave Sydney for Saigon in 1965 was small. Sydney traffic training instructor Frank Corcoran, aircraft engineer Brian Chadwick and security officer John Healy would work with American forces at Saigon's Tan Son Nhut airport on the coordination of aircraft parking, unloading, refuelling, security and anything else needed to guarantee a quick turnaround. The aim was to have the Boeings spend as little time as possible on the ground.

Chadwick was chosen as an engineer who had all the necessary technical qualifications to sign out a 707. Corcoran says his 'recruitment' for the task was a fairly arbitrary one. His boss, traffic manager Jim Ledger, at first asked him how 'fast' he could turn a 707 around at an airport. 'Obviously satisfied with the answer he then told me the airport was at Saigon.'

Corcoran, Chadwick and Healy made their first flight in with two of Qantas's most experienced captains, World War II veteran Captain 'Torchy' Uren and Alan Morris, aboard a Pan American 707. Frank Corcoran commented:

Apparently there had been a mortar attack the previous day and the skipper announced, because of that, the normally steep approach profile would be increased and not to be too worried. At that stage we must have been at about 20,000 feet. Morris was up the front on the flight deck and Torchy was in the seat across the aisle from me in first class.

As we started down I got the feeling this was all too steep and too fast as the ground was coming up very quickly.

I looked across and noticed Torchy was gripping the arm of his seat really tightly and was as white as a ghost.

After we landed Morris told us the first officer was calling out the wrong rate-of-descent figures to the captain. I'm certainly glad we didn't know about that at the time.

While Uren and Morris left after a few days, Corcoran, Chadwick and Healy spent more than three weeks in Saigon establishing ground arrangements for the Qantas charters. They were given a Land Rover and a driver for travel to the airport each day to wait for the Qantas arrival.

To avoid the danger of hand grenades being thrown into the Land Rover, the trio sat inside a cage built on the back of the vehicle. While they appreciated the extra security the cage offered they would soon learn that it wasn't foolproof. Apparently the Viet Cong had devised a method of throwing grenades with hooks attached so they anchored themselves to the sides of cages.

The war itself was never far away, with the rumbling of artillery constantly in the background and mortar attacks on the airport itself not uncommon. Billeted three to a room on the first floor of a hotel in the city, and with the frequent explosions in mind, Chadwick took the precaution of taping up the windows at the front of their room. It was as well he did.

'Several days later, at about 5.30 in the morning there was an enormous explosion and a gun battle broke out outside the hotel which was situated opposite a bus station where hundreds gathered each morning,' says Corcoran.

'The bus station had the misfortune of being midway between an American officers' mess and a sergeants' mess and we learned later that a motorcyclist had detonated explosives in his bike's saddlebags.

'The guards at each mess opened fire believing the VC would be on the buses and their bullets literally perforated the heavy metal bus shelters.'

The only injury in the hotel was to an RAAF officer who received a cut from glass fragments; the taped-up windows saved the Qantas trio from serious injury.

All those who had anything to do with Tan Son Nhut in the following years would describe it as 'organised chaos'. Most remember just about every military aircraft they had ever heard of either parked, taxiing for take-off or landing, from the smallest single-engine spotter planes to Hercules transports, an assortment of helicopters and every type of fighter or ground-attack aeroplane in the US military inventory.

By mid-1966 the charter flights were weekly as troop units were rotated to and from the war.

Early flight crews were briefed by Torchy Uren before the charters started, but even then they might have been excused for not totally realising the job in front of them until they approached Tan Son Nhut. 'I'm sure you'll find it exciting,' Uren had said as he ended his briefings.

Many of the military aircraft approached the airport in a narrow, descending spiral, then pulled out sharply and landed, a procedure designed to limit their exposure to small arms fire from Saigon and its airport surrounds. But the Qantas 707s were required to follow a glide slope on the airport's instrument landing approach that started 16 kilometres out at 2500 feet, a trajectory bringing them well within the range of small arms fire.

As the flights increased there were numerous 'surprises' for Qantas crews.

Ken Lewis, then a flight steward and later to become the airline's safety officer, was sitting behind Captain Bunny Lee as they approached Tan Son Nhut. Lee was just about to prepare for touchdown when a US air force Hercules suddenly appeared directly in front of them.

'I'm talking around 100 metres away. Bunny took the 707 around again. It turned out the C-130 had something wrong and had to get down quickly.'

The level of aircraft movements around the airport meant the air traffic controllers' instructions were 'like continuous bursts of machine-gun fire'. Crews needed to listen carefully as there was no break in the nonstop transmissions to allow anyone to ask for a repeat. And any doubts one may have had about the precarious nature on the ground at Saigon were graphically evident by the number of burnt-out, roofless buildings near where they were told to park the 707s.

'We were held up once on approach because the strip was being mortared at the time and it seemed to me more dangerous on the ground with all that was going on . . . choppers whizzing around, holding while taxiing while a bunch of Phantoms went past and trucks seemingly roaring all over with no regard for how bloody dangerous the ass-end of a 707 actually was,' says crew member Alan Ross.

Michael Collins's 707 was at 3000 feet with its undercarriage down on final approach to Tan Son Nhut when the American air traffic controller began shouting into their earphones. 'The rest of the crew were having trouble understanding him but I had been there before and I could tell he was telling us not to deviate as there was an air strike going on somewhere. So we kept on course and the next minute a couple of ground-attack Skyraider aircraft appeared diving almost vertically alongside us firing rockets into the ground.

Despite a natural tendency to get as far away from the Skyraiders as possible, the crew held firm on their landing approach but, as they reached 500 feet the air traffic controller began shouting again: 'Qantas. Qantas. There's an F-4 coming in underneath to land in front of you. Continue your approach. Don't go around. Land behind him.'

'With that the Phantom fighter bomber comes in from the right, slides underneath, lands right in front of us, then halfway down the runway deploys his braking chute and drops it onto the runway just as we're about to use reverse thrust. I have no idea what happened to the parachute.'

Les Hayward, who also flew into Saigon as a second officer, remembers tracer bullets appearing off to the left of the 707 as they approached.

'We were only at about a hundred feet and the captain, Dick Otway, who had been a bomber pilot in World War II, immediately took evasive action. For a moment or two I wasn't quite sure whether he'd had a heart attack!'

All pilots and cabin crew operating the flight were volunteers, but Hayward, like others, soon became concerned when the pilots' union discovered that their superannuation scheme didn't cover war risk as part of their insurance.

'At the same time the government was telling us as we were civilians they weren't covering us either.'

The issue was quickly referred to the Arbitration Commission at which the government produced a major from army intelligence as a witness who described Saigon as the 'Paris of the east', painting an image of mothers and their children strolling down tree-lined boulevards. When pilots' union representative Don Gray queried why, if that was the case, the crews were required to adopt such unusual take-off and landing procedures, the major admitted that was so the approaches to the airport could be kept free of mortar and machine-gun fire!

'That fixed that,' says Hayward. Qantas was required to and did provide insurance cover.

The issue of small arms fire during approach to landing was raised on several occasions, with one captain suggesting that if the authorities were worried about fire coming from one particular area then why didn't they just seek out the Viet Cong shooter and put an end to the problem. The answer that came back suggested that he had proved such a lousy shot they had decided to leave him there in case the Viet Cong replaced him with someone more accurate!

Not that crew tensions were allowed to ease once they were on the ground. Unlike any normal airport, Tan Son Nhut appeared to be devoid of any ground control, with vehicles of all descriptions crossing the runway from all directions in front of the 707s as they taxied to their parking position. 'No one seemed to be in charge of anything on the ground,' says Ray Heiniger, later to become a senior management pilot. 'You just had to avoid them.'

Often the diggers on board would be confronted by tractors carrying trolleys of body bags past the aircraft as it came to a stop. 'Just the insensitivity of it must have been pretty hard on the lads down the back who were just about to step into this war,' says Michael Collins.

And stepping into the war was just what they were doing. When one cabin crew member asked a welcoming sergeant major whether the disembarking diggers would be treated to a good meal after disembarking, the reply came back: 'No. Straight into the trucks and into the jungle.'

As the Australian commitment lengthened, the flights changed from the early one-way loads into Vietnam to carrying replacement troops in and rotating troops out back to Australia. By then, most flights operated out of Richmond, Townsville and Darwin via Singapore, where one of the bizarre aspects of the charters occurred. Because of the inter-country politics of the region in relation to the war, the Australian troops were required to land in Singapore dressed in civilian clothes then change back into military uniforms once they reboarded for the short last stage into Saigon.

With the increased frequency of the charters and to minimise disruption to Qantas's regular worldwide schedules, as well as meeting crew flight-time limitations, the charters operated differing patterns. Some taking troops both to and from Vietnam would fly into Singapore where a new crew would take over for the final delivery of the in-bound troops to Saigon and the uplift of home-bound troops back to Sydney or Darwin.

The nonstop Vietnam-to-Australia routing required an aircraft to take on enough fuel at Singapore to enable a quick turnaround at Saigon and still have sufficient fuel for the long flight back to Australia. But while it might have suited the airline's scheduling commitments, the pattern often presented crews with considerable difficulties during the Saigon departures.

Despite its iconic reputation as one of history's great aeroplanes, the Boeing 707 had severe limitations when it came to operating fully loaded out of hot climates, particularly under wartime conditions. Take-offs from Saigon in the middle of the daytime heat could at best be described as 'character building' for pilots and other crew members as their Boeings struggled to clear the markers at the end of the runway.

There are numerous tales of heart-in-the-mouth take-offs, along with some inventive initiatives to get the Boeing into the air and homeward bound. Alan Terrell recalled lining up for take-off one midday to have the air traffic control order him to execute a sharp right turn immediately after take-off. 'Apparently there was a fire fight in the area and he wanted to get us around it.'

Despite being an experienced captain on 707s, Terrell was acutely aware of his aircraft's limitations. 'The 707 was a wonderful aeroplane to fly but its ability to do steep turns fully loaded and at low level after take-off was not something I was happy about.' But orders were orders. Terrell remembers telling his crew as they began their take-off roll: 'If you feel this thing starting to shake, then for Christ's sake tell me about it immediately.'

Terrell though obviously had enough confidence in the aeroplane's ability to meet the challenge, as another incident remembered by Mike Collins attests. Flying as second officer with Terrell on a direct Saigon–Brisbane flight it was Collins's job to compute the take-off data, factoring in the aircraft's passenger and fuel weight, outside temperature and therefore the length of runway they would need.

On this occasion, with the temperature around 40 degrees Celsius and a full load of troops and fuel, Collins's numbers were telling him they were just too heavy. He passed his card of calculations to

Terrell with: 'Skipper, I can cheat with the best of them but with the best will in the world I just can't make this work.'

Collins watched as Terrell took the take-off card, did a few scratches here and there, then put the card back in the middle of the cockpit.

'When I looked at it I saw a load of bollocks, but I wasn't about to say anything as the alternative was to unload the troops, and that wasn't going to happen.'

'So we took off eventually and I think we were still at 3000 feet twenty miles [30 km] from the airport. Any self-respecting Viet Cong could have shot us down,' Collins laughs.

Demands for tight turns immediately after take-off were common. With his fully loaded Boeing just airborne, Ian Macdonald was ordered to turn left immediately. It was the last thing Macdonald wanted to do at such a critical moment but the sight of a swarm of helicopters blasting away at targets on the ground quickly helped him make the decision.

Flight engineer Frank Amy, who did several trips to Vietnam, says not only was it a volunteer assignment but in the early days of the charters they were not even permitted to tell their family where they were going. 'Actually it wasn't the type of trip you went out of your way for. I'd much rather have been sitting on the beach during a Waikiki stopover.'

According to Amy, not all the diggers were looking forward to it either. 'One bloke locked himself in the toilet and wouldn't come out. At one stage the sergeant in charge was going to use an axe to break the toilet door down but we used some piano wire to trip the lock.'

Flight steward Alan Kitchen, who in later years would be instrumental in establishing Skippy Squadron in recognition of the work of the troop charters, volunteered six times between 1965 and 1972. Kitchen, like others involved, remembered the sharp contrast in the mood of the troops when the two-way charters began to operate. 'Leaving Australia the mood was often subdued, particularly on the Singapore to Saigon leg, but coming back they were much more animated.'

Les Hayward agrees and says Qantas made sure there was plenty of beer on board on the way home. 'Sometimes we'd fill the toilets with extra beer and the cabin crew made sure by the time we got to Sydney they'd drank us dry,' says Hayward proudly.

Often too Qantas crews were mindful of the desire of their passengers to return home as soon as possible from the war zone, a situation which could often encourage aircraft captains to improvise when necessary. Another highly respected captain, Norm Field, had a well-honed ability to improvise when it became necessary. It was December 1970 and Field was ready to depart with a full load of diggers who would be home for Christmas, when the air traffic controller changed his runway take-off direction because a fire fight had broken out at that end of the airport.

Field now found himself faced with the age-old airman's problem of having to take off downwind, a less-than-ideal situation in a fully loaded 707, particularly as the controller was telling him the tailwind was up to 15 knots (28 kilometres per hour) and the absolute maximum downwind component allowed for a 707 was 10 knots (18 kilometres per hour).

'Looks like you'll have to stay the night,' was the controller's helpful suggestion over the radio.

Field didn't need much imagination to know what the reaction would be when he made that announcement to the troops down the back, so he headed off to the control tower. 'I vividly remember that control tower. It was well ventilated with shrapnel and bullet holes which doubtless helped the air conditioning,' says Field.

Using a mixture of guile and pleading, Field managed to persuade the traffic controller into 're-assessing' the wind factor at 'ten knots—gusting to twelve' which now put Field within the 707's 'legitimate' take-off limits.

'We got off the ground okay but when we reached around 300 feet we got the real tailwind and were stuck there for miles and at one stage were actually flying under the helicopters which were heading for the fire fight.

'Helicopters are not a nice sight when you're underneath them in a Boeing,' was Field's wry comment 45 years later.

For the troops themselves it was an exercise in contrasts. Michael Jeffery, who, in a distinguished military career would win the Military Cross in Vietnam, later serve as commander of an Australian Special Air Service Regiment and eventually be appointed Australia's governor-general, still remembers the Saigon 'weather report' over the airline's public address system as they approached Tan Son Nhut. 'Well folks, we've begun our approach to Tan Son Nhut where the weather is quite hot, around one hundred degrees [38 °C] and the enemy fire is light and variable.'

Bill Gray, who served with the SAS in Vietnam, has a similar memory of that weather report before arrival: 'What struck me first was the porthole view of an air base in full war mode, with F-4s cradled in revetments, other war planes of all shapes and sizes and armed troops everywhere. Then when the doors opened came the overpowering humidity and smell of the local fish sauce, nuoc cham, as it wafted into the cabin.

'The Qantas cabin crew on the *Freedom Bird* coming home were typically irreverent and friendly and after weeks of anticipation it was all light-headed plotting about what we would be doing on our first night back on Australian soil and the excitement of seeing family and mates again.'

Russ Properjohn, who did a twelve-month tour with the RAAF in Vietnam, experienced a contrast of another type.

Within an hour or so of arriving on Qantas into Singapore in December 1966 Properjohn had changed into civilian clothes and was sitting in a hotel beer garden sipping cold Tiger beer and listening to a Chinese girl singing.

Next day he boarded a Pan American 707 for Saigon where he watched the hostesses sitting at the front of the cabin chatting and painting their fingernails, rarely venturing into the cabin. As they disembarked at Saigon, Properjohn couldn't resist commenting: 'A cup of coffee would have been nice.'

'You got here didn't you, Mac?' was the reply.

A year later he was hardly in his seat on a Qantas 707 when there was a fresh, cold beer in his hand and loud cheering as they were airborne and Vietnam faded into the distance. 'In those days we had a very proprietary view of Qantas. It was our national airline,' he says.

One of the flights too would be something of a family affair, with Captain Stu Archbold flying the 707 that took his son Jim to war as a digger. On several occasions during his twelve-month tour in Vietnam, Jim managed to make it to Tan Son Nhut to greet his father as his 707 arrived with a planeload of fresh troops. Jim also believes his father, himself a decorated World War II fighter pilot, was the only captain to be photographed posing in front of his 707 proudly holding a combat rifle (borrowed from Jim).

Crews operating the charters weren't the only ones to get a close-up view of the Vietnam War. What is not often acknowledged is the fact that the normal international air corridor between Hong Kong and Europe took the regular scheduled Qantas 707s over Vietnam. Approaching Da Nang after take-off from Hong Kong they would descend to around 26,000 feet as they crossed Vietnam towards a checkpoint near Bangkok.

During the crossing they would often catch sight of the giant US air force B-52 bombers coming in above them to bomb Vietnam from around 30,000 feet.

'There would be big gaggles of them above you as they flew on to where their navigation co-ordinates told them to let their bombs go,' says Peter Raven.

Since the flights out of Hong Kong were at night, crews would occasionally see patches of flickering light on the ground below as the Special Forces fired constant flares to protect their camps from attack. 'Somehow it seemed strange to be sitting up there with a cup of tea in hand whilst there was a full scale war taking place just a few thousand feet below,' Gordon Power reflects.

**

No account of the Qantas involvement in Vietnam should be written without reference to the uplift of war orphans out of Bangkok by a 707 under the command of Captain Alan Bones.

It was mid-1975, the war had been lost and South Vietnam was in the throes of being overrun by North Vietnam forces. Bones, at the time a relatively junior captain, was told his QF180 from Bangkok to Melbourne was to pick up orphan children being brought in from Saigon aboard an RAAF Hercules.

When Bones's chief steward saw RAAF personnel from the Hercules carrying cardboard boxes across the tarmac towards the 707 he immediately assumed it was food, shouting to them that

QF180 had already taken on its catering supplies. Then he noticed the first box contained two babies, head to toe. The following boxes also contained very young children and by the time loading was completed Bones had 74 of them on board, plus several Australian military nurses.

Bones soon learnt that two of the children had already died on the flight from Saigon and many more had been airsick but when he requested a clearance to taxi Thai authorities refused. He would not be allowed to move until the names of all on board were listed on the paperwork. Since no one knew the infants' names, Bones thought about it for a moment then told the chief steward to start writing.

QF180 duly left with a complete list of names on its passenger list. They included a Donald Duck, a Mickey Mouse, a Sydney H Bridge and many other imaginative nom de plumes.

Approaching Australia, Bones was told that both Sydney and Melbourne were closed due to fog but with a welcoming committee of politicians and other VIPs waiting to receive the orphans at Melbourne. Bones requested a special clearance to approach through the overcast conditions.

He later admitted that it was not until he had reached the absolute lowest height he could legally descend to that he suddenly caught sight of the runway and landed safely.

All 74 children were admitted to the Fairfield Infectious Diseases hospital, some with serious illnesses. Many years later two young Vietnamese women, now married and living in Australia, came looking for 'Captain Bone' to thank him for what he had done.

By the time the last Qantas 707 rose into the air from Tan Son Nhut in February 1972 the American air traffic controllers had christened them the Red Tail Rats or the White Tail Rats, largely because they struggled to understand what a kangaroo was. By then the airline had flown more than 300 charters and carried around 30,000 troops into and out of the war zone.

Anxious to ensure that the deeds of the Qantas volunteer aircrew and ground staff would not go unrecorded, Alan Kitchen's team formed Skippy Squadron in 2000, its members also becoming eligible for the award of the Australian Active Service Medal 1945–75 with Clasp Vietnam and the Vietnam Logistics and Support Medal. They have marched under their 'Skippy' banner on every Anzac Day since 2003. 'It's our way of recognising an airline which paid a high price in lives during World War II and served this country so well in other wars,' Kitchen says. We didn't lose any in Vietnam but lives were lost in World War II.

6
CYCLONE TRACY

The cyclone warnings had begun a few days before Christmas 1974 but, like most of Darwin, the Qantas manager for the Northern Territory, Ian Burns-Woods, took little notice of them. Anyway, he had memorised such tips as opening and closing windows to equalise air pressure, filling the bath with emergency water and retreating to the bathroom for safety. Although there'd been a similar alert several weeks before, nothing had come of it.

Burns-Woods may have been in Darwin only nine months but his Christmas cheer commitments were heavy as he began his rounds visiting the airline's numerous travel clients and industry contacts and joining in the festivities. Around midday on Christmas Eve, as Burns-Woods set off to buy his wife Gabrielle a pearl necklace as a Christmas present, a message came through from Qantas head office that all international operations were being diverted away from Darwin due to cyclonic activity within the region. Burns-Woods still wasn't concerned. It was a normal precaution in the airline business.

By later in the afternoon, Burns-Woods received word that the airport had been closed to all commercial traffic and that some airline operators like Connellan Airlines were taking the additional precaution of flying their aircraft south to Katherine, just in case. Then word came from Darwin's weather station that the cyclone had in fact altered course away from Darwin and he feared the monotonous warnings over the radio might turn into another cyclone 'fizzer.'

By then Burns-Woods was enjoying a few drinks at the office of Darwin's largest travel agency, oblivious to the wind build-up and the dark threatening clouds that had developed outside. Then his wife phoned. Gabrielle, two months pregnant, had just received a call from the local naval chief, Eric Johnston, that his own people were telling him the cyclone had changed course again and was now heading directly for Darwin. Burns-Woods decided it was time to head home.

Once there Burns-Woods called Johnston for any latest news. Johnston reconfirmed his earlier report and suggested they join him at Naval Headquarters, a solid brick building on Darwin's waterfront. Burns-Woods declined, believing they would be safe where they were. After all their two-storey, architect-designed home was constructed mainly of brick and glass from the ground up, unlike most Darwin residences built as single storey fibro dwellings mounted on brick pillars.

Burns-Woods spent the following few hours confirming that all passengers had been advised and rebooked on later flights and checking in with his airport manager, Peter Snelling. Snelling had already told Peter Auld, on duty at Darwin airport, to close down and head for home.

Then the phone went dead and the Burns-Woodses decided to

take their two cats and the dog upstairs and to try to get some rest as Christmas Eve now had all the portents of a long night.

But soon any rest was out of the question. By 11 p.m. the wind was howling, rain was pouring through the rattling louvred windows, the floor was vibrating and the walls were shaking. With Gabrielle carrying one of the cats, two pillows and, fortuitously, a bottle of cognac, and Burns-Wood the dog and a torch, they headed for the bathroom, just as the lights went out. While Gabrielle huddled in the shower recess trying to calm the animals, Burns-Woods went back for the second cat and was in the passageway heading towards the bedroom when there was a violent shudder and a blast of air as the brick wall of the bedroom blew out and the bed and side tables went out with it.

Back in the bathroom they huddled together, sustained on occasions by the contents of the cognac bottle via a glass Gabrielle had found in the bathroom closet.

Before long there was a violent wrench and a grinding sound as the roof was torn off and, as the house disintegrated around them, part of the bathroom ceiling crashed into the bath alongside them. Placing the pillows on their heads as protection from falling debris they jammed their feet against the bathroom door as the storm now ripped through what remained of the house. Ears blocked from the wind noise and air pressure, they had to shout to each other to be heard, although words were hardly needed when Burns-Woods realised he still had Gabrielle's Christmas present in his pocket. She opened the soggy envelope and placed the pearl necklace around her neck as the cyclone raged on.

Hours went by and then suddenly there was silence, as if the huge wind machine had been turned off. Stepping gingerly through bits of timber and plaster they made their way downstairs to the still-intact laundry and decided to spend the rest of the night there. On their way they could hear the plaintive cries of the missing cat coming from somewhere inside the debris.

Morning revealed an almost unbelievable sight. Looking out through the opening left by the missing wall, Burns-Woods wondered out loud how anyone could have survived the night's events. Houses were shattered as far as the eye could see, steel stanchions twisted and bent, roofing iron, fibro and house contents blocking streets.

A shout from a neighbour told them it was over and the cyclone had moved further inland.

'Who told you that?' asked Burns-Woods.

'My dad,' the neighbour replied.

'I believe you,' said Burns-Woods. 'Merry Christmas.'

Peter Snelling and wife Rosalie had also been partly lulled into the belief that Tracy would pass Darwin by. When the wind began to increase, Snelling at least tied the Christmas tree firmly into the corner of their lounge-room wall. The next morning, the tree and the wall had both gone.

Crouched under the kitchen table, the Snellings sat out the howling winds and shattering glass as their house blew to pieces around them.

Snelling recalls a smell of alcohol everywhere after the liquor cabinet collapsed and bottles emptied onto the floor. At one stage the children wanted to go to the toilet but Snelling told them: 'Just go where you are.'

Quiet came briefly with the cyclone's 'eye', then it was back to howling wind and more flying debris until morning when they saw for the first time the extent of the damage. 'But we were alive and the first thing we did was check on the neighbours.'

Snelling had around a dozen bottles of Qantas port as give-aways. 'Every neighbour got one and I can attest they didn't touch the sides!' he remembers.

The only casualty appeared to be their cat which went missing. But it survived and returned several days later.

Snelling linked up with Burns-Woods and the pair went off to check on as many of Qantas's 112 staff as they could locate with the aim of getting together at Darwin's Travelodge, which had weathered the storm—although with five cars in its swimming pool. But now, along with feelings of great relief, Burns-Woods found himself experiencing pangs of helplessness, inadequacy and even hopelessness. 'After all, who would expect such violence and intensity from Mother Nature to occur on Christmas Day, the time for peace on earth and goodwill toward men?'

Meanwhile, unknown to Burns-Woods and Snelling at the time, were a small group of Qantas employees who were not listed on Darwin staff numbers. They were cabin crew transiting the city when Tracy hit. Robert Lindsay and his crew had arrived on 23 December and were scheduled to operate a service to Singapore on Boxing Day. New to the job, it would be Lindsay's second-only flight as cabin crew, on a schedule known as the 'milk run' from Sydney to Darwin via Brisbane, and a two-day stopover to wait for their onward flight to Singapore.

Booked into rooms on the fourth floor of the Territorial Hotel, Lindsay and his team noted a decline in weather conditions but didn't think too much of it. Anyway, someone had mentioned there'd been an earlier alert but nothing had happened. As usual, before turning in for the night they called reception to make sure their early morning calls had been logged for the next day.

'The weather then got gradually worse and it became a horrendous night. I don't think anyone can really describe that noise. Then a window blew out and things were actually sucked out of my room.' Risking a glance out the window Lindsay saw the roof blow off a bus shelter on the street below and crash into a transformer, sending sparks into the night. He locked himself in the bathroom.

'Finally the hotel people gathered all the crew together and took us down into the basement, steering clear of the lobby as the glass frontage was blown in and the front awning had crashed down.'

For Burns-Woods and Snelling, Christmas Day was occupied with gathering staff, assessing what they needed and trying to collect thoughts, at the same time wondering whether the rest of the world realised what had happened. In the middle of it all, Eric Johnston arrived to break the news that the naval headquarters he had offered as a sanctuary the night before had been evacuated as it began to collapse.

Early next morning Burns-Woods's concerns as to whether the rest of the world knew of their plight were answered in an emotional moment as he and some of his staff prepared to leave the Travelodge again for the airport. Suddenly, over the top of the Travelodge, loomed the underbelly of a Boeing 707. As it circled around low in the sky above them the red tail with the flying kangaroo came into view. 'Some of us had tears in our eyes and the thrill of that moment remains with me today. We waved and cheered before jumping into the cars to drive as quickly as possible to the airport to meet it, hoping to hell it would be able to land.'

The man at the controls of that Boeing just below the clouds, Captain John Brooks, was also hoping he would be able to land and his first sight of what was left of Darwin that morning hadn't filled him with confidence. Boxing Day was already turning into a long day for Brooks, who had been called out by Qantas Operations and was on his way to the airport shortly after 3 a.m. for a pre-flight briefing. Not that there was much information to be briefed about, merely that little had been heard from Darwin and his instructions were to make his own assessment, land if he could and, if not, he had enough fuel on board to return to Sydney.

Other Qantas people were gathering at Mascot, among them a medical team comprising two doctors, Harvey Dakin and Tommy Thompson, a nursing sister, six engineers and staff from personnel, line maintenance, general services and the airline's traffic department. On the suggestion of the airline's director of engineering and maintenance Ron Yates, Brooks's Boeing would be one of only six in the company fitted with a single side-band (SSB) radio. It would subsequently prove invaluable in allowing direct contact between Darwin and Sydney to assess what was urgently needed. Also aboard were 8 tonnes of food, including baby food, drinks, ice and several thousand blankets.

The Boeing was ready to leave by 4.30 a.m. but then bureaucracy intervened, and getting his aircraft airborne became a frustrating experience for Brooks, his first officer Bryan Griffin and flight engineer Norm King. Even after explaining it was an emergency flight with a medical team and emergency supplies on board, Mascot air traffic control refused an engine start-up on the grounds they were still inside the curfew period between 11 p.m. and 6 a.m., forcing an exasperated Brooks to suggest they call the Minister for Transport and request a clearance. When told the minister would be asleep, Brooks suggested curtly: 'Well, wake him up.'

But, despite other efforts by Qantas operations, it was to no avail. Brooks and his crew sat cooling their heels until just before 6 a.m. when their start-up clearance came over the radio.

Brooks says he will never forget the descent towards Darwin that Boxing Day morning, with no radio communication, no air traffic control and no idea what was ahead of him: 'We were at about 30,000 feet [9000 m] when we started the descent and even though it was daylight, without any communications it was as if we were on the dark side of the moon.'

At his briefing Brooks had been told there 'might have been a problem with the cyclone' but it was all pretty much guesswork—until he broke out of the cloud at around 8200 feet. 'My first thought was: "Christ, it looks like it's been hit by a nuclear device" as it was just flattened. Surely a cyclone couldn't have done that?'

Brooks took the Boeing out over the sea to lose altitude then flew over the town to have a closer look and it was at this point Burns-Woods and people spotted him. A false run low across the airport convinced Brooks the runway surface was clear so he climbed the Boeing back into the circuit and did a normal landing. Later, on the ground, Norm King discovered the runway had been littered with roofing nails. 'How they didn't pierce one of the tyres I'll never know,' he confessed years later.

Once on the ground, Brooks found the airport deserted and without radio had no idea where to park the Boeing so he merely headed for a cleared section of the tarmac. Neither was there any ground power, which meant he would have the leave the number four engine running to provide power for the Boeing on the ground and to use it to start the other engines in the event they had to leave again. Later they would locate a ground power unit among the airport debris and were able to shut down the engine, but not before Brooks's start-up dilemma resulted in a clash of wills between Burns-Woods and the man in charge of Darwin's disaster relief, Major General Alan Stretton.

While Brooks's Boeing and its SSB radio maintained a contact point with Qantas's Sydney head office, Burns-Woods raced back to town to announce the aircraft's availability at a disaster meeting called by Stretton, but by the time he entered the room the meeting was in the middle of a discussion on re-erecting the town's power lines. Realising time was critical with the engine still running on the 707 Burns-Woods put his hand up at the back of the room and started to explain there was an aircraft that could take anyone who was seriously ill out of Darwin.

Appearing miffed at the interruption, Stretton responded: 'When I'm ready to hear from Qantas I will let you know.'

Undeterred Burns-Woods waited a few more minutes then stood up again: 'I don't want to be rude but the aircraft is currently idling on one engine because we have no serviceable ground-start equipment and as it cannot be refuelled it will have to leave very soon.'

Once again Stretton shut him down, suggesting what was of interest to Qantas was not his concern. By now Burns-Woods, realising he was getting nowhere, bluntly announced that unless some action was taken the aircraft would have to leave with no one on it.

That appeared to get Stretton's attention: the meeting was adjourned and the Northern Territory medical service people began to nominate patients for evacuation. The two Qantas doctors would remain to assist.

Doctors Dakin and Thompson soon found themselves attending to the injured at Casuarina High School, where thousands of refugees from Darwin's northern suburbs had been sheltering since the cyclone. Despite the fact that they had been there for 24 hours without power, running water or toilets, Tommy Thompson was impressed by the 'morale and orderliness' that prevailed.

'Maybe it was the relief at survival that produced a good-humoured acceptance of the conditions. As one medical worker told me: "paradise was a corner to sleep in and a roof over your head."' Thompson later recalled how ingenuity fixed the toilet problem: the backs were ripped off several filing cabinets and they were stretched across a trench.

While the two doctors treated the injured, Salvation Army and Red Cross men and women moved through families, keeping them fed, watered and as comfortable as possible. As the days wore on, Thompson would reveal a disappointment to which only a doctor could confess—there were no babies to deliver! 'They are coming here with babies only a few hours old or just about to have them, but I've been out of luck,' he explained to a Qantas colleague at the time. 'The number we had, however, would make me think the whole of Darwin had been pregnant.'

Extraordinary too there were no births on any of the subsequent flights out.

While the two doctors had been threading their way through debris-strewn streets on their way into town to offer what medical assistance was needed, the Boeing was unloaded. Norm King noted that the most popular items on board were the 50 cans of WD40 for starting saturated equipment and cartons of Benson & Hedges cigarettes. 'I've never seen so many men lighting so many cigarettes all at once,' recalled King.

Meanwhile, Snelling and other Qantas staff began arranging for the most urgent cases to gather at the airport until finally, with 266 on board, more than double the normal seating for his Boeing—including Robert Lindsay and his cabin crew, who had been helping the loading—Brooks took off for Sydney.

'People in seats had children lying across them, people were on the floor in the aisles, cabin crew were sitting on the floor in the galley. I sat on the knee of one of the nurses on the flight deck during the take-off,' Lindsay says.

As for Brooks: 'I confess I didn't want to know what it was like in the cabin as I thought the civil aviation people might come down on me for what I did.'

Brooks's flight marked the start of the Qantas involvement in the largest airlift in Australia's history, when airlines, the RAAF and other aviation units evacuated more than 20,000 people out of the shattered city.

For those handling the situation on the ground, it was a case of making do with what you had or could scrounge. More ingenuity came to the fore when it came to providing departing refugees with food without the availability of power. Snelling and his staff gathered all the barramundi from the airline's shattered catering centre, turned two large filing cabinets on their back, strung a sheet of arc mesh between them and lit a fire underneath. Every passenger was issued with a freshly cooked barramundi fillet once on board.

Over the coming days Qantas alone lifted 5000 evacuees. One Boeing 747 carried 673 people, a world record. In-bound 707s and 747s from Sydney flew in relief teams and 63 tonnes of emergency supplies and equipment, including several motorbikes to help Snelling and his team navigate the piles of debris across the roads. Qantas facilities at Sydney and other centres were used as clearing houses to process evacuees, arrange accommodation or move them on to other areas free of charge on scheduled services, while providing ground handling for a succession of RAAF aircraft arriving in Sydney from Darwin.

Sixty-six people had died as Tracy flattened Darwin and, despite their personal trauma, Burns-Woods, Snelling and other local

Qantas staff, quickly supplemented by others flown in on the Qantas emergency flights, stayed the distance while the airlift continued.

Snelling has fond memories of how Qantas looked after its people afterwards. 'If they didn't want to stay in Darwin, they were offered relocation to any Qantas office in Australia.' But, like others in Darwin at the time, Snelling still harbours deep resentment over the way the Federal Police moved in, presumably to prevent looting or other misdemeanours.

The Burns-Woods and Snelling families had taken an offer of rooms in the Travelodge while they went about organising the airlift on the ground, only to be arbitrarily thrown out when Federal Police arrived. Like other decisions made at the time by Major General Alan Stretton, the man sent to Darwin to oversee the immediate aftermath, Snelling regarded it as an overreaction. 'You needed to consider people had nothing but what they stood up in and were pretty well trying to survive.'

And when Stretton announced a ban on any celebrations for New Year's Eve, concerned any such functions would get out of hand, Burns-Woods suggested they'd all worked non-stop for days under appalling conditions and ignored the order.

Still, there were occasional 'good news' stories. The only Qantas staffer injured during the cyclone, Eric Palisa, had been sent south with a dislocated shoulder and severe cuts. Eric's house had been demolished and he had had to leave without finding any trace of his blue cattle dog pup, which he assumed had died in the wreckage. Even if it had survived, orders issued by Stretton for any stray dogs to be shot on sight threatened a limited future. Several days later Burns-Woods and cabin services man Mike Field were looking at the remains of Palisa's house when they heard a whine. Out from under a collapsed wall crawled the pup, alive and well. Its only problem was a tick, removed back at the Qantas office. Two days later the pup flew out to join Eric in Melbourne.

Ironically, few in Darwin knew that only a few weeks before Tracy hit, Qantas head office had ordered Burns-Woods to close down Darwin as a Qantas base as the airline's own movements through there were minimal and its major role had been the servicing of other international airlines passing through. He had not relished the task of breaking the news to the staff.

In the end, Cyclone Tracy did it for him.

SAFETY IS NO ACCIDENT

7
TRAINING AT THE BAY OF PIGS

Motorists driving along the highway between Melbourne and Geelong in the 1960s and 1970s often would be treated to an unforgettable sight as a Qantas Boeing 707 appeared at low level out of the north and began to weave erratically from side to side as it approached to land at Avalon airfield. At the last moment it would flare and briefly touch down, then the engines would roar as the throttles were opened and the Boeing would once again climb away to the south towards Corio Bay, to return a few minutes later to repeat the performance. For those who stopped along the roadside to watch, it was an impromptu air show, made all the more spectacular because it was all done at low level and the whole flight pattern was within eyesight of those on the ground.

Avalon has a special meaning for many former Qantas aircrew and, when mention is made of it, several things immediately spring to mind. The first is the role it played in establishing Qantas's much-admired safety record; the second is the belief that the Boeing 707, perhaps more so than any other aircraft, is the one most identified as forging the Qantas we know today. The 707 not only transitioned the airline into the jet age, but was also the representative of an era of tough, professional airmen who were passing on their hard-won skills, both at training sessions and while flying the line, to the flight crews of the future.

But Avalon was hardly a home away from home for those whose very flying future depended on how they got through their training there. It was more like a battle of survival. While those spectators standing below them on the roadside enjoyed the nonstop spectacle, several of those in the cockpit might be looking at their very future as a Qantas pilot.

Basically, Avalon was there because hands-on flying training on a big jet was all there was. The sophisticated simulators at the Qantas Jet Base in Sydney, where pilots would be able to call up a computer image of any major airport in the world, were still some years away. Thus, during periods of heavy training demand, 707s would be based at Avalon for weeks at a time as second officers, first officers and captains undertook licence renewals or promotions through the various stages of their careers. Time actually spent at Avalon varied. In the case of a second officer's licence renewal, it could mean a flight down from Sydney in the morning and return the same afternoon.

In fact, a brief circuit at Avalon was often the only time a second officer had the opportunity to take off or land a 707, as his normal role was one of monitoring what was happening on the flight deck and standing in for the flight engineer while he took a break. Even then his Avalon exposure was brief, often just a quick take-off, a short time in the air, then a letdown and landing. He could be out of the seat within 30 minutes.

But the transition from second officer to first officer and into the cockpit's right-hand seat was a quantum leap and could mean a four- or five-day stint at Avalon, depending on how many were due for promotion. For first officers undergoing training for captaincy particularly, those days at Avalon were demanding, with much of the time spent flying around the circuit area specifically designed to test their ability to handle the aircraft at low level and in poor weather conditions. While flying conditions in Australia might have been relatively benign as far as weather was concerned, approaching Frankfurt or London in mid-winter was a different story altogether. The trainee's hours in the air would not end until the training captain was convinced he could handle the worst weather conditions Europe could throw at him.

It was a structured process, starting with a briefing about the characteristics of flying a swept wing jet aircraft, its handling peculiarities at low level and the performance differences between piston engines and jets. The jets, after all, were a new breed to master, particularly when it came to engines and aerodynamics. In the old Constellations, if power was needed to retain a safe airspeed, the airflow swept over the wings by the propellers provided almost instant lift as the speed increased. The jet engine, slung underneath and blasting its airflow away behind the wings, took longer to 'spool up' and increase the aircraft's speed, a critical consideration when flying at low level.

Not that this was new to all of those who were being checked at Avalon for the first time. Some had already accumulated hundreds of hours flying jets with the RAAF or the Fleet Air Arm, so for them the emphasis on the piston/jet comparison by training captains who had grown up on propeller-driven aircraft would often be received with a degree of cynicism. 'While the word "dinosaur" might spring to mind, no one was game enough to say it out loud,' recalls one former military pilot.

The briefing was followed by a walk-around ground inspection of the 707 before take-off, all designed as part of a learning curve. Once in the cockpit, however, the serious business began.

First officers undertaking command training often had another first officer as a 'crash mate', hardly the most flattering term for the colleague who was undergoing a similar test. If your 'crash mate' was the first chosen to occupy the right-hand seat alongside the training captain, you sat behind them in the 'jump' seat until your own turn came in the right-hand seat.

To suggest the cockpit might be filled with tension would be something of an understatement as these were the days when remaining a permanent second or first officer for the rest of your career was certainly a possibility. Most first officers from Avalon times will admit to a high degree of nervousness when it came to their turn at the controls, always conscious that 'big brother' captain, while limiting you to low altitude, was assessing every move you made.

As the emphasis was on approach and landing, all flying was at low level and even in clear skies if the trainee bumped above 600 feet he was likely to be met with a shout: 'Too high. Too high. We're in cloud,' all designed to force you into a situation where you had to make the right decisions in approaching to land.

Norm Field vividly remembers how his particular training captain, Ted Harding, took him through his conversion from first officer to captain. 'Coming around and turning to line up for the final approach, you put the flaps out—which made the aircraft balloon—and you risked losing your aiming point on the runway because the nose would come up. Ted would hammer it home that this is what is going to happen in a bad-weather situation anyway, and you needed to handle it.'

'When it was your crash mate's turn you watched closely and if he made any mistakes you learned from him and vice versa. (As it happened Field's 'crash mate' did experience some difficulty countering the ballooning effect, with Field hoping he wouldn't have a similar problem handling it.)

'You might be several hours in the air, with a requirement to do twenty cross-wind landings, exchanging seats with your crash mate when it was your turn, after which came the on-ground debrief, which could be another harrowing experience,' says Field.

One training captain, Eric Robinson, had a booming voice and Field remembers waiting outside the room listening to Robinson debriefing one of his crash mates: 'As long as your arse points to the ground you'll never make it,' came the voice from behind the door, probably largely designed to shock the unfortunate trainee into performing better.

'I wondered if I would cop it next,' recalls Field.

While acknowledging it was tough, Field acknowledges the Qantas training was excellent, although there are those who will admit Avalon had its 'dark' side, which perhaps had more to do with the personalities of some of the training captains than the nature of the training. Avalon, in fact, would become known among Qantas aircrew as the Bay of Pigs, something of a play on both the adjacent Corio Bay and a small group of its training personnel who appeared to go out of their way to make life difficult for the newcomers, sometimes for not quite the right reasons.

What needs to be remembered here is that the senior pilot ranks of the Qantas of the 1960s and early 1970s were dominated to a large extent by former World War II airmen, many of them highly decorated.

The majority of these men flew the line on the airline's international route, were excellent mentors to their first and second officers and were only too happy to pass on their vast experience. This was also true of some of the check and training captains, but like any such community, there were the exceptions who stood on ceremony to the point of pomposity, were prone to place a high value on their status, took themselves very seriously and tended to treat their cockpit comrades as somewhat lower forms of life. The good ones, of course, went out of their way to assist and instil confidence; others went out of their way to make life miserable for those 'brought before them'.

Trevor Merton claims every Qantas pilot who had the misfortune to go through a promotion or training program with several of the less desirable captains would reach a point where he would wonder to himself whether it was all worth it. 'It was perfect misery. They absolutely delighted in taking you to the breaking point.' At the same time Merton admits it was legitimate to test people to a certain degree, but not beyond the degree of practicality.

Merton was not alone. Field, already an experienced captain on DC-4s, remembers arriving at Avalon for his conversion to the 707 to be met by training captain Graham Lance as they climbed aboard: 'I just want to let you know I had a tough time being checked out myself and I have never passed anyone on their first attempt.'

'Well, thanks for letting me know that at this stage, Graham,' replied Field, hardly thankful for the offering.

Gordon Power admits aviation can be a cruel profession and a pilot needed to have superb confidence in his ability if he was to survive. 'A pilot's performance is constantly being judged, often harshly by others who indicate either audibly, usually loudly, or by body language that our abilities are non-existent and would be unlikely to qualify as the driver of a night cart, the latter being delivered in a language that would make a ship's stoker blush.

'I have seen several pilots, including captains, who have been psychologically destroyed by these types of verbal attacks and their careers lost.'

David Howells, an experienced former Fleet Air Arm pilot is even more scathing about the ability of several of the captains assigned to the training role: 'There were some people who should never have been senior training checks at all,' says Howells, citing incidents where an aircraft had been taken down to as low as 100 feet on a non–precision landing approach in poor visibility.

'The first time they couldn't see anything and the next time they landed halfway down the runway and came to a juddering halt against a pile of rocks at the end of it. Ten minutes later there was hardly a cloud in the sky. The Department of Civil Aviation would have had a field day.'

As in the case of Norm Field, prior experience often didn't account for much when it came to several members of a close-knit cartel of training captains. Ken Lewis, who joined the airline as cabin crew and would later become the airline's highly respected safety chief, puts it bluntly:

'If they didn't like the "cut of your jib", it often didn't matter much how well you performed,' he says. Lewis cited the case of Bunny Lee, a highly decorated World War II pilot and experienced DC-4 captain, who arrived for command training on the 707. Lee qualified at his first attempt but, not one to mince words, took the opportunity over a beer that evening to tell them what he thought of their methodology. 'The next day he was given another check ride and referred back to the DC-4. It was several years later before he made it onto the 707.'

Perhaps a comment by Trevor Merton goes some way to explaining life as it existed in the hierarchy of Qantas cockpits in those days: 'You could tell a joke as a second officer and no one would laugh. Same joke as a first officer—a polite titter of laughter. Same joke as a senior check captain and everyone roared laughing.'

Airmen being airmen, Merton wasn't the only one who could see the funny side. Old pilots remember New Zealand-born Roly Probert, who at one stage controlled the training program, having a tendency to take himself extremely seriously, often to the point of pomposity. Gordon Power recalls flying on a Boeing 747 as a passenger with another captain and a first officer to Avalon for their final command checks, with Probert at the controls of the aircraft out of Mascot. Halfway to Avalon, Power delegated the first officer, as the most junior, to take cups of tea up to those on the flight deck. A few minutes later the first officer was back, still with one cup of tea, which turned out to be that originally destined for Probert who had apparently declined the offer with words to the effect: 'I'm flying.'

When quizzed why he hadn't left Probert's cup of tea there anyway, the first officer replied: 'Would you interrupt Rembrandt when he was creating a masterpiece?'

Such character traits aside, the lessons learnt in training would become part of a culture that had existed in Qantas from its earliest days. Those early check captains would be responsible for transitioning the airline into a jet era during which Qantas would create an impeccable record for safety in the air, an era where it would be fatality-free, where new challenges and hazards would be overcome.

The attrition rate for pilots might have been high, but so were the consequences of landing short in a loaded Boeing 707 buffeted by violent cross-winds.

David Shrubb, who would later follow them as a training manager, is convinced pilots like Eric Robinson, Roly Probert, Alan Emmerick, Len McNeil and Dick Lucas, names the public have never heard of, were the main reason Qantas did not have a serious undershoot accident like most of the 'great airlines' did in those transitional days.

Many would suggest also it was through engineering and maintenance, areas that are vital if an airline is going to be not only safe, but also to maintain an operational culture the envy of many other world airlines. In Qantas's case, it was a culture that dated from its very earliest days.

8
'QANTAS NEVER CRASHES'

It's a pivotal, four-minute scene in the Academy Award–winning movie *Rain Man*, starring Dustin Hoffman and Tom Cruise.

Hoffman, playing the role of Raymond Babbitt, an autistic savant, panics when Cruise, playing his brother Charlie, tries to get him to board a flight from Cincinnati to Los Angeles. Raymond has memorised every airline crash statistic and refuses to board several airlines suggested by Charlie, insisting: 'Qantas never crashes.'

Faced with the dilemma that Qantas doesn't fly from Cincinnati to Los Angeles, the characters are forced to drive. Although Hoffman's statement is only true to a point, it further cements the Australian airline's reputation for safety and demonstrates the value to be gained publicly from an aspect of airline operations that most airlines themselves are reluctant to talk about.

But the fact that Hoffman speaking those three words actually became the chosen extract to be watched by millions during the 1989 Academy Award presentation was an advertising coup any airline in the world would have paid a fortune for.

It all had the most innocent of beginnings.

American Ernie Beyl's job as public relations manager for Qantas in the United States was to do all he could to promote the airline in one of the toughest markets in the world, a world where this relatively small foreign carrier had to compete for passenger revenue with some of the largest airlines of the world. There could be no comparison in size. Over the years the United States had thrown a succession of airlines on the US-to-Australia route, giants like Pan American, Continental and American Airlines to name a few. Achieving public recognition of the Australian minnow against such opposition in the vast US market often called for some bizarre tactics. Easy-going Beyl had even found himself on occasions squeezing his two-metre frame into, of all things, a koala suit, in an effort to make some impact at an airline promotional function. In fact, beyond the large kangaroo on the Qantas logo, the koala was one of the few images that appeared to resonate with Americans, a situation that dated back to a series of advertisements launched by the Australian carrier in the 1960s.

Groundbreaking in its negative concept, it was known as the 'I Hate Qantas' campaign and was the brainchild of the airline's regional chief for the Americas, Hugh Birch, and Qantas's advertising agency in the United States, Cunningham & Walsh. Hugh Birch was one of those colourful characters an airline colleague once described as 'straight out of central casting'. He had come to Qantas with an impressive record as a pilot in World War II, flown numerous pioneering flights in the airline's flying boat days, had the looks of Errol Flynn and the personality to match—all factors which made him instantly popular with Americans.

With the sheer marketing 'spend' of the major US airlines swamping the market to Australia, Birch and Cunningham &

Walsh turned to that other unique Australian marsupial, the koala, to supplement the Qantas kangaroo. But their chosen koala would be the grumpiest version you could find and would be prepared to go to great lengths to 'discourage' American tourists from disturbing his peace and tranquillity. And it was all Qantas's fault!

For Qantas, which had six Boeing 707 services out of San Francisco to Sydney when the campaign was launched on television and print in 1967, it was an instant success.

Here was this cuddly koala, under a quote: 'I Hate Qantas', appealing to Americans: 'I am an Australian. A very sensitive Australian. What I like is peace. And quiet. And ferny places and secret trees. Which is mostly what I've gotten up to now.' Over subsequent years he would appear wearing a mask and a snorkel, a backpack, a Hawaiian shirt with a camera clung over his shoulder and even holding an Australian Rules football, all the time complaining about what Qantas was doing to make his life miserable.

Nothing about Qantas was sacred. When the airline boasted about the fact that it now had more Boeing 747s on the route than any other airline, Teddy, as he was known, countered with: 'How about a little modesty?' Under another print advertisement showing all nineteen crew of Qantas pilots and cabin crew standing in uniform in front of their 747, he complained: 'Looks like four cops, three meter maids, a desk clerk and an eleven-piece band.' But it would be the television commercials that would steal the hearts of Americans as Teddy voiced his complaints while sitting in the cockpit, in the cabin, or staring down from the overhead luggage rack.

The original Teddy commercial starred an American-born koala from the San Diego Zoo, one of the few places outside Australia ever to breed them. Later, as the commercials had him on site at Australian beaches, the Great Barrier Reef, the Sydney Opera House and even Alice Springs, Australian koalas were used, but creating these television commercials presented significant challenges for film teams.

For a start, there's no such animal as a trained koala and although some are accustomed to being handled by humans, getting them to actually 'act' is far from easy. They found giving the chosen animal a eucalyptus leaf to chew could be enough to move his mouth to approximate speech to enable American comedian Howie Morris to voice-over the 'I Hate Qantas' line. The authenticity of an Australian accent had to be abandoned as the use of an American accent was considered to provide better clarity for Americans, who would be hearing it everywhere from Brooklyn to South Carolina.

Getting Teddy to turn and look over his shoulder with a 'disdainful stare' was achieved by rattling a bunch of keys behind him, while a trail of broken gum leaves leading to a bigger pile at the end was often enough to get him moving in a particular direction.

Although a number of koalas from San Diego would be used over the time of the commercials there was an America-wide public reaction when the original Teddy died in 1976. The final measure of success came in a letter from a Bronx, New York, schoolteacher who told how she'd been giving a lesson on animals to her class. When she held up a picture of a koala, the children broke out in unison: 'That's a Qantas.'

But, in 1987, the 'I hate Qantas campaign' was little beyond a plaque on Ernie Beyl's wall as he rifled through some paperwork in his San Francisco office one afternoon, when the phone rang.

Someone was calling from Hollywood. He was working on a film and wanted to know whether it was true Qantas had never had a crash or a fatality.

'Yes, but why do you ask?' Beyl replied. He received no answer to the question but at least managed to gouge out of the caller the name of the film's producer, Mark Johnson.

Good public relations people, particularly those who have a journalistic background, have a 'sniff antenna' that reacts when it detects there might be a background story in there somewhere. Ernie Beyl found his own antenna was starting to prompt him to take this further.

It took days to track down Mark Johnson on the telephone but it was time well spent. 'He was charming, told me about a film called *Rain Man* and said the director, Barry Levinson, was considering a scene where Dustin Hoffman, who was playing an autistic savant, says he wants to fly Qantas from the Mid-West to Los Angeles.'

'When his brother, played by Cruise asks why, Hoffman can say, "because they never crash."'

Johnson explained that both he and Levinson liked Australia and the idea of Qantas flying on such a sector had a humorous aspect to it in the script. By this time Beyl's 'antenna' was starting to flutter as he could see the value if it all worked. Tentatively, because his promotions budget was extremely limited, he asked what he might have to do to have that line put in the movie, expecting the answer might be more than he could afford in US dollars.

'Tell me all about Qantas and I'll see what I can do,' was Johnson's reply.

Within hours a screed from Beyl containing the entire Qantas history was on its way to Los Angeles. Johnson called with a quick thank you and then—silence.

It was almost a year later before Johnson called again with one of the shortest phone calls Ernie Beyl had ever received. 'Go see the movie,' he said. 'You'll like it.' He didn't say anything else.

Beyl went to see the movie and there it was.

'I was something of a hero. I called Mark Johnson and thanked him, offered him a free trip first class anywhere on the Qantas network but he politely declined, saying he was too busy. I promised the offer would remain, so maybe some day. He said maybe.

Twelve months later when Beyl heard *Rain Man* had been nominated for an Academy Award, he called Johnson again, acutely aware of the fact that, as each film being nominated in the Best Picture category was announced, a short scene was played. Could Beyl live in hope it might be the airport scene?

Johnson explained there were many factors that went into that choice—timing, emphasis, showing the actors to best advantage. And of course, Dustin Hoffman would have to approve.

Beyl and his boss, Qantas regional vice president for the Americas, George Howling, along with every other Qantas employee within reach of a television, was glued to the screen that night in 1989 and there it was—the Hoffman airport scene and the line 'Qantas never crashes', followed by four Oscars: best picture, best original screenplay, best director and Dustin Hoffman as best actor.

Perhaps understandably, it took Beyl some time to track down Johnson at the Beverly Hills Hotel next morning and, after thanking him profusely, he reminded him of the travel offer. 'In an embarrassed tone, he said it wasn't necessary and, besides, he was still too busy.' When Beyl asked what he was going to do when he took some holidays, Johnson said he would probably fly out Mid-West to visit family.

Months went by and Beyl called again. This time Johnson gave in and said he would perhaps take the family to Tahiti. Four first-class return tickets were on their way within hours.

It was a small price to pay for exposure that Qantas's San Francisco staff estimate netted the airline more than a million dollars in marketing exposure in the vast US market and one for which any US carrier would have paid a high price. As it turned out, their reaction was palpable, with the *New York Times* reporting that at least fifteen major US airlines actually cut the scene from the version being shown on their in-flight movie channels, a decision Levinson described in the *Times* article as 'ridiculous'.

'It's a key scene to the entire movie. That's why it's in there. It launches their entire odyssey across country—because they couldn't fly.'

Not that Ernie Beyl and the Qantas team cared much. They just sat back and watched the movie surge at the box office, along with Qantas's image across the world.

9
DANGEROUS SKIES

Dustin Hoffman's *Rain Man* line: 'Qantas never crashes', while achieving invaluable credibility for the airline, also presented its own challenges in separating myth from reality. Not only has Qantas had its share of accidents over its 95-year history but it has also managed to kill a few people along the way. In fact, the whole air safety issue in relation to Australia's national carrier has been plagued by a mixture of half-truths and misconceptions that have confused the issue in the minds of some.

What is fact is that, between its formation at Longreach in 1920 and 1934—its earliest days as an outback airline—crashes cost the lives of four passengers and three crew while more than 40 of its passengers and eleven crew died during the war years, either through accidents or enemy action. Between the end of the war in 1945 and 1951 thirteen passengers and eight crew died, ten in a Lancastrian that disappeared without trace over the Indian Ocean in 1946 and seven in a de Havilland Drover off Lae, New Guinea, in 1951.

What is also fact is that the airline has never 'lost' a paying passenger since the advent of the jet age with the introduction of the Boeing 707 in the late 1950s, although it's been a close run thing on several occasions. Such a record has had much to do with training and airmanship, augmented by that other essential—luck.

Although an airline's excellent safety record has obvious public relations advantages, handling such an advantage is a complex issue and one fraught with risks. While the temptation might be there to highlight those advantages, they have the capacity to change dramatically in an instant the next day, next week or in the year ahead, should your luck run out. But a continuing value is there, in the public's image of an airline with the highest engineering and operational standards, part of the consequence of which is a subtle message of safety. There is no doubt Qantas has been the beneficiary of this for decades, but just how slender the margin between life and death has been is little short of remarkable.

A Constellation crash at Mauritius is an appropriate place to start because it demonstrates the requirement for split-second decision-making in the cockpit and the exemplary performance of the crew in the minutes after the crash.

Light rain was falling outside the terminal building at Plaisance airport, Mauritius, in the late afternoon of Wednesday, 24 August 1960, as the 28 passengers sat waiting to board their Super Constellation *Southern Wave* for the next stage of their flight to Australia, twelve hours through the night to a refuelling stop at Cocos Island.

The Mauritius to Cocos sector was then the longest overwater flight without any alternative landing field on the Qantas network and *Southern Wave* was fully loaded with 25,000 litres of highly inflammable aviation fuel, including 2275 litres in each of her wingtip tanks.

The crew of twelve, under 48-year-old Captain Ted Ditton, included first officer Dennis Patrick; two second officers, Ray Miller and Graham Quinn; two flight engineers, Eric Chuter and Maurie Pickens; navigator, Len Sales; and radio operator, Doug Hocking. Hocking's role was unique, as, although radio operators had been phased out of all Qantas sectors by 1960, they were still necessary on the Mauritius–Cocos flight, which would be out of range of voice communications and require the use of Morse code.

Ushering passengers to their seats as they boarded shortly before 5 p.m. was senior flight steward Pat McGann and his cabin crew: Alan Mackie, Neville Foster and Marion Stewart-Dawson.

Maurie Pickens, who would be the operating flight engineer on the sector, was closely monitoring his instrument panel as Ditton, a 25-year flying veteran, began the sequence of starting the four Wright Cyclone engines one at a time, while McGann and his team ran through the safety drill with the 33 adults and five children down the back.

A light misting of taxi-way water could be seen flicking up behind the aircraft as Ditton turned *Southern Wave* and lined up at the end of the runway, then, with all throttles open and all four engines producing 13,000 horsepower, they were on their way.

The take-off run is when an aircraft is at its most vulnerable, when gravity, speed and the weight of the machine all enter the mix, along with the available length of runway. All need to be carefully calculated to provide the crew with two critical speed markers—known in aviation parlance as V1 and V2. This night at Mauritius V1 had been calculated at 112 knots (207 kilometres per hour) and V2 at 115 knots (213 kilometres per hour).

Cockpit procedures dictate that, while the captain's total attention is directed to flying the aircraft, the first officer monitors the speed and calls V1 when that speed is reached. If an engine failure should occur before V1, then the take-off should be aborted, but if a failure occurs after V1 it is then considered too late to stop on the remaining length of runway and the aircraft is lifted off, the engine feathered and fuel dumped to bring the aircraft's landing weight down before returning to the airfield.

Flight engineers like Pickens and Chuter were well aware of the idiosyncrasies of the Wright Cyclone engines, which sometimes performed in a peculiar manner in the tropics, with a tendency to briefly drop horsepower for a second or two then quickly snap back to normal. As the aircraft reached towards 100 knots both saw the brake pressure gauge on the No. 3 engine drop slightly although the oil, fuel and temperature gauges all appeared normal.

But when the gauge hadn't flicked back up again as the aircraft reached 110 knots, Pickens waited no longer, shouting the call no pilot ever wants to hear: 'Failure engine No. 3.'

What happened next is a classic example of how everyone can be performing perfectly but circumstances intervene.

Pickens's 'failure' call came the very instant first officer Dennis Patrick was about to call 'V1', and in the several seconds that followed Ditton, who had not heard the call 'V1,' did what he was trained to do, closed the throttles, threw the engines into reverse pitch and slammed on the brakes.

But for the 50-tonne aircraft, it was too late and *Southern Wave* overran the end of the runway, ploughed through a grass safety strip, bounced over a low embankment and, with its undercarriage collapsing, plunged nose first into a rock strewn gully and burst into flames.

As fate would have it, three Qantas representatives—Jim Cowan, a former navigation officer, and two ground engineers, Ron Barrett and Don Kennedy—had been watching the take-off from a balcony on the terminal building and heard the scream of the engines into reverse thrust as it skidded off the end of the runway. They ran to their car and headed off down the centre of the airstrip, passing the airport's fire tenders on the way. Ahead of them smoke was rising from the Super Constellation.

Senior flight steward Pat McGann, sitting beside Alan Mackie on the right-hand side of the cabin towards the front of the aircraft, knew something serious was about to happen even before the aircraft skidded off the runway.

'There was a young child sitting in a seat just a few feet from me, and as the plane swerved to the right I unbuckled my harness—telling Alan I was going to protect the child—it was purely an instinctive movement—but, as I got up, the port undercarriage collapsed and I was slammed into a map of the world on the cabin wall!' McGann recounted years later.

Within seconds of the aircraft stopping, McGann was shouting 'Evacuate! Evacuate!' at the top of his voice and struggling rearward through passengers and scattered in-cabin baggage to the galley door behind the wing on the left-hand side of the aircraft, only to find it blocked by heavy frozen-food boxes and an American passenger trying to open the door. McGann, a big man, grabbed the panicking passenger and shoved him away from the door, but as he began to clear the boxes the American was back again, shouting in terror and again trying to get to the door. McGann, now conscious of flickering flames outside the aircraft, pushed him violently back out of the galley and onto the floor, yelling to Mackie: 'Grab him, and don't let him back in. If he tries to come back in here again, hit him.'

Clearing a path through the boxes, McGann had to use all his strength to open the jammed door just as a tongue of fire leapt through the opening and over his arm. He was now faced with every cabin crew's nightmare—a fire at the exit.

McGann later confessed at that moment he felt there was little chance of survival, fully expecting the aircraft to explode and kill them all. But training and survival instinct took over and that door was their only chance to get people out alive. 'Although we were scared witless, we couldn't afford to *be* scared,' he recalled.

These were the days before elaborate escape slides on aircraft. With Marion Stewart-Dawson ushering passengers towards him, McGann stood in the doorway making sure they jumped to the ground below. Anyone who hesitated at the prospect of the 3.6 metre drop received a shove in the back. Despite the incredible chaos, fear and noise, McGann forever recalled seeing one older gentleman, when told to get out, slowly stand up, take his jacket out of the coat locker and put it on before strolling to the exit—as if he had all the time in the world.

Stewart-Dawson was now shouting at McGann to get out himself but there was no way he was going to leave yet. When she continued to protest he grabbed her by the collar and her backside and literally threw her out of the exit, only later to learn she had broken an ankle in the fall.

Once outside and making his way along the outside of the fuselage, McGann heard flight engineer Chuter shout there was a woman who had suffered a fractured leg after jumping to the ground.

'I grabbed her by the arms and Eric took her feet. She was so heavy we could hardly move her.' McGann shouted for help, Alan Mackie arrived and the three of them carried the woman up the embankment to safety.

By now ground engineers Ron Barrett and Don Kennedy had reached the aircraft and although told everyone was off, both courageously clambered aboard and made a final check, then, with the Constellation now burning and the grass around it catching fire, they made their way to safety.

Up in the cockpit at the same time a separate drama had been unfolding for Maurie Pickens. With the collapse of the Constellation's undercarriage as it plunged into the gully, Pickens could now smell the fuel that was escaping from fractured fuel lines in the wheel well. Then Ditton said: 'All out quick, we're on fire.'

But despite fire-warning lights and bells ringing everywhere across his panel, Pickens couldn't see any fire from where he sat and began to go through his normal shut-down procedure. When the light and bell went off for No. 2 engine he fired the suppression bottle for that engine and the bell stopped.

Then the bell for No. 1 engine started ringing so he fired that bottle too and the fire went out. Score two to Pickens. But when a third bell went off Pickens found he had run out of suppression bottles to use and now began to realise for the first time how serious the fire outside might be. Turning in his seat, he saw Ditton standing there. 'You better go,' he said to the captain.

'No, I'll go when you go,' replied Ditton and, as they reached the nearest open door, Pickens saw the extent of the fire for the first time.

'It was horrendous,' he recalls. 'The whole left wing was on fire with a sheet of flames rising about 50 feet [15 m] into the air.'

At the time he was just running from the aircraft, Pickens heard someone shout: 'Grab her!' He turned to see a child aged about three being held by the arms from a door. Pickens ran back, stood under the door and caught her as she dropped, then headed off again with the little girl under his arm. Once they were a safe distance away Pickens stopped and looked back, just as a fuel cap was blown off and an arc of burning fuel, 10 centimetres in diameter, lit up the right side of the aircraft.

Chuter arrived and told Pickens everyone was out of the aircraft. They stood and watched, as within minutes the only recognisable sections of the burnt-out wreck were the three signature Constellation tail fins.

A headcount revealed that all the passengers and crew had survived, although sixteen people suffered injuries, including broken legs, ankles and burns, most sustained while jumping from the aircraft onto the burning grass. The injured were treated at hospital and the following day another Constellation arrived to take the passengers on to Australia. Before leaving, they compiled a telex to Qantas general manager C.O. Turner, expressing their gratitude for the 'prompt and efficient emergency actions of the crew'.

The same aircraft also brought in Qantas and Australian Department of Civil Aviation investigators to interview crew members on the spot, although most of them didn't mind the wait.

'We were treated like royalty by the locals,' says Pickens, who tells of offers of luncheons, golf days, water skiing, tours of Port Louis and a day on a plantation as the guest of its owner.

Fortunately, the fire-fighters had managed to douse the flames on the No. 3 engine before they ran out of foam and the investigation began in earnest, concentrating on those critical seconds on the flight deck when the engine failure had been identified. Several months later the Qantas Air Safety committee handed down its report, which found that no blame could be attached to any member of the operating crew.

Maurie Pickens continued to serve on Constellations until Qantas phased out the aircraft in 1963 and Pat McGann went on into the Boeing 747 era as a flight service director and become one of the company's best-known and highly regarded members of its cabin crew.

IT'S ALL IN A NAME—OR IS IT?

Research into such events even many years later often reveals interesting sidelights. In the case of the Mauritius Constellation, it relates to the earlier war service of first officer Dennis Patrick. When war broke out, his initial application to join the RAAF in 1942 was rejected because he didn't have his Intermediate certificate for completing Year 9. So, borrowing his father Rupert's Intermediate certificate, he waited a short time and reapplied under his father's name, using his Intermediate certificate instead. Rupert Patrick himself served on ground staff with the RAAF while son Dennis flew with Bomber Command in Europe until the end of the war. RAAF bureaucracy never tumbled to the fact that they both had the same birth date: 16 April 1916. In fact, RAAF records still show two Rupert Bert Patricks, one finally discharged as a flight lieutenant and the other as a leading aircraftsman at the end of the war. Sadly, Dennis was struck down by a viral infection to his liver and died within twelve months of the Mauritius accident.

Some media reports suggested at the time that with no lives lost, 24 August 1960 was a 'lucky day' for Qantas, but it's a moot point. Certainly luck played its part, but rather it was the training and professionalism of Pat McGann and his crew that saved the day and resulted in only burns and a few broken bones.

The Lockheed Constellation's twitchy engine performance called for intense monitoring, although former flight engineers like Jeff Donaldson will tell you not all the risks were in the air. According to Donaldson, crews operating out of Cairo in those days not only faced the problem of poor engine performance in hot weather conditions on take-off, but the risk of colliding with a train as well.

As the aircraft gathered speed down the runway, the crew would have to briefly open the cowling flaps slightly to cool the engine, with the result that the extra drag would cause the speed to drop off. The flaps were then shut again to ensure lift-off speed was achieved and, as Donaldson puts it, 'the fully loaded Connie would stagger into the air with the help of the curvature of the earth.'

'They had to check to make sure there wasn't a train going past the end of the runway when they took off so they used to have a train timetable to make sure that wasn't the case.'

***

Whether you were in a Constellation or a jet, flying through foreign skies meant other dangers lurked, not only problems with aircraft performance but also the varying degrees of competence when it came to such areas as air traffic control. They delivered some frightening moments.

John Fulton's Constellation had been directed into a holding pattern at 10,000 feet while waiting to land at Rome when they burst out of the clouds to see a US military Convair flash over the top of them.

'He had seen us, we didn't see him.'

Obviously experiencing as big a fright as the Qantas crew, Fulton heard the Convair pilot query air traffic control: 'You have any traffic at 10,000 [feet]?'

'No, no extra traffic,' was the reply from the ground. At which point Fulton grabbed his own mike to remind the controller he'd told them to 'hold' at that altitude.

'That was the end of the conversation and we had to get ourselves down to land by talking to other traffic. We put in a report but never heard another word about it. Not that we expected anything, as to anyone in Rome or the Middle East it was just another piece of paper.'

In 1963 Norm Field was in a Boeing 707 over France en route from Cairo to London with Captain Ron Ballard when Ballard's quick reaction saved the aircraft. Over Abbeville in France the French air traffic controller suddenly came on the air: 'Qantas descend immediately 1000 feet.'

'Ron disconnected the autopilot, down we went and an Air France Caravelle charged past so close we could see the passengers looking out windows.

After the shouting stopped, Ballard turned to Field, sitting in the right-hand seat: 'You have my permission to swear at that ATC bastard.'

Alan Terrell remembers climbing out of Beirut for Rome early one morning: 'I was going through 32,000 feet when this bloody great Air Canada DC-8 appeared, cruising the other way at 35,000 feet. I know it was Air Canada as I could see the writing on the side!'

Terrell immediately reported the incident to air traffic control but heard no more. 'Some idiot had made a mistake and he wasn't going to tell us about it.'

Such 'near misses' have remained a constant threat through 707s and into the jumbo era as civil air corridors have juggled with military zones and even war zones. In fact, what might appear on the map to be a straightforward route between, say, London and the Middle East, can involve zigzagging around the military airspace of sovereign countries, some of them neighbours who don't like each other much.

Qantas Captain Fred Phillips's 747 hit the headlines back in 1977 in a near miss with a batch of German air force fighter jets while flying out of Frankfurt for Bahrain. Tangling with German fighters was hardly a new experience for Phillips, one of the airline's most respected captains. As a master bomber with the RAF's Pathfinder Force, Phillips completed 64 missions over Europe, ending the war with a DFC and Bar, and the French Croix de Guerre.

Phillip's Boeing had reached 30,000 feet when air traffic control warned that a group of unidentified aircraft, believed to be military, had strayed out of their airspace and were approaching him head on. With the air traffic controller unable to communicate with the fighters, Phillips suffered anxious minutes as the controller gave him several more alerts that the aircraft were still closing on him, but there was nothing Phillips could do until he could see where they were coming from.

Suddenly, out of a clear, moonless night, Phillips saw three flashes go by, very close in the opposite direction. Recounting the experience in 2015 Phillips added: 'All I could do was hang on and hope they'd miss.'

Phillips reported the near miss to Ground Control immediately. The incident made headlines in Australia the following day. Sydney's *Daily Mirror*, in its renowned style, under a banner headline 'Jumbo Buzzed', had Phillips wrenching at the controls and diving his aircraft 10,000 feet to avoid a collision!

Other press reports quoted air traffic control admitting they couldn't do much as they had no way of knowing what the fighters would do. They estimated that the nearest of the fighters passed within 700 metres of the Boeing, not a great margin at closing speeds around 1600 kilometres per hour.

The incident prompted European aviation authorities to express concern at the number of near misses in Europe's crowded skies, although nothing much was heard from the military until some weeks later Phillips received a letter from the general in charge of the German Luftwaffe explaining 'such risks were the price we have to pay for peace keeping in the Cold War.'

Fred Phillips was less than impressed. 'That didn't cut much ice with me, but at least it was my last brush with the Luftwaffe,' he says with a smile.

But it wasn't to be his last brush with his former allies, however.

In November 2014, at a ceremony at Sydney's Hyde Park war memorial, the French government awarded Fred Phillips, now 91, with the Legion of Honour.

**

But while any near miss is serious, the near mid-air collision of a Qantas Boeing 747 and a huge US Air Force C-5A transport over Thailand in 1990 can cause experienced former Qantas captains to take a deep breath when they think about it.

For Captain Geoff Westwood, in command of Qantas flight 10 from London to Singapore on 13 September 1990, it had been an uneventful trip. It was now dark, just after 7 p.m., and his Boeing was approaching Phuket in Thailand. Soon Westwood and his crew would begin their gradual descent into Singapore.

For business-class passenger Cris George, one of the 360 people on board, the last two hours of the flight had been something special. Commander of the air wing at Nowra Naval Air Station, south of Sydney, he was returning from talks in London prompted by growing concerns in the Middle East. Earlier that month Saddam Hussein's forces had invaded Kuwait; France and the UK were announcing troop deployment to Saudi Arabia. All the signs were there that the United States was gearing up for war.

Although the previous days had seen George's involvement in these critical international concerns, George was now thinking how he might be able to talk his way up front to get a firsthand look at the cockpit layout of Boeing's latest -400 version. 'Being an aviator myself I was always so impressed with Qantas, the height of professionalism,' he says.

Though unknown to George at the time, Westwood himself had family roots in Nowra and, noticing George's name and military attachment, sent a flight attendant to ask him if he'd like to come up for a look. 'Would I ever. Clear a path,' was George's excited reply.

George was still there when the flight attendant came back and told him meals were being served and he had just sat down to eat when a violent vibration ran through the aircraft.

'A short time later the first officer came out the cockpit door and his face was ashen,' George says.

He had reason to be.

The Qantas Boeing was cruising in scattered cloud at 37,000 feet when suddenly, heading north and filling the cockpit

Passengers and cargo are transferred between a motor launch and a Qantas Catalina flying boat. Not an unusual sight in Papua New Guinea in the 1950s where Catalinas were used to service remote areas without airstrips. Photo: Charles Wade

Qantas captain Mal Shannon (left) and Gordon Power standing under the wing of their DC-3 in Papua New Guinea in 1958. Power described Shannon as one of the best 'bush pilots' he had ever flown with because of his uncanny ability to handle Papua New Guinea's weather and dangerous terrain. Photo: Gordon Power

A typical flying scene in Papua New Guinea in the 1950s as a Qantas DC-3 slips through the Bena Gap before it is closed completely by gathering clouds. On seeing this photograph one old Qantas pilot was heard to mutter: 'I think I can recognise some of those trees.' Photo: Qantas

Romney Marsh sheep are jammed into a single engine Qantas de Havilland Beaver in 1955 for a flight from Lae, New Guinea into a patrol post at Menyamya, 95 miles away. With few roads throughout Papua New Guinea all such cargos went by air. Photo: Qantas

An aircraft interior familiar to anyone who flew in the Qantas DC-3s in Papua New Guinea in the fifties. The ex-wartime DC-3s boasted what were known as 'hard arse' seats along the inside of the fuselage. Note also the lack of interior cabin lining. Photo: origin unknown

The converted Lancastrian became known as 'Yates' Pregnant Pup' after Qantas engineer Ron Yates. He designed the original bomb bay hinged faring to enable the aircraft to carry spare engines up the Kangaroo Route to replace the frequent engine failures experienced by Lockheed Constellations in the late 1940s. Unfortunately the addition of the faring created dangerous instability in the Lancastrian and was soon abandoned. Photo: Qantas

This photo, taken by an engineer inside Boeing test pilot Tex Johnston's prototype Boeing 707, shows the aircraft in the middle of a barrel roll over Seattle's Puget Sound in 1954. Johnston's unscripted aerobatics, performed in front of a gathering of airline chiefs, horrified his boss, Boeing Chairman Bill Allen. Photo: source unknown

The Qantas Royal Flight crew parting with Queen Elizabeth, the Queen Mother at Malta in 1958 after the oft-delayed journey home to England from Australia in 1958. The aircraft captain Fred Phillips stands on the right behind the Queen Mother.
Photo: Elyse Phillips

One of the most recognisable Qantas captains of the post World War II era, R.F. 'Torchy' Uren OBE. DFC. While serving with the RAAF's No 30 Beaufighter squadron on Papua New Guinea, Uren featured prominently in cinematographer Damien Parer's footage of the squadron's low level attacks on a Japanese convoy during the Battle of the Bismarck Sea in 1942. Parer filmed the action from behind Uren in the cockpit. Photo: Qantas

An unusually formal photograph of Captain Ross Biddulph, one of the characters of the Qantas post war era, renowned for his antics in the air and his imaginative practical jokes on the crews of other airlines.
Photo: Norm Field

A Qantas Constellation on the tarmac at Iwakuni, Japan, during the Korean war.
Photo: Argus Newspaper Collection of Photographs, State Library of Victoria

As seen through Qantas captain Norm Field's 707 cockpit window, the flight line at Saigon's wartime Tan Son Nhut airport in December 1970 with its array of military helicopters, C-54 transports and a Douglas Skyraider ground attack aircraft.
Photo: Norm Field

A great character of Qantas's 707 days, Captain Stu Archbold poses with son Jim's assault rifle during one of Stu's flights into Saigon airport. Jim, second from left, would occasionally arrange to meet his father's charter flights while serving in South Vietnam. Photo: Jim Archbold

Captain John Simler (left) whose DC-3 crashed at Wau during Qantas's New Guinea years. This photograph was taken in the 1960s after Simler had transferred to flying TAA Catalinas in Papua New Guinea and captained the last Catalina flight to Samaria, an island community on the remote south-east of the country. Photo: Author's own

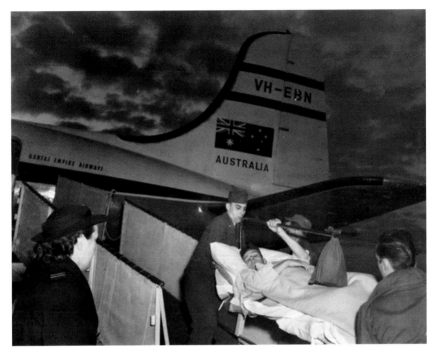

An unidentified casualty from the Korean War is being loaded onto Qantas Empire Airways aircraft for evacuation back to Australia. Photo: Phillip Hobson, Australian War Memorial

The burnt out remains of the Qantas Constellation after the aircraft crashed on take off from Mauritius in 1960. Prompt action by the Qantas crew saved the lives of the twenty-eight passengers on board. Photo: Qantas

The Qantas bag, one of the iconic symbols of the Qantas Boeing 707 era, being offered as a promotional prize at a function in the USA in the 1960s. Photo: Qantas

Qantas DC-4 Pacific Trader after suffering a nose wheel collapse during an emergency landing at Port Moresby in February 1969. The sixty passengers on board, mostly school children, escaped injury. Photo: Barry Flood

Qantas Manager (Darwin) Ian Burns-Woods and wife Gabrielle alongside a car which ended up outside the Qantas office during the cyclone, killing its occupant. Gabrielle is wearing a bandage after suffering cuts to her leg during the cyclone. Photo: Qantas

The famous 'I hate Qantas' advertising campaign in America in the 1960s featured the 'disgruntled' koala complaining that the Australian airline was interfering with his peace and tranquillity. It was a runaway success in the United States and it gave Qantas a high profile against the major US airlines. Photo: Qantas

Young evacuees get some Qantas service during the Darwin uplift after Cyclone Tracy. One Qantas Boeing 747 carried 673 people, a world record at the time. Photo: Qantas

An impressive Chinese welcome awaits as the Qantas Boeing 707 touches down at Beijing for the historic visit of Prime Minister Gough Whitlam in October 1973.
Photo: Rolf Gschwind

One of Qantas's most respected captains Alan Terrell rose through the ranks to become the airline's head of operations and a senior executive of the company. Along with flying the Concorde, Terrell featured in many of the airline's major achievements during his
years with the company.
Photo: Qantas

Qantas engineers, above left, Kevin Walters, Ken O'Neil and Peter Thomas, inspecting a grounded Continental DC-10 at Mascot. Although only required to check part of the aircraft, Thomas' team decided to extend their checks and found serious corrosion in the aircraft. Photo: Peter Thomas

Obviously the days before clean aeroplane engines! A Qantas Boeing 707 leaves an exhaust trail as it takes off for a training session at Avalon. Photo: Noel Dures

Qantas engineers work on a fuel control unit on a 707 in the hanger at Avalon.
Qantas 707s were often based at Avalon for some days during training programs.
Photo: Noel Dures

Captain David Howells, seen here at the controls of a Boeing 747, was instrumental
in the recovery of the Boeing 707 which would become known within the company
as the 'Bahrain Bomber' after it dived out of control over the Middle East in 1969.
Photo: David Howells

During serious fuel crises Qantas was forced to review every item carried on an aircraft so it could reduce weight and therefore reduce burning expensive fuel. This photo, taken in a Mascot hangar, shows every item normally carried on a Boeing 747 even before any passengers are boarded – from heavy galleys and food trolleys to baby nappies and in-flight magazines. Photo: Qantas

The Special Performance version of the Boeing 747. The aircraft's entry into Qantas service in the early 1980s was the catalyst for a serious strike because of the number of cabin crew staffing the aircraft. Photo: Boeing

Former Qantas executive Brian Wild with the autographed photo and cake box sent to him by the royal couple following their wedding. Wild had been instrumental in 'smuggling' the future Princess Diana onto a Qantas flight to London under the noses of the Australian media in January 1981. Photo: Brian Wild

Qantas Manager (Greece) Jim Brad-field battles violent wind gusts to join Greeks planting gum trees on the hillside outside Athens. The trees were a gift to Greek authorities after they agreed to remove other gum trees near Athens Airport which restricted the take off weight of Qantas Boeings flying non stop from Athens to Asia. Photo: Qantas

One-time chairman of Qantas, Sir Lenox Hewitt (centre), and Qantas Board member, Sir Jack Edgerton (right), enjoy a laugh with West Australia's Sir Charles Court. Photo: Qantas

The Qantas crew who flew the ANZAC veterans back to Gallipoli for the 75th Anniversary in 1990 gather on the steps after their arrival in Istanbul. Photo: Qantas

The final resting place of the Qantas Boeing 747-400 which overran the runway while landing in a rainstorm at Bangkok International airport on 23 September 1999. The aircraft was extensively damaged but none of the 410 passengers and crew was injured. Photo: Australian Transport Safety Bureau

Members of Qantas's Skippy Squadron, who took part in the airlift of Australian troops to and from Vietnam, march together for the first time on Anzac Day in Sydney in March 2003. Known as the 'Red Tail Rats' they operated more than 600 charters in and out of the war zone. Photo: John Stanley

Qantas Boeing 747-400 'City of Canberra', which established the non-stop record between England and Australia in August 1989, landing for the last time at Albion Park, NSW, on 8 May 2015. The aircraft is now on permanent display at the Illawarra Regional airport's Historical Aircraft Restoration Society Museum. Photo: Lee Gatland

windows, came the massive shape of another aircraft, its bow wave sending the Boeing on a 15 degree roll to the left.

It was all over in an instant. Although Westwood's first instinct was to put the Boeing's nose down, he had no time to react. Even if he had, the other aircraft would have taken the tail off his Boeing.

Westwood and his crew estimated the other aircraft had passed no more than 50 feet above them. For most of the passengers the near miss was merely a momentary bout of turbulence and only later would it become apparent just how fortunate those aboard the Boeing had been that night.

The Boeing 747's flight management system allows for the aircraft's autopilot to be engaged on either the captain's or the first officer's altimeter settings, and although the difference may be only a few feet, the aircraft will fly at the chosen system's altitude. On this night's flight, Westwood had selected his own system. Had he chosen the first officer's system, the Boeing would have been flying 75 feet higher and although that was within the limits allowed for this type of aircraft, there is little doubt the two aircraft would have collided.

Renowned as a fairly cool character, Westwood pressed on to Singapore, debriefed the cabin crew on arrival, went off to dinner with some of his own crew, then went to bed early. In the middle of the night the realisation of how close they had been to disaster suddenly snapped him awake and, as he later recounted to his colleague Roger Carmichael: 'I got up, went out and got smashed.'

Immediately word of the incident reached Sydney, disgusted with what appeared to be a serious air traffic control mistake that could have cost the lives of hundreds of passengers, Qantas's air safety chief Ken Lewis started to investigate why the Galaxy had been there in the first place.

Lewis tracked down the commanding officer of the C-5A squadron in Hawaii, and gave him a piece of his mind over the phone. He was shocked at the response: 'Well, there's a war on you know.'

Lewis, never one to take a backward step when it came to prosecuting his case, responded: 'I know that. I just didn't realise we were the bloody enemy.'

The Americans later claimed they had tried to contact Thai air traffic control but received no response and came into Thai airspace at the wrong altitude. For their part Thai air traffic control confirmed they didn't know the C5-A was there, but Lewis has his own theories about the incident.

With tensions rising in the Middle East, he remains convinced the US Air Force directed its aircraft not to use identification transponders when flying near Muslim states, particularly across Asia. Thus the Thais, even if they knew an aircraft was there somewhere, might have had no idea who he was or how close he might go to Qantas flight QF10.

No doubt prodded by Lewis's sharp exchange with Hawaii, it wasn't long before two US lieutenant colonels arrived in his office from the US embassy in Canberra to discuss the incident, although—as the months went by and the US launched Operation Desert Storm—the Iraq War was then in full flight and interest in the issue had started to fade.

**

Near misses aside, the jet age has provided other examples where Qantas has touched the edge of disaster either through mechanical, system or human failures.

On 4 June 1966, Stu Archbold and Norm Field were climbing

out of Sydney for Brisbane when their Boeing 707 suddenly started to 'porpoise' into a series of violent up-and-down manoeuvres. Startled, Field turned to Archbold and asked him what he was doing.

'It's not me,' was Archbold's reply, taking his hands off the control column to prove it, and both pilots watched in amazement as the column continued to move forward and back on its own, the noise in the cockpit now reaching a crescendo from the effect of the airflow breaking away over the flight deck as the aircraft lurched through the sky.

'I tried to send a "Mayday" call when I got my voice down to a shriek and told Alf Coyle the flight engineer to get the thrust off as the nose was coming up.'

Gradually the aircraft began to stabilise and Field requested a return to Mascot via the coast. Neither he nor Archbold wanted the aircraft to be over a populated area if the phenomenon returned.

After reporting the incident to engineering they were given a replacement aircraft and they resumed the flight to Brisbane, then on to Honolulu, although not before Field had requested an inquiry into the incident. Field later regretted not insisting on an inquiry that same day as it was three weeks before he was interrogated by a small panel including two senior captains, Torchy Uren and Max Bamman, and representatives from Qantas engineering and Boeing.

As the questioning went on, Field soon became aware that two factors were working against him, the first being the fact that Stu Archbold was based in Melbourne, leaving Field on his own to face judgement. The second came when engineering announced they had erased the cockpit voice recorder in use on the 707 that day. Field knew its recording of his and Archbold's conversations would presumably have settled the issue but now detected the panel was coming to the conclusion that the incident resulted from pilot error caused by Archbold and Field moving the control column in opposition to each other. Fortunately for Field, Max Bamman dissented and the subsequent investigation showed that balance panels installed in the aircraft's horizontal stabilisers on the tail had malfunctioned, sending the aircraft into what was becoming known as a 'Dutch roll', a combination of yawing and rolling motions that could occur in swept wing aircraft. Although aircraft like the 707 had been fitted with yaw dampers to improve stability and techniques for recovery were part of pilot training, it needed correcting as soon as possible.

While Boeing had originally identified the problem during its early development of the 707, its consequences could be fatal. During an acceptance flight by Braniff Airlines over the Boeing plant at Seattle several years before Norm Field's incident, poor recovery from a Dutch roll at low level resulted in three of the 707's four engines being ripped off its wings before it crashed, killing all eight on board.

But while the investigation finally absolved Archbold and Field, they had experienced what became known in Qantas as the 'blame game', a belief among some aircrew that no matter what the real or contributory causes of an accident might be, the initial response by their more senior management and corporate colleagues was to blame the pilot. According to the aircrew it would be a recurring theme for many years and a retrospective view of some of the accidents and incidents experienced by the company makes one tend to believe they might have been right.

John Simler had firsthand experience of it when his DC-3 ended in a ditch after landing at Wau, Papua New Guinea in the 1950s.

Simler had not been warned about water from a typical tropical downpour on the runway and his attempts to deal with the aircraft's lack of traction had taken him into the ditch.

Once the Qantas safety inspector arrived at Wau to investigate it didn't take Simler long to get the impression he was being blamed for landing too far down the strip, an accusation he vehemently denied. Adding to his woes was the fact that a Department of Civil Aviation plane carrying their own investigators had landed two hours after him, although Simler was able to point out by that time much of the airstrip had dried. 'He landed at least a further hundred yards [metres] beyond my touchdown point without a problem.'

As he had predicted, the Qantas Board of Inquiry, which, says Simler, lacked anyone who had ever operated under Papua New Guinea conditions, found him responsible for the incident. He was demoted to first officer and ordered to once again take all the written examinations necessary to return to requalify as a captain. 'Bill Taylor, as first officer, was criticised for not taking over control when the aircraft started to aquaplane—an absolutely ridiculous suggestion,' Simler says with obvious cynicism.

But, as it turned out, the DCA did not accept the Qantas findings; their report stated the blame should not fall totally on Simler's shoulders. Simler soon returned to captaincy, later transferring to Catalina flying boats. He was one of a small group of pilots chosen to remain in Papua New Guinea to train TAA crews after TAA took over the PNG Qantas operation there in 1960.

One of the more bizarre examples of the 'blame game' surrounded an incident that took Qantas's impeccable safety record close to disaster over a little-known Middle Eastern town called Jiwani. Those close to the company's operations in those days still wonder at the combination of luck and the Boeing 707's incredible ability to survive stresses far beyond what it had been designed to withstand.

It became known as the 'Bahrain bomber' incident.

10
TWO MINUTES OF TERROR
OVER THE MIDDLE EAST

As the Qantas Boeing 707 *City of Canberra* slid through a pitch-black sky over the Arabian Sea on the night of 21 February 1969, en route to Bahrain, everything appeared normal. The passengers who had reboarded at Bangkok had been served their supper, the heavy meal carts had been tucked away and John 'Buddha' Greene and his cabin crew had dimmed the cabin lights to allow the passengers to sleep as his own crew began to take turns at their rest breaks.

That there were only 62 passengers on board, one of whom just happened to be Australia's renowned nuclear physicist Sir Mark Oliphant, had not only made the Bangkok-to-Bahrain sector of the flight to London relatively easy for Greene's crew but meant the Boeing itself was very lightly loaded, a factor that, in the minutes ahead, would help determine whether they lived or died.

Those flying the Boeing were an experienced crew. The aircraft's captain, Bill Nye, had flown Catalina flying boats in the Royal Australian Air Force during the war and had accumulated thousands of hours in command. On this London pattern, Nye's first officer David Howells was on the second stage of his command training before himself qualifying for his own captaincy.

As is the captain's prerogative, Nye decided who would command each particular sector and had given Howells the first—out of Sydney to Perth the previous day. Nye then elected to fly the second sector from Perth to Singapore. Howells was given the short Singapore-to-Bangkok flight for training and had also handled the take-off from Bangkok earlier that night.

David Howells was already an experienced airman, graduating as a pilot in the Royal Australian Navy in 1954. He had flown piston-engine fighters off aircraft carriers HMAS *Sydney* and *Melbourne* until the demise of the Fleet Air Arm. Since joining Qantas in 1960, he had flown Lockheed Electras throughout the Far East and across the Tasman to New Zealand. Second officer Ian Watkins and flight engineer Bob Hodges made up the rest of the crew.

As was normal procedure, before departing Bangkok, Bob Hodges had inspected the aircraft's technical log, which notes any previous history of defects and, although there had been earlier notations of comparison warnings between the artificial horizons for the captain and first officer, the aircraft was, for all practical purposes, serviceable. There are actually three artificial horizons on Boeing 707s, instruments that show the Boeing's flight attitude at any given time, vital in determining whether the aircraft is flying straight and level through cloud or at night. There are two in the centre of the instrument panel in front of both the captain and the first officer, plus a third on the central console between the two pilots.

Now, near midnight local time and cruising at 35,000 feet, the Boeing had passed overhead Karachi and was heading towards a navigation beacon at the coastal town of Jiwani, near the

Pakistan–Iran border. Like the cabin crew, the pilots were also rotating their rest breaks in the crew rest area back in the cabin near the galley. Nye had been the first to go, to be replaced by Howells who was dozing in the bunk when he felt the aircraft start to turn to the left. Initially such a turn would be of no concern to Howells, assuming it would probably mean they were altering course slightly to avoid some bad weather ahead.

But when the aircraft's turn increased, Howells began to think perhaps the weather had deteriorated in Bahrain and they might be diverting to Karachi to take on more fuel. It was a thought that only lasted a few seconds as the aircraft kept turning to the left and he heard the cockpit speed-warning bell begin to ring, a warning that the aircraft was exceeding its legal maximum speed.

There are numerous cockpit alarms to warn pilots of problems but the speed-warning bell is one they never want to hear. It means the aircraft is approaching a speed at which it is likely to suffer serious structural damage. Realising he had to get to the cockpit quickly Howells tried to climb out of the bunk but ended up sprawled on the galley floor and unable to get to his feet due to the gravitational forces created by the Boeing, now spiralling downwards and almost on its back.

Unable to rise, Howells began crawling along the carpet, at one stage climbing over senior steward Ed Kirkland and flight hostess Maureen Culey who were also pinned to the floor and trying to get up. By now the noise was deafening, with the warning bell ringing incessantly and the screech of the airflow rushing over the groaning aircraft mingling with the screams coming from the passenger cabin.

One can hardly imagine the sight that confronted Howells when he had crawled far enough to open the cockpit door and claw his way into the vacant second officer's seat directly behind Nye.

By now the aircraft was heading straight down in an inverted dive, approaching the speed of sound with Nye and Watkins trying to regain control.

Howells's arrival in the cockpit had one critical advantage, an advantage that helped to save their lives. In a matter of seconds, from where he sat, back a little from both crew members, Howells could clearly see a discrepancy in the three artificial horizons, noticing Nye's was still stuck on a 30 degree bank to the right while Watkins's artificial horizon and the stand-by horizon on the central control panel agreed with each other.

Here Howells's experience flying military aircraft on instruments also came to the fore and he shouted to Nye to raise the nose of the aircraft to stop the airspeed increasing, applying the proven theory that the moment the speed increase stops is the moment when the aircraft is flying level.

By now, less than a minute since Howells had been tipped out of his bunk, the aircraft had already fallen through 19,000 feet to around 16,000 feet and it began to porpoise wildly as it climbed again to 21,000 feet before its nose dropped again and it descended to 17,000 feet before finally coming under full control. Gradually Nye began the slow climb to return to 36,000 feet to reset course for Bahrain. The whole death-dive sequence had taken two minutes in what had been a horrifying experience for those in the cabin.

Maureen Culey had just completed a 'walk through' the cabin to check the passengers when she remembers feeling an enormous force against her as the aircraft turned and she had the presence of mind to head for the jump seat near the forward door where she managed to strap herself in.

'This is it. I'm dead. This aircraft is going to crash. So this is how it ends,' flashed through her mind.

She vividly remembers Howells crawling along the carpet and over the top of her. 'It must have been a mighty effort for him as the force was phenomenal.'

Ed Kirkland, meantime, found himself pinned to the Boeing's ceiling for a few seconds then, as the gravity eased towards another gyration, came crashing down on Sir Mark Oliphant seated below him. (Oliphant later admitted to Howells that, in keeping with his scientific bent, he had used part of their downward spiral to calculate how many seconds it would take before they hit the sea!)

As soon as the aircraft recovered, Kirkland and Culey set off for the rear of the aircraft to help John Davis, the senior economy class steward, but found the concertina door separating first class from economy jammed. Ripping the door off its mountings they were met with the sight of bags, pillows, blankets, broken duty-free bottles and other debris stacked against the forward part of the cabin.

'Everything had been just turned upside down, although strangely enough the passengers were much calmer than I had thought they would be,' a situation Culey attributed to sheer shock.

Fortunately nearly all passengers had their seatbelts on, although one who didn't, a Royal Brunei policeman, hit the ceiling and slammed into the seat-rest ashtray as he came down again, later requiring the wound to be stitched in Bahrain hospital. Robert Edy and his wife had their daughter Chrissie lying across two seats and at first thought they had merely hit some turbulence until they saw Chrissie floating about a metre above them. Chrissie was unharmed. Another passenger also remembers hitting the ceiling and 'watching all the stuff in the cabin floating around below'.

But another bizarre event was in store for the cabin crew. A woman seated towards the rear of the aircraft suddenly became distressed, telling the crew the baby she had been carrying in her arms had disappeared. After a frantic search the crew located the infant under the pile of debris at the front of economy. It had floated the length of the aircraft and when negative gravity had come off, descended to the floor, to be then covered with cabin trash. Miraculously, it had been fast asleep the whole time and was uninjured.

With the aircraft now stabilised, the cabin crew used their medical kits to treat any minor cuts and bruises and began to clean up the aircraft.

After making a brief calming announcement over the intercom, Nye went back to talk to the passengers while Howells slipped into the first officer's seat. Several minutes then passed before Howells, realising that the Boeing's engines were still set at cruising speed, and now alarmed at the stress damage the aircraft may have suffered, told Hodges to reduce the speed by 25 knots (45 kilometres per hour) to ease the strain on the aircraft. He could not know at the time but it would be a decision that would later have serious consequences for him.

By now the shaken crew in the cockpit began to realise what had happened with the artificial horizons. When Nye had returned to the cockpit after his rest period, he had noticed with alarm that his artificial horizon was showing a 30 degree bank to the right. With pitch darkness outside and therefore no external references, he reached forward and switched off the automatic pilot and, without first cross-checking the other two horizons, 'corrected' with a 30 degree bank to the left, thus sending the aircraft into a downward spiral dive earthwards.

Later investigation showed the Boeing's speed had peaked at 885 kilometres an hour in the dive, close to the speed of sound;

Qantas flight 739 (QF739), the 'Bahrain Bomber'

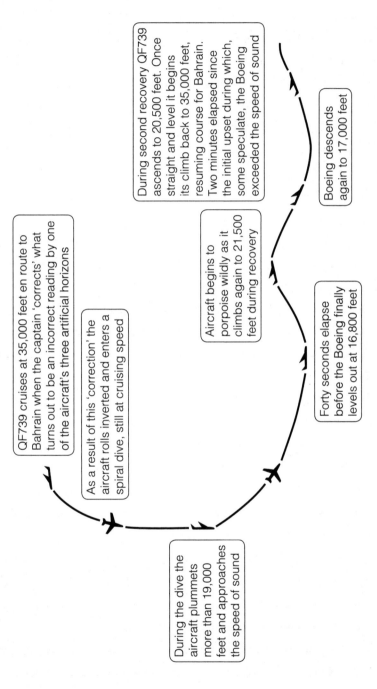

QF739 cruises at 35,000 feet en route to Bahrain when the captain 'corrects' what turns out to be an incorrect reading by one of the aircraft's three artificial horizons

As a result of this 'correction' the aircraft rolls inverted and enters a spiral dive, still at cruising speed

During the dive the aircraft plummets more than 19,000 feet and approaches the speed of sound

Aircraft begins to porpoise wildly as it climbs again to 21,500 feet during recovery

During second recovery QF739 ascends to 20,500 feet. Once straight and level it begins its climb back to 35,000 feet, resuming course for Bahrain. Two minutes elapsed since the initial upset during which, some speculate, the Boeing exceeded the speed of sound

Forty seconds elapse before the Boeing finally levels out at 16,800 feet

Boeing descends again to 17,000 feet

Drawing not to scale

From the original drawing courtesy of John McHarg

although some of the Qantas experts involved in the investigation would claim that at some point the aircraft had actually exceeded the speed of sound, as compressibility around the pitot tubes that measure an aircraft's speed can cause airspeed indicators to under-read. What was without doubt though was that the Boeing had rolled onto its back in the first part of the dive, eventually to end up pointing in the opposite direction to which it had been flying when Nye first rolled it to the left.

None of the investigators was in any doubt as to the critical factors that had saved the lives of those on board. One of the main reasons was that the aircraft had been relatively lightly loaded. Had it been carrying a full load of passengers and fuel, the Boeing would probably have broken up in the air as it pulled out of the dive. Even allowing for the light weight, it was a tribute to the robustness of the Boeing's construction that it hadn't started to break up anyway.

After landing at Bahrain at around 1 a.m., the Brunei police-man was taken to hospital and arrangements were made for onward flights for the remaining passengers. Several, still badly shaken, opted to remain in Bahrain for several days before moving on to London.

As is normal under such circumstances, Nye, Howells, Watkins and Hodges were stood down pending an inquiry, *City of Canberra* was grounded awaiting the arrival of a technical team from Sydney and both crews headed for local hotels. Buddha Greene had the presence of mind to relieve the aircraft's bar of several bottles of whisky, but Howells can't remember touching a drop before he went to bed, only to wake up later in the afternoon shaking uncontrollably. They spent five days in Bahrain while Nye compiled his written report on the incident, and the Sydney team assessed the damage, removed the flight data recorder containing all the details of the flight and prepared the Boeing for an empty ferry flight back to Mascot.

At one stage during their stay Nye and his crew returned to the airport to watch one of the Qantas engineers crawl into the bowels of the aircraft below the cockpit, tinker for a while, then call out: 'Is this what you saw?' They watched as Nye's artificial horizon showed a 30 degree bank to the right and the other two remained level. The cause: a loose wire at the power source to the captain's artificial horizon.

Even more than 40 years later several of the crew, including Kirkland, Culey and Davis remain critical of their homecoming treatment by the airline. Apart from the two people in charge of the male and female crews, John Davis says there was no one else to meet them when the aircraft parked at a remote section of the airport. Davis is convinced the company did all it could to avoid publicity about the incident as, although there had been press coverage in the UK immediately afterwards, virtually nothing had appeared in Australia.

Culey, now Maureen Bushell, agrees: 'We were met by the passenger service people who said "How are you, dear?" and that was about it, although I did get a fairly limp letter from Customer Services. They seemed to have successfully swept it under the carpet although I did receive some clippings my parents found in the London papers. 'There was no such thing as counselling in those days, although I never had any nightmares. I guess we were fairly young and you just move on.'

Culey left the airline eighteen months later to marry. But for the technical crew, particularly David Howells, the saga was far from over. As the investigation progressed, it became clear that, in common with many aircraft accidents or incidents, there are often multiple links in the chain of events that lead to the eventual occurrence. The unfortunate combination of the captain's faulty artificial horizon, the crew's lack of awareness of any prior problems with the instrument and that the failure occurred on a pitch-black night without outside situational references were obviously part of the problem.

There was also the fact that in the very first seconds of the incident, second officer Ian Watkins was busy transmitting a regular position report to Karachi air traffic control, reading from an A4 sheet clipped to an aluminium board with the help of a map light, which would have obscured his instrument panel. By the time the aircraft rolled on to its back and started to dive, neither Watkins nor Nye would be cross checking artificial horizons as they fought to control the aircraft.

But what was incontestable was that Nye omitted to observe one of the basic tenets of instrument flying, which is to immediately check the authenticity of the horizon's readout with the other instruments. The arrival of Howells in the cockpit, bringing with it his extensive night-flying experience as a former fighter pilot and his ability to read all three instruments, helped close that loophole—not that this was going to help Howells much when the company's investigation report was handed down. While Ian Watkins and Bob Hodges were absolved of any blame, Bill Nye was sent off to do some refresher training and David Howells received a reprimand—for reducing the speed of the aircraft after the incident without the consent of the captain! Howells was shocked, not only because he wasn't even on the flight deck when the trouble started, but it appeared he was the only one being punished, with a permanent mark against his flying record.

The whole process was reduced to farce when Howells presented himself before the investigation committee to hear the official inquiry results before he could return to flying. By now the Australian Federation of Air Pilots (AFAP) had taken an interest in Howells's predicament, insisting he be accompanied to the hearing by another of their members, Captain Barry Ellis, an old friend of Howells from when they had both been based in London. Both sat there stunned as the captain handling the process spent the first few minutes haranguing 'engineer officer Hodges' until it was pointed out to him that the chap before him was actually first officer Howells. Duly corrected, the captain went on—to repeat the whole harangue word for word—only this time addressing it to 'first officer Howells.' By now Ellis and Howells could see the funny side of it and could barely contain their laughter.

With the reprimand still on his record the AFAP insisted on taking the matter further, resulting some months later in a union delegation to Canberra to bring the matter to the attention of the Minister for Civil Aviation, Senator Robert Cotton, before the reprimand was expunged from Howells's record. Howells went on to become a training captain on Boeing 747s and, like Ian Watkins and Bob Hodges, had a long and successful career in Qantas.

Bill Nye continued his training but after a subsequent landing incident in Singapore, he was relegated to first officer, a position he held until his retirement.

Boeing 707 *City of Canberra*, later to be renamed *Winton*, flew with Qantas into the 747 era, and was eventually sold to an international aircraft leasing company in 1977. Needless to say, old hands at Qantas still talk in hushed tones of her role as the 'Bahrain bomber' and those minutes of terror over the Middle East.

11
BATTLING THE ELEMENTS

In the years before the attacks on the World Trade Centre on 9/11, inviting passengers forward for a look at the flight deck was a common practice. Inevitably some would come away with the impression that 'not much was really happening,' as 'George', the automatic pilot, was doing all the work.

Experienced airline captains will tell you nothing is further from the truth. Everywhere pilots fly, they must have a 'safety height', or a limit to where you can descend before you hit a mountain, as things can get complicated when you have a range of mountains reaching up to 20,000 feet below. As one Qantas check and training captain puts it: 'I get very cross if a pilot I'm checking can't tell me without looking at the flight plan what his safety height is at any given moment, as the action required in a decompression must be instantaneous.'

Because a rapid decompression is capable of sucking all the maps and other charts out of the cockpit in a split second, it's essential that pilots keep ahead of their aircraft and know what their 'safety height' is at all times. 'You might be sitting there a little fatigued for fourteen hours but your brain's situational awareness needs to be working,' says another.

Duty dispatchers like Richard Cantor factor this safety height into every flight plan they deal with, while at the same time making sure their flights are well out of range of what military activity might be taking place on the ground below.

Cantor says particularly after 9/11 there were three routes through the danger area presented by Afghanistan: one that opened up on a day-to-day basis; another that went fairly close to Kabul; and a third further south. A US military AWACS aircraft in the vicinity of the day-to-day route operated in conjunction with a ground station and Qantas could work with the latter to make sure everything was safe. The problem with the other two routes was created by so many aircraft converging on the relatively narrow 'gates' at either entrance to them. Not that the 'gates' were the only concern. Often air traffic control would re-route the aircraft at short notice, meaning Cantor's people back in Sydney would have to quickly determine which was the most acceptable route to, say, Singapore, without sending the Boeing over a live rocket-firing range in India.

Flying into and across China presents other challenges beyond high ground, particularly with communications. For instance, if a service was crossing Chinese airspace from Afghanistan en route to Bangkok, all communications modes such as satellite and data links, in addition to voice, had to be working because it would be passing through areas of Chinese military airspace and where controllers had limited English. If there was a glitch in any one of these, the aircraft would be diverted to Hong Kong. 'It's not that the Chinese are uncooperative but rather if you want to change a routing due to a cyclone or weather effect the process can be quite labour intensive at their end, possibly due to their hierarchical culture,' Cantor says.

Cantor credits Qantas with pioneering route development through to Europe over many years and it's still a truism that every flight plan for every route has its own idiosyncrasies, often causing people like Cantor to wonder whether even some of the aircrew realise what's really going on behind the scenes. 'It's a bit like the duck. There's a lot of paddling going on underneath,' he says.

On occasions that 'paddling' involves skirting the dust from volcanic eruptions that can cause havoc with a jet's engines. It was an issue dramatically brought to the public attention when a British Airways Boeing 747 flew into a cloud of volcanic dust thrown up by Indonesia's Mount Galunggung in June 1982.

Despite flying through clear night skies at 37,000 feet, the first sign of trouble was the appearance of St Elmo's fire on the Boeing's windscreen—a strange light created by an electric field around air molecules occurring under certain weather conditions—soon followed by an accumulation of smoke and a pervading odour of sulfur within the cabin. A short time later all four engines stopped.

The following minutes have earned a place in aviation history as they record how British Airways captain Eric Moody and his crew methodically went through repeated attempts to restart the engines as the Boeing, now little more than a 300 tonne glider, gradually lost altitude towards 11,000-foot mountains on Java's south coast. If the engines couldn't be started by then, they would have to contemplate turning the Boeing towards the sea for a crash landing.

Moody's announcement to the passengers has all the hallmarks of classic British understatement: 'Ladies and gentlemen. This is your captain speaking. We have a small problem. All four engines have stopped. We are doing our damndest to get them going again. I trust you are not in too much distress.'

Finally, after losing more than 20,000 feet, the crew's repeated attempts to restart were successful when first one engine fired into life, then was followed by the other three, allowing Moody to climb again out of harm's way. His troubles were far from over though, as damage to the windscreen from the St Elmo's fire effect meant Moody had to squint through a remaining narrow strip of the glass to see the runway.

Investigation showed that, because the volcanic ash was dry it had not been detected on the Boeing's weather radar, which is designed to detect moisture in cloud. Entering the hot engines, the dust had melted, clogging intakes and causing the engines to fail. Fortunately, as the aircraft reached lower altitudes, the molten particles solidified and began to break away, making it possible for a restart.

The incident caused serious concern within the industry, particularly with airlines like Qantas, as the majority of its routes cross volcanic regions. The worry was accentuated by a lack of established warning procedures that could alert airlines to the danger. Everyone knew where the volcanoes were but advice needed to be gathered when an eruption took place.

In the case of Indonesia, Australian authorities detected a reluctance to put even the most basic measures in place, the first of which would be to set up radio outposts in suspect areas to raise the alert—a difficult decision for a country that had its own security concerns about equipping people with radios in remote parts of the country.

One of Qantas's most experienced captains, Bill Cape, led the Qantas team that eventually established an early warning system advising operators of imminent eruptions. The phenomenon itself is now known as Convective Available Potential Energy and describes the amount of energy a parcel of air has as it is lifted vertically through the atmosphere. Bill Cape's deep involvement in the process remains in its acronym—CAPE.

NARROW CORRIDORS

If you asked an international airline pilot to list the world's most dangerous skies, the Middle East would probably rate high on the list. It's up there with such things as the vagaries of weather and other unpredictables, including volcanic eruptions.

As for the Middle East—for decades now conflicts have moved back and forth in this part of the world, bringing with them the requirement for airlines to be constantly aware of the dangers below and to adjust their operations accordingly.

Arguably one of the most significant effects has been the narrowing band of safe airspace a multitude of airlines need to fly through as they transit the region, requiring a constant change to flight plans as wars break out between foes below, are settled, then break out elsewhere across this conflicted landscape.

Often it's not simply a question of a large number of airline jets crisscrossing narrow corridors within easy sight of each other, but an air traffic control problem that brings with it language difficulties and often confusing interpretations of English.

For many Qantas crews, it has been standard procedure to have every one of the available crew on the flight deck during Middle East over-flights. As with approaching busy airports like Los Angeles or Heathrow, any extra pair of eyes in the cockpit is a bonus. Extra ears can be helpful too. One Qantas captain, heading through the night sky one evening, heard an Egyptian air traffic controller clear another Qantas Boeing 747 flying in the opposite direction onto the same altitude. Quickly asking the other aircraft to turn on its landing light, he was horrified to see it heading straight towards him. Both crews immediately took steps to avoid each other.

Such violations were relatively commonplace, as Roger Carmichael can attest. 'We would keep our wing lights on all the time in some areas and most of us had multiple incidents over the years where we had to call air traffic control to prevent breaches or warn of head-ons.'

On one occasion Carmichael had to call up another oncoming aircraft, telling them to climb 500 feet while he descended 500 feet until they passed.

Over the more notorious areas like northern India and Iran, pilots would often opt to fly one nautical mile to the right of their normal track to avoid the risk of a head-on collision.

Richard Cantor said one airway—known as the Chitral route as it crossed northern Pakistan—was particularly disliked by crews for several reasons. He recalls one captain recounting how he was flying along the route one night when another aircraft turned on its landing lights. 'Immediately, others followed suit and they realised just how many other aeroplanes were out there,' says Cantor, explaining these were the days before aircraft were fitted with traffic collision avoidance systems (TCAS).

Another reason for the Chitral route's unpopularity was the proximity of the mountain ranges through the Hindu Kush, highlighting a little-known factor when it comes to the general public's appreciation of the hazards of international flying—sudden decompression. Should decompression occur, the pilot must get the aircraft down quickly to an altitude where oxygen isn't needed, usually around 10,000 feet. He therefore needs to know immediately whether he might need to avoid mountainous terrain which might be higher than 10,000 feet as he dives his aircraft to a lower level.

Despite such initiatives, it would be far from the last brush airlines like BA and Qantas would have with the dreaded invisible ash cloud.

Almost exactly three years later, flying through the night towards Sydney from Hong Kong, Captain Graham Crowther's Boeing filled with smoke as St Elmo's fire began to dance across the windscreen. The culprit this time was Soputan, a volcano situated near Manado on the northern tip of Sulawesi, Indonesia.

Crowther told the 287 passengers on board he suspected the sulfur-ridden smoke was due to atmospheric conditions and no cause for concern, but the conditions lasted for around four to five minutes, one of the engines faltered briefly, and dust settled across everything in the cockpit. At one point he contemplated diverting to Darwin but, as conditions returned to normal, he decided to continue on to Sydney. As dawn broke, he saw the windscreen had been sandblasted to the point where forward visibility was restricted but he was still able to land safely.

But damage to the aircraft amounted to much more than replacing Crowther's windscreen. All four engines had to be removed and more than 5000 man-hours were expended on bringing the 747 back into operation—at a final cost of $500,000.

Once again a Qantas team would be dispatched to Indonesia, this time led by Qantas safety manager Ken Lewis, who had by now identified the problem as a lack of coordination between Indonesia's meteorologists and vulcanologists. He confirmed this situation soon after his arrival when he invited the vulcanologist and the meteorologist concerned to dinner and found they'd never met! Things improved after that, although Qantas took the extra precaution of closing the direct route over Soputan and directing all its aircraft well to the east. Crews operating the sector were also advised to contact Sydney by radio for updated information before reaching the area.

Not all Qantas's volcano crises have been in the air. Passengers on Qantas flight QF20 were buckled up and ready to depart Manila on the evening of 15 June 1991 when Captain Derek Tomasetti suddenly noticed that his windscreen was covered in sand. Just then the airport manager Ernesto Fray appeared in the cockpit with his hair filled with a sand-like substance.

Mount Pinatubo, 87 kilometres away to the north-west, had exploded in what was one of the most cataclysmic eruptions since Indonesia's devastating Krakatoa in 1883.

In the following minutes, while arrangements were made for the passengers to be ferried to hotels, Tomasetti's crew and Qantas airport staff gathered sheets of plastic and whatever other materials they could to protect the 767's engines from the abrasive volcanic ash, as heavy rain began to turn the ash and sand to mud. Several other aircraft were less fortunate, a Boeing 747 and an Airbus A-320 suffering damage to all their engines. It was four days before conditions had improved enough for the airport to open and flights to get under way again. One of the first to leave was the Qantas 767, saved from serious damage by the quick thinking of the Qantas staff.

And then, of course, along with near misses and volcanoes, there's always the weather. Despite sophisticated onboard weather radar and the introduction of weather satellites, climatic extremes are often impossible to avoid as changes of altitude or diversions may be limited by other traffic or airspace restrictions.

That was the dilemma that faced Qantas captain Geoff Rees, flying over Yugoslavia when he was confronted by a weather build-up that extended many kilometres ahead and above his 747. With no chance to climb out of the storm, Rees asked for permission to divert either side of it, only to be told there was gunfire on one side and conflicting air traffic on the other. Forced to maintain track, Rees flew through it and into hailstones so large they tore the radar dome off the aircraft and smashed against the leading edges of the wings with deafening force, as if someone was battering the 747 with a giant hammer.

So damaged was the aircraft that Rees decided to return to London. Eventually the damage would cost more than a million dollars to repair.

Being closer to the ground provided its moments too, particularly at airports like Rome and Kai Tak at Hong Kong, where vicious cross-winds would appear out of nowhere. Geoff Westwood, whose 747 went within metres of being taken out by the US Air Force C-5A over Thailand in 1990, was in the middle of flaring the aircraft to a touchdown at Rome on a clear night when Rome's notorious south-westerly cross-wind picked it up and thrust it towards the edge of the runway. Westwood managed to regain control but not before damaging the landing gear and some of the runway lights to the extent the Boeing had to be ferried back to Sydney for repairs.

Cliff Viertal's experience flying a 747 Special Performance aircraft into Seattle in the United States highlights some of the unusual external factors that must be taken into account by a pilot when landing in poor weather. Viertal was delivering the latest version of the SP, which had been fitted with more powerful Rolls Royce engines, into Seattle at night. The weather was appalling but a diversion was out of the question as conditions at other nearby airports were no better. Not only did he have to constantly operate the de-icing equipment on the wings and engines, but the little extra fuel he had in the wings was close to freezing and creating its own external ice on the wings as well.

Added to that, as Viertal approached Seattle, he was having trouble slowing the SP down during the descent due to a combination of opposing forces—the light weight of the empty SP and the required thrust on the more powerful Rolls Royce engines to keep it in the air. It was a problem that could normally be handled by deploying the Boeing's speed brakes and putting the wheels down early but in this case Viertal knew extending brakes and the wheels was likely to generate large ice blocks capable of killing someone on the ground. 'Somehow I managed to get it down on a flooded runway but it did create one of the "memories" in the life of a pilot,' he remembers.

***

In more recent times, it was another flooded runway that took a Qantas 747 to the very edge of disaster and caused the airline to take a long hard look at its operational standards and emergency training. It also highlighted the lengths to which some at the top of the airline would go to protect the airline's reputation as one of the safest in the world.

Thunderstorms and heavy rain were lashing Bangkok's Don Muang international airport as Qantas flight QF1 approached to land late on the night of 23 September 1999. Although ground control told the Boeing 747 crew that visibility was 4 kilometres, they hadn't been told of another weather observation that estimated the visibility was down to 1500 metres. The crew were also unaware that, only minutes in front of them, another Qantas Boeing—QF15—had abandoned its first attempt to land and gone around for another approach. Air traffic control did tell them that another aircraft had reported that, although the runway was wet, braking was good, something that would have been reasonably reassuring to the crew. Although it may be difficult for the layman to comprehend, a 300 tonne aeroplane is still capable of aquaplaning on a drenched runway.

By the time the Boeing was within metres of touching down, the rain was so heavy that the captain told the first officer who was flying the aircraft to abandon the landing and go around. As the first officer shoved the thrust levers forward the aircraft's main wheels touched the runway and, without announcing his actions, the captain pulled off the thrust levers. It was to be a critical decision.

By now, the Boeing was more than 600 metres beyond its normal touchdown point on the runway and still travelling at its touchdown speed of 154 knots (285 kilometres per hour), having already used up almost half the runway length.

A later detailed report on the accident pointed to confusion in the cockpit leading to the crew not using the aircraft's reverse thrust but relying on the brakes to stop the landing roll, now seriously affected by the Boeing's tyres aquaplaning on the runway. Under these conditions and without reverse thrust the crew had no chance of stopping the Boeing on the remaining runway length available.

As chance would have it, sitting in seat 4K in first class was the airline's former director of engineering, Mick Ryan, then working for Australian publishing magnate Kerry Packer and on his way to Amman, Jordan, to check out a new aircraft Packer was looking to buy to replace his ageing DC-8 executive jet.

Ryan realised something was wrong when he heard an unusual change in engine power before the nose wheel touched down, followed by a shuddering action that became more intense as the aircraft's fuselage started to shake violently. Panels from the ceiling broke away and crunching noises from outside told him the aircraft was hitting solid objects and tearing apart.

Then there was a jolt. Ryan was thrust forward against his seatbelt. The aircraft stopped. Suddenly there was deadly calm. It was pitch black outside and still raining heavily.

Ryan released his seatbelt and was preparing to evacuate but the crew told everyone to stay calm and remain seated, causing Ryan concern as the cabin filled with a strong smell of hydrol (the hydraulic fluid) and the pungent odour of burning electrics.

Minutes went by. Passengers began to use their mobile phones and Ryan started to wonder what was happening. Numerous times during his long Qantas career he had watched cabin crew training exercises demonstrating the urgency of getting people off the aircraft. This was the opposite to what was happening here and the crew didn't appear to know what to do. So he sat and waited as the time ticked by.

Although they didn't know each other, one of Ryan's former engineering employees, Peter Thomas, on the ground at Bangkok, had been watching and listening to the drama unfold. Thomas, whose job it was that night to check over the Boeing during its transit of Bangkok, had been listening to the company radio frequency so he could keep track of the aircraft's movements after it landed.

He saw the Boeing touch down—then watched it disappear in the gloom of the torrential rain. There followed some confused chatter over the radio until someone said the aircraft was apparently stuck at the end of the runway with no brakes and suggested he go and have a look. When QF1 didn't respond to Thomas's calls on the company frequency, he headed off towards the runway in the Qantas vehicle.

'When we got to the end of the runway there it was, sitting alone and silent, three hundred yards [metres] away on the golf course, still out of reach.' Fortunately Thomas played golf on the course so he knew how to get there, driving across an active taxi-way and along a road verging the course.

By now the rain had stopped but the Boeing's nose, firmly jammed into the mud, now prevented him from using the front attachment on the aircraft to plug in his phone and communicate with the crew. He was making his way towards another plug on one of the engines when he heard a crew member shout whether it was okay to use the aircraft escape slides.

'I shouted back it was okay but not to use the rear ones as back of the fuselage was so far off the ground the slides wouldn't have reached it.'

Passengers then began coming off, but soon there were more than Thomas could handle as they gathered on the roadway alongside the aircraft while Thomas kept urging Qantas ground control to get buses to the scene and allow passengers to get well clear of the aircraft.

As passenger numbers dwindled Thomas climbed up the raft to be told there was no power in the aircraft and therefore no communications. Thomas checked the battery switches in the cockpit to make sure they were off, then went to look for the captain and the first officer, finding them down the back shepherding the remaining passengers forward.

Passengers already on the ground outside the aircraft were remarkably calm as they were coaxed under the forward section of the Boeing towards the golf course road to where buses would arrive. Mick Ryan might have been calm, but was singularly unimpressed by the whole process. He says it was 5 or 10 minutes before the fire engines arrived. 'We could have been incinerated as it was impossible to tell from the inside of the aircraft if a fire was under the wing. The crew acted like stunned mullets but at least the emergency floor lighting worked,' Ryan recalls. He says another 10 minutes went by before the order to deploy slides was given.

'There was no real hurry to get off and, at the bottom of the slides, people just wandered around and had to be encouraged to move away from the aircraft. When the bus arrived 20 minutes later, they were boarded but didn't move as the drivers had to work out how to navigate the one-lane golf course track, finally backing up the road to a turning area.'

Four hours later Ryan and other passengers were in Bangkok's Emerald Hotel with what they stood up in, while Ryan's son Andrew, also a Qantas engineer, was already on his way to Bangkok on a relief aircraft to help in the recovery of the Boeing.

By now, as lights began to arrive, Peter Thomas could see the state of the aircraft. Unable to stop in time, the Boeing had crossed the end of the runway, its nose gear and right-side undercarriage collapsing almost immediately, taking with them an airport navigation aid that had been mounted on a concrete base.

Thomas believes that, had the aircraft crossed the road, the remaining landing gear would have been torn off and the Boeing would have been totally destroyed with the loss of lives. 'Qantas certainly dodged a bullet that night,' he says.

In Australia the next morning, the crash made front-page news as Qantas went into damage-control mode, although that didn't go according to plan either. Ben Sandilands, one of Australia's leading aviation writers, remembers a visibly shaken Qantas chief executive, James Strong, appearing on a morning television show.

'He showed clear signs of being rattled or shocked,' recalls Sandilands, who clearly remembers Strong describing the crash as 'a safety enhancing incident' to the show's female presenter. Sandilands acknowledges that, as this would have been only hours after the accident, Strong could not have been in possession of all the facts, but what struck Sandilands as strange was the choice of the word 'incident' rather than 'accident', particularly when live pictures were coming through of the crippled Boeing on its nose on the golf course. Speculation later arose that to use the term 'accident' would have meant a part admission by the company that the aircraft had to be written off, which in airline terms means a hull loss, something no airline wants on its record. Perhaps there are grounds for this in the fact it would cost more than $100 million to repair the aircraft, not far short of replacing it with a new one.

However, given that aircraft purchases by airlines can be complex arrangements, there is a counter argument suggesting that the probability of costly adjustments to special tax arrangements covering its purchase, added to the high book value of the aircraft at the time, made the decision to repair it still cheaper than writing it off.

The Australian Transport Safety Bureau's final report eighteen months later was highly critical of many aspects of the accident—even well beyond the performance of the flight crew and the cabin crew—to deficiencies in training and operational procedures.

Although Mick Ryan was offered a free trip for two anywhere on the Qantas network as compensation, he was still annoyed enough to pen a letter to James Strong outlining some of the shortcomings he'd witnessed. Two months later the former Qantas director of engineering received a three-page reply from Strong addressed to a Mr 'William' Ryan, apologising for the disruption to his travel plans and acknowledging there were 'lessons to be learnt from every stage of the process'.

'I suppose there's not much you can say from a passenger point of view. You approach, you crash, you get out and consider you were lucky that the aircraft didn't crash into the trees, rupture the fuel tanks and incinerate all of us,' Ryan concludes over a decade later. But while he and others believed it had been Qantas's lucky day, in the weeks and months that followed, the airline went to extreme lengths to move the mishap as far away from the public's view as possible, creating severe tensions between the media and the airline that were tending to affect the airline's image.

The aviation writer for *The Australian*, Steve Creedy, says problems surfaced immediately after news of the crash reached Australia. 'They [Qantas] wouldn't even tell us where the passengers were staying so I rang a few hotels close to the airport and found some of them there.' Creedy acknowledges that, with an accident inquiry pending, the airline certainly couldn't be expected to detail too much about what may have happened. But, as only the bare minimum was offered, this led to the press continuing to fill the void with whatever facts they could find. In turn this led Strong at one stage to describe the media reporting as 'outrageous.' Throughout the process Strong appeared to take the whole issue personally, at once threatening Creedy that if he ran a particular angle of the story he would go on radio the next day and refute it.

Creedy ran the story anyway. Strong didn't follow through with his threat.

Much of the debate between the two kept coming back to the description of an 'incident' rather than an 'accident' but, as the months went by, Creedy says it even became difficult to get any information as to where the aircraft was being repaired. So the media continued to look for it themselves and the story, much to Qantas's chagrin, developed a life of its own, leading at one stage to the *Sydney Morning Herald* publishing a photograph of a Boeing 747 in a hangar in Xiamen, China, only to have to admit several days later it was the wrong aircraft!

Finally, when repairs to the aircraft were completed, Strong himself flew back into Sydney on the Boeing with the aim of assuring the public it was now safe and back in Qantas's service.

Creedy believes that both Qantas and Strong learnt a valuable public relations lesson from the incident (or accident). In the interim, when the undercarriage of another Qantas jumbo collapsed through structural failure while on the ground at Rome, one of the airline's most highly respected engineers, David Forsyth, provided the media with detailed explanations of what had occurred. Although the two incidents were radically different, Creedy adds: 'The result was the Rome incident disappeared off the media agenda after a few days. Bangkok went on for two years.'

CHANGING SKIES AHEAD

One of the earliest signs appeared over the Atlantic Ocean on the night of 31 May 2009, when Air France flight 447 crashed into the Atlantic Ocean while flying from Rio de Janeiro to Paris. It took several years before the wreckage was located and an inquiry revealed what many in the aviation industry had been fearing for some years: that 225 people had died because of the failure of the pilots to control one of the world's most sophisticated aircraft when part of its automated systems failed.

As with most aircraft accidents, a sequence of events came together—weather, the absence from the flight deck of the aircraft's captain in the vital first minutes of the disaster, along with lack of proper communication between the two remaining crew. But what would stun many in the industry was the sheer inability of the pilots to apply basic airmanship to overcome the crisis they found themselves in.

In fact, they did the complete opposite. With faulty instrument readings telling them the aircraft was stalling, instead of lowering the nose to regain airspeed and recover, they consistently pulled back on the control column and the Airbus A-330 kept stalling, with fatal results. One can imagine the surprise when some of the older Qantas pilots learnt of the incident—pilots who had a simple recovery technique: set the thrust and the aircraft's attitude and you know you must be flying, no matter what the airspeed indicator is telling you. It had been drummed into them from their earliest training days.

Little more than two years later the Korean crew of an Asiana Boeing 777, approaching San Francisco airport in broad daylight, crashed short of the runway, killing three and injuring 180 of those on board, simply because the pilots were not able to approach and land visually. The subsequent investigation pointed to cultural influences where not only was the pilot 'very concerned' about having to land an aircraft without full automation but because other Asian pilots were able to do them 'he could not say he could not do one'.

The ethos on the Qantas flight deck, where every crew member was encouraged to speak up immediately—and even take control—if he considered a landing approach was not being executed properly has been probably best summed up by Roger Carmichael's advice to any newly promoted captain or first officer: 'Just keep thinking everyone in this cockpit is trying to kill you.'

Several more recent disasters—the disappearance of Malaysian Airlines MH370 on a flight from Kuala Lumpur to Beijing in May 2014 and the loss of an AirAsia Airbus A-320 with 162 people on board on a flight between Surabaya and Singapore in December 2014 are also causing concern throughout the industry, although for differing reasons.

In the case of the mystery of what happened to MH370, and with the search concentrating on an area in the southern Indian Ocean, serious questions are being raised about an alleged lack of transparency shown by the Malaysian government and its authorities about what they knew of the aircraft's possible flight path, information that would have been critical in concentrating the search in the days immediately after its disappearance.

A report on the loss of AirAsia will be looking at the

possibility of pilots once again being unable to compensate once a fully automated aircraft demanded they correct it themselves.

Whatever the outcome of these tragedies, the industry is taking a good hard look at a training regime that may have led to an over-reliance on complex automation that, while reducing costs and certainly bringing generally safer skies, has, to a large extent, fallen short of making sure pilots retain the ability to fly their aircraft as their predecessors did in what were known as the 'stick and rudder' days.

Then there are those cultural factors, particularly in Asia, where caste differences or respect for authority discourage any challenge that may cause a loss of face, bringing into play a dichotomy dangerously out of place in an aeroplane cockpit where it is absolutely essential that a crew member communicates concerns the instant he sees something might be wrong.

It is Asia, too, that has seen an unprecedented surge in air travel in recent years, where rapidly growing national carriers are being joined by new start-up operators, and hundreds of new Airbus and Boeing aeroplanes are due to enter already crowded skies in the years ahead.

Experienced pilots from some of the world's leading airlines who have assisted some Asian carriers with their training have been watching these developments with increasing alarm, although they are not surprised.

One former Qantas check and training captain was particularly blunt in his assessment of the Asiana accident at San Francisco: 'It's just unbelievable. The aircraft was so nose high it was basically falling out of the sky and they probably had some difficulty seeing the runway. Yet no one was calling it or grabbing hold of the situation and saying "Hey, what's going on here?"'

As for aircraft stalling, as occurred with Air France and may have been a significant factor in AirAsia's accident over the Java Sea, he points out that part of a pilot's basic training traditionally related to stall recovery at low altitudes to avoid ground contact, with the idea of minimising height loss. Since both Air France and AirAsia aircraft were flying at over 35,000 feet, adequate altitude was available if the proper procedures were implemented. But here, other factors are involved: namely, the relationship of the weight of the aircraft and the thinness of the air at high altitudes.

According to many experienced pilots much of this goes back to how technological advances have affected training.

As aircraft like the 707 and the Douglas DC-8 were superseded and computerised flight simulators reached unprecedented levels of sophistication, the prohibitive cost of taking an aircraft the size of a Boeing 747 out of the fleet for training gradually became uneconomic.

'Things had to change for many reasons,' explains one former senior Qantas captain. 'Safety and training had to be rationalised, particularly against a background where accidents were rare and profit margins were narrowing as competition increased dramatically. Simulators were the answer, nowadays able to dial up any contingency likely to confront a pilot in the air.'

But somewhere along the way, as fully automatic training has matched fully automated aircraft, where a flight can be programmed from the airport of origin to the destination, often with only limited input en route by the pilots, the importance of manual flying has been degraded to the point where some members of the crew rarely normally actually 'fly' the aircraft.

Since the Wright Brothers, part of flying has been the ability to land an aircraft using a visual approach to the airport, carried out when a pilot is able to see the airport, then, by looking out the window, eyeball himself onto the threshold of the active runway, similar to the way the Qantas crew did when they landed the Boeing 747 *City of Canberra* on its last flight to Albion Park's short runway in 2015. There's nothing terribly complicated about it but, as one old airman suggests, it does require judgement and training, along with the necessary manual skills of manipulating throttles and the control column, rather than sitting back and allowing the automatics to work it out for you. Light aircraft pilots do it every day when landing at airports around Australia and it was a critical part of that training on Boeing 707s during the days when Avalon functioned as a training base for Qantas. Many is the Qantas pilot under training to become a captain who suffered damaged eardrums from his instructor if he deviated from his angle of approach while landing at Avalon, all to emphasise the importance of low-level handling skills.

While automation has improved economics, enhanced some safety aspects and lessened the workload for pilots of today, traditional 'stick and rudder' skills have in many cases been almost totally erased from the training agenda. Reports from Asia, where there is a limited general aviation industry for pilots to gain flying experience, indicate that some prospective pilots come from university or an air force and into the first officer's seat on a commercial airliner with only several hundred hours flying experience, much of it in a simulator. And don't get the impression that this is purely an Asian problem as some of the world's leading airlines have pilots who are not confident of making a visual approach even into cities like Melbourne.

Neither can the responsibility for this be restricted to the airlines. Some experts believe organisations like the International Civil Aviation Organisation and the International Air Transport Association have recognised the problem and are taking steps to drive the solution.

AN AIRLINE FULL
OF CHARACTERS

12
LIFE WAS NEVER DULL

The aviation industry has changed to such an extent that it's difficult to imagine some of the characters who worked in Qantas in years past ever holding down a job at the airline today. Most would not take offence if you suggested they would find it hard to reconcile themselves with either the advances in technology or perhaps the pressures of doing business in an increasingly competitive world. Broadly speaking too, in aviation and most other industries, the days of the characters have passed because the very traits that made them such colourful people would no longer be tolerated in an environment of shareholder interests and 24-hour media scrutiny. But, even though they may be gone, the airline industry owes much to them. They were people of the times who provided that spark that further illuminated an industry that, along with its dangerous side, already had an inherent romantic appeal.

They were a mix of personalities: some painfully formal, others irreverent, some natural practical jokers. The contrasts appear stark. One could hardly imagine those iconic captains of airline's formative days, men like Russell Tapp, Lester Brain or Bill Crowther, steeped as they were in the business of flying, encouraging a humorous atmosphere in the flight deck. Rex Senior, who flew with them on the wartime Catalina Double Sunrise service between Perth and Colombo during the war noted there was always a very 'naval' overlay when it came to crew status, probably a hangover from the Empire flying boat days pre-war. Thus the captain was known only as 'Captain' or 'Skipper', never by his first name, while the first officer was only ever referred to as 'Mr' by the captain.

Much of the change to a less-formal atmosphere can be pinpointed to the years immediately after the end of the war in 1945 as former wartime pilots joined the ranks, men who had faced death every night for months in the air over Europe or flew against the Japanese in the South-West Pacific. While a few carried their consciousness of rank into civil aviation, still others knew how to let their hair down out of working hours or spear pomposity with a sharp retort, although often it depended on where they were flying at the time.

Papua New Guinea certainly provided a unique training ground in the late 1940s and 1950s, when pilots, traffic officers, engineers or ground staff were all tossed together in cramped living quarters with few modern facilities, but few stood on ceremony when off duty.

Gordon Power's account of the exchange between Captain Geoff Piggott and his roommate, newly minted first officer Alan Ross, later to become a senior check captain, doesn't surprise. Part of the household roster in the pilots' accommodation at Lae was the requirement to defrost the refrigerator, so when Piggott arrived home one evening to find there was water all over the kitchen floor, he confronted Ross. 'Well, what are you going to do about it, Alan?' inquired an irate Piggott.

'I think I'll drill a few holes in the floor and let it all drain out,' was the reply.

In a hardship posting where living conditions were anything but normal, reports of such exchanges had an almost 'domestic' family-like flavour to them, further demonstrated by pilots visiting major centres down on the mainland often taking time to shop for essentials for some of the Qantas families serving on remote stations. One captain even agreed to shop for a bra for the wife of a station manager while taking a DC-3 south for maintenance. Bill Forgan-Smith was known to make an occasional unscheduled diversion to Madang to deliver delayed mail to staff, tossing the mail out the window then roaring off into the Highlands again to resume his flying schedule for the day.

Thanks to such characters, life was never dull. Some remember the company man in Lae, part of whose responsibility was to organise the laundry. Since he had well-trained local staff to ease his load, he tended to spend a great deal of his free time at Ma Stewart's notorious Hotel Cecil, occasionally ending the day's drinking session with a dip in the Cecil's pool until one evening, in one of his more exuberant moments, he dived in, only to find Ma Stewart had drained most of the water out for maintenance. With his departure to Australia for treatment, Qantas Lae had to find a new manager for the laundry.

Others were credited with showing more initiative, such as the traffic officer in Madang who became known as the 'Black Trader'. Traffic officers in those days earned little money, so the idea was to supplement their incomes any way they could, particularly when Burns Philp were in the process of organising 'boi' charters to Rabaul for twelve months' work on their plantations.

Thus, when a Highland native would arrive in Madang with a bag of coins to purchase a ticket to visit a relative or 'wontok' in

Rabaul, our man would deliver him to Burns Philp on the back of the Qantas truck where he would join the other natives heading off on the charter, soon finding himself in Rabaul working a twelve months' contract but with ample time to keep in touch with his 'wontoks'. Not that one should get the wrong idea here. A year's pay with accommodation and all meals provided was usually a welcome relief from the daily grind at home in the Highlands. Meantime our man pocketed £16 as a 'facilitation fee'.

Beyond Papua New Guinea, even crews flying the long-haul Constellations and, later, Boeing 707 services around the world placed their own stamp on a side of the company rarely referred to in its own records.

Unlike the international air routes of today, where crew slips at various ports are measured by hours rather than days, the crew of a Constellation freighter might spend more than twenty days in each other's company before returning home to Sydney. Since much depended on the personality of the captain, old hands will tell you trips of such duration could either be a highly enjoyable experience or an interminable hell.

One Qantas pilot remembers flying as a first officer with Marsh Burgess as captain out of London to New York. While Burgess had proved an exceptional pilot, he could be difficult in the cockpit of a 707. The first officer received two tongue-lashings even before they had left the ground at Heathrow; the navigator copped it shortly afterwards. By the time they reached New York, the flight engineer remained the only member of the crew who had escaped Burgess's ire and wore a smug smile on his face as they approached the parking bay. Suddenly, to the rest of the crew's delight, something tripped Burgess and the flight engineer joined the club as well.

When Burgess asked them to join him for drinks at the hotel that night they all declined, pleading they needed an early night. After Burgess repaired to his room, they all went out on the town without him.

Flying as a second officer was part of a steep learning curve; second officers spent hours in the air, hoping to have the captain pass on to them any morsel of wisdom to help with their flying. But much depended on the captain's personality.

Early in his career, one very junior second officer remembers being excited when he was told he was rostered with Ken Meares, an experienced flight captain, on a trip to Hong Kong. Apart from the necessary operational comments, nothing was heard from Meares during the nine-hour trip until shortly before they began their approach into Hong Kong, when, out of the blue, Meares said, 'Don't put any charts on the glare shield as it reflects off the windscreen and makes it difficult to see any other traffic.'

'I was mystified!' the second officer recalled years later. 'I had never placed anything on the glare shield but it appeared that this gem of wisdom was to be my total reward for flying with the Fleet Captain.'

Such instances aside, there can be no doubting the value gained from learning from captains who were very willing to pass on their experience. Some became characters largely because they left others in awe of their flying ability.

While based in Bermuda in the 1970s, Roger Carmichael often flew as a first officer with Tony Jennings as captain. 'Tony was one of a few people in the airline who when they got into an aeroplane they strapped it onto their back. The rest of us strapped ourselves into it.'

London's Heathrow was being lashed by a gusting 50 knot (90 kilometre per hour) cross-wind as their 707 approached to land one March morning, a wind so bad no other airlines were taking off or landing there. Carmichael, sitting in the right-hand seat, says by the time they were down to around a thousand feet, the wind was forcing the Boeing's nose off at an alarming angle to the direction of the runway.

'In fact I could look out my right side window straight at the runway,' says Carmichael, so he offered: 'Tony, if I was doing this landing I would be diverting to Prestwick.'

'Son, that's the reason I'm doing the landing,' was Jennings's reply.

'I think all of Heathrow had come out that morning to see the aircraft crash but at the last moment he put his great boot down on the rudder pedal and straightened it out. It was magical flying,' Carmichael says.

Other captains appear to have had difficulty when it came to mixing with crew outside flying hours. Although he had earned respect for his war record and status within the airline, some found Torchy Uren difficult to mix with. After landing in Honolulu on one occasion, Alan Terrell asked Torchy if he would like to join his crew and the cabin attendants in Terrell's room for a drink after they signed off. Appearing surprised, Uren asked Terrell whether it was his normal practice to invite the cabin crew. When Terrell told him it was, Uren replied: 'I find I have little in common with them.'

Others became known for their idiosyncrasies. Hughie Hemsworth had a high-pitched voice that often startled the traffic officer responsible for handing him the aircraft's load sheet immediately before departure.

After a quick scan of the sheet Hemsworth would exclaim for all to hear: 'Are you bastards trying to kill me?'

It might have been Hemsworth's idea of a joke but marketing director George Howling remembers receiving a frantic call from the Singapore regional director, Bob Low, to tell him Hemsworth was delaying the departure of his 747 Singapore to Sydney flight because the chocolate frogs that were part of the crew meal had not been loaded. Howling, who had known Hemsworth since his London days in the late 1940s, was quickly on the phone to Singapore. 'I pointed out he had a full flight and to delay it while catering went and found the chocolate frogs was not the wisest attitude to take. He reluctantly agreed and I promised the frogs would be available on future flights!'

Any close study of Qantas's history leaves little doubt that the 707 era marked the emergence of many of the real characters, be they aircrew, traffic officers, cabin crew or those on the ground. While many have gone to that great landing ground in the sky, a select few still hold legendary status when old pilots gather, their efforts written into Qantas folklore. In fact, there are probably very few gatherings where Ross Biddulph's name doesn't come up.

Biddulph flew RAAF transport aircraft in the South-West Pacific before joining Qantas in 1948 and it was in the Qantas New Guinea years that his legend was born. One of his earliest escapades occurred while he was flying a DH-84 Dragon out of Kainantu for Lae one morning when he realised he'd left his tin of 50 Craven A cigarettes down the back of the aircraft.

Unknown to Biddulph, Qantas's chief pilot in Papua New Guinea, Bill Forgan-Smith, was flying a DC-3 1000 feet behind and above him when Biddulph decided he was desperate for a cigarette. As there was no cargo or passengers, his idea was to quickly dart down the back, get the cigs and smartly return to the driver's seat.

Years later, in a letter to his old mate Norm Field, Biddulph described what happened next:

Winding full nose down on the trim, and holding up straight and level with one hand I scrambled out of the seat and did a 'Usain

Bolt' towards the after region. Apparently Dragons don't like people rapidly appearing behind the centre of gravity because the wretched plane reared up like a Wodehouse salmon and set course for Jupiter. Almost immediately it stalled and, forgetting all about Jupiter, screamed straight down towards Nadzab.

Shortly after I arrived in the flight deck area, spreadeagled against the instrument panel like a butterfly and covered in thousands of Craven As.

Biddulph then describes how he gets the aircraft under control only to look out the window, 'straight into the apoplectic face of Bill Forgan-Smith, ten metres away, flying in formation with me and trying not to stall as he eased the DC-3 past.' Biddulph said the subsequent conversation in the chief pilot's office was 'fruity'.

As Biddulph worked his way through the Qantas pilot ranks via DC-4s, Constellations and finally 707s, even the achievement of reaching 'Captain' status provided the inevitable 'Biddulph moment'. In those days, once a first officer had been selected for command level, he was paraded before director of flight operations Alan Wharton to be officially 'knighted'.

Wharton, renowned for his dry sense of humour, later described greeting Biddulph when he arrived at his office with: 'Christ, they've reached the bottom of the barrel this time.'

'No, boss,' replied Biddulph, 'they just started a new barrel.'

The achievement of such rank didn't seem to curtail Biddulph's escapades, either in the air or on the ground. Having several days to spare during a lay-over in Rome he decided to take his whole crew to Napoli 'to uplift some culture,' as he later told Field. Becoming aware that a fabled collection of pornographic art could only be accessed by genuine researchers and academics, Biddulph left the bus outside the gallery in the persona of one 'Professore Bindolpo' travelling with his group of 'studentees'.

Genuflecting and with clasped hands, they were duly accepted into the building by the abbot and all went well until the radio officer gave the game away when he made a lewd reference to a carved image of a soldier and a goat. They were promptly asked to leave.

Unfortunately the local BOAC representative in Rome filed a report on the incident and Biddulph once again found himself summoned before his chief pilot, this time in London, who opened the batting with 'Do you know a Professor Bindolpo?'

'I knew then I was dead,' Biddulph later admitted.

But it was on the Kangaroo Route to London, where Qantas crews operated in close company with those of BOAC, that most of the Biddulph stories had their origins. These were the days when Qantas crews stayed at premises known as Speedbird Houses, BOAC-owned accommodation at night stops along the route.

Bringing some of the Mother Country's best and brightest pilots down to size seems to have appealed to Biddulph's colonial streak. When they discovered the British had erected a bar tent for their own exclusive use at Speedbird House in Karachi, Biddulph and Andy Young managed to collapse the guide ropes, leaving a bunch of BOAC pilots' heads poking up through the roof.

On another occasion in Karachi a BOAC crew suddenly realised the waiter dressed in Arab robes and offering them camel steaks was our man Biddulph.

There's also the story of the cold winter's day at Speedbird House at Heathrow when the British pilots had their chairs strategically positioned around the fireplace, blocking the Qantas pilots from the warmth. A short time later Biddulph appeared dressed in the uniform of the cleaning staff. Carrying a bucket and shovel, he proceeded to pile the fire's contents into the bucket and set it up in the room next door for his own crew.

Not only BOAC pilots were at risk. During one stopover in Cairo, Biddulph noticed all the drivers of an approaching camel train were asleep. Waiting until they reached him, he slipped across to the lead camel, grasped its bridle rope and turned the animal around, watching with glee as the whole of the train followed it off in the opposite direction.

On other occasions, while the crew stood on the pavement somewhere in the world waiting for transport to their hotel, he would announce: 'Anyone who can't tap dance is a poofter.'

It's hard to conjure the image of a present-day Qantas crew, dressed in flight uniforms, going through a dance routine outside one of today's international terminals!

Sadly, Biddulph's career with Qantas ended at a relatively early age when he landed his Boeing at Perth. It appears that although the runway was fully serviceable, the final paintwork had not been applied at the threshold and a management pilot travelling as passenger reported Biddulph for 'landing short'. Never a large fan of officialdom, Biddulph refused to accept the landing was anything other than safe and, after telling the company what it could do with some of its rules and regulations, resigned.

Unlike the salary levels of today, pilots in the Constellation and early 707 days weren't all that well paid and even captains like Ted Harding occasionally supplemented their income from other sources. In Harding's case he had part-ownership of a fruit-and-vegetable barrow at Manly wharf.

On one occasion on his way home after a trip away, Harding arrived at the wharf to find his barrow man having difficulty handling all the customers waiting to be served. So Harding, still in uniform, spent the next hour or so helping out.

When director of flight operations Alan Wharton heard about

it, he called Harding to his office: 'Ted, I believe you were seen working in your Qantas uniform on a barrow at Manly wharf.'

When Harding confessed, Wharton continued, 'I'm afraid that's not a good image for a Qantas captain. I'll tell you what, either you give the barrow up or you can leave Qantas.'

Quick as a flash Harding replied, 'Can I have a week to think about it?'

With today's senior Qantas A-380 captains reputedly on salaries exceeding $500,000 a year, Wharton's anecdote today has an odd ring to it!

Adelaide-born Harding had joined the RAAF in 1941 and flew 78 missions on Hudson bombers in the South-West Pacific. His squadron suffered heavy losses, with 70 per cent of their officers killed and half their aircraft lost to the enemy or in crashes. Their attacks on enemy shipping, aerodromes, troops and installations earned his squadron a Presidential Unit Citation from Franklin Roosevelt for 'outstanding performance of duty in action'.

Harding joined Qantas in 1945 and, after the introduction of the 707, became a training instructor at Avalon where several of his pupils would later remember him as 'tough, but fair'. Rumours persist that during his time at Avalon Harding achieved what few others have—barrel-rolling a Boeing 707 over Corio Bay, off Geelong.

Barrel-rolling a large commercial airliner like the 707 wasn't recommended for obvious reasons, but experienced pilots can confirm it could be done quite safely, with little stress on the aeroplane, if the aircraft was properly set up and the manoeuvre was executed the right way. Boeing's chief test pilot Tex Johnston was the first to achieve it when he barrel-rolled the very first production 707 over Lake Washington in 1954, much to the dismay of his boss, Boeing Chairman Bill Allen.

Allen had gathered senior airline executives from all over the United States aboard the Boeing yacht, hoping to impress them into buying their aeroplane of the future with a traditional Tex Johnston low fly-past over the Sound. But Johnston, without pre-warning Allen, arrived overhead and executed two barrel rolls in front of the awestruck group.

When Allen later berated Johnston for putting the whole of Boeing's future at risk, Johnston insisted it proved just how good the aircraft was. Although Johnston's effort was recorded for posterity by a spectacular photo of the Boeing engines above the wing while it was upside down, there are apparently no such records of Harding's performance. It's just as well. If the story's true, it probably would have cost him his job.

Harding helped introduce the 747 into Qantas service and retired in 1975, reputedly always willing to joke how he was once the only person who could sell Qantas founder Hudson Fysh a pound of peas at the Manly barrow in the morning then fly him to Singapore that night.

Stories about Hugh Birch have also reached legendary status in the Qantas lexicon. Much decorated during World War II, Birch held the honour of taking part in the first air-to-air combat between two flying boats near Gibraltar. Birch's Sunderland managed to get a few shots away at a Dornier, which replied in kind, blowing part of the hull out of Birch's flying boat.

After the war, Birch pioneered many of Qantas's Pacific routes flying Catalina aircraft before joining the company's management ranks. Perhaps his most famous story involved him and his co-pilot Mick Mather, both renowned for their party tricks throughout the islands, and hinged on Mather's ability to place a billiard ball in his mouth. That was until one night in Noumea when, bets having been taken, Mather repeated the performance, only to find he and Birch hadn't realised that French billiard balls were larger than the normal variety. A doctor had to break Mather's jaw to get the billiard ball out and the telex to Qantas Sydney next morning explaining the reason for the delay of that day's service has also become part of Qantas folklore.

Stu Archbold was no less a legend. His worldwide network of celebrity acquaintances stretched from the Shah of Iran to High Court judges and even the cream of Australia's horseracing fraternity.

Right from his earliest RAAF flying training days, Archbold was in the public eye, running into a fence and smashing his Tiger Moth's propeller at Yarrawonga during a cross-country navigation exercise. The prop replaced, he took off immediately on the next stage of the exercise to Corowa but ran out of daylight and buzzed the town often enough for locals to organise a dozen cars to light the aerodrome runway so he could land.

Archbold's wartime superior officers expressed some doubts about his future but he was to prove them wrong, winning acclaim flying Kittyhawk fighters in the Western Desert and the Italian campaign, during which he undertook dangerous experimental work developing Hawker Hurricanes into rocket-firing fighters for ground attacks.

First flying for Australian National Airways after the war, Archbold joined Qantas in 1959 and, by the time he retired in 1975, he had become one of the best-known Qantas pilots of his era, largely due to his extensive range of international contacts. Peter Raven, who first flew with him in 707s on the Kangaroo Route to London in 1967, says it was not unusual to have the Australian High Commissioner's Rolls Royce waiting to pick up

Archbold from Heathrow on arrival and a Buckingham Palace garden party invitation waiting at the hotel.

Raven recalls, during one slip in London, Archbold rang him in his room and asked him if he wanted to go to the races. When Raven agreed, Archbold told him: 'Well, hurry up, Scobie and I are downstairs in the car.'

'So off to the races we went in Scobie Breasley's car and though I knew nothing about horses I backed the Australian jockeys riding that day and won,' Raven says.

During a stopover in Teheran in the 1960s, Archbold and his crew were playing at a bowling rink when the shah arrived with a group of minders and took over an alley nearby. Raven says it wasn't long before Archbold had introduced himself to the shah and was providing his Highness with a few tips on the sport. 'After that Stu would often be invited into the royal presence whenever we went through,' says Raven.

Much of Archbold's networking was done in the air and those who flew with him remember the most 'open' cockpit they ever experienced, with an endless stream of visitors, many of them VIPs, invited onto the flight deck. Archbold was often used by Qantas for publicity purposes and was a natural choice to captain the first Boeing 707 into Melbourne for the opening of Tullamarine airport in 1970.

Retiring with 22,000 hours in his logbook, Archbold continued consulting for sections of the aviation industry, only to lose his life while acting as a technical aviation adviser during filming of a glider operation at Bacchus Marsh in Victoria in May 1980. He was the passenger in a Janus glider when something went wrong with the towing sequence, resulting in the glider diving vertically into the ground, killing instantly Archbold and his companion.

While Archbold's cockpit was apparently open to all on board, most cockpits were workplaces where rank was acknowledged when it came to the serious business of flying, although some crew members didn't hesitate to prick the status balloon. Flight engineer Jeff Donaldson remembers one captain who had a habit of half-turning after he'd finished his tea break and placing his cup on the navigator's table immediately behind him.

Tired of his captain's habit, the navigator decided to teach him a lesson while at cruise over the Pacific. First requesting they alter course about 10 degrees to the right, he then called for another course 10 degrees to the left, then a third request back to the original course.

'What the hell is this all about?' asked the confused captain.

'I'm navigating around your bloody cup and saucer on my nav chart,' was the reply.

'The skipper never did that again,' confirms Donaldson.

Another navigator Howard 'Joe' Bartsch, ever the perfectionist, would recount his frustration that pilots could never be bothered to alter a heading by one degree at his request—a situation Bartsch would overcome by saying: 'Request alteration of heading of five degrees left'; to be followed shortly afterwards by a further request saying 'Change of heading four degrees right'. Problem solved.

It goes without saying that pilots were not alone in the 'character' stakes, some cabin crew adding a rich vein of experience, and numerous examples of humour, to the Qantas story.

GETTING THE AVRO 504K
IN YOUR LOGBOOK

There's hardly a pilot anywhere who can resist the opportunity to add a new aircraft type to his or her logbook.

For most airline pilots, it could be a Boeing or an Airbus version; for general aviation pilots, a new Cessna or Piper.

Imagine the dilemma faced by Qantas 747 captain Bill Taylor when in 1982 he was assigned to taxi a replica of the first aircraft that went into service with Qantas back in 1920 for a film commercial.

The Avro 504K was a two-seater biplane from World War I, similar to the original Avro 504K flown by Qantas founder Sir Hudson Fysh in the airline's earliest day and which had long been on display as the pride of the airline at Mascot. But, unlike the original, the aeroplane Bill Taylor would taxi along the ground had never been intended to fly, having been built as a 'spare' and as a labour of love by a handful of veteran Qantas engineers who were the last at the Qantas jet base who had any knowledge of the art of wood, wire and fabric aircraft construction.

While the team had worked from the original aircraft's specifications, some 'compromises' had to be made with the materials and although it was never intended to fly, it would provide the airline with a second aircraft for publicity and photography purposes.

When Qantas's advertising people came up with the idea of a series of commercials revisiting the airline's past and chose the Avro as the centrepiece, Taylor found himself as part of the film team on a grazing property just outside Coonamble, in central western New South Wales.

Taylor's assignment was to taxi the aircraft around the property while the cameras rolled, re-enacting those early days of the airline's birth at Longreach in outback Queensland.

But by late afternoon, as the breeze dropped to dead calm and as the repeated film 'takes' required Taylor to taxi even faster and faster along the ground, Taylor obviously couldn't resist the temptation.

In front of the assembled trio of engineers, whose structural efforts had never been designed for flight, Taylor suddenly opened the throttle and roared across the paddock and into the air. It might have been only a few metres above the ground for 75 metres or so but advertising manager Bruce Tregenza vividly remembers the reaction of those watching: 'The three engineers nearly died when the wheels left the ground. None of us had any idea what he had in mind.'

Taylor himself later confirmed it was something of a risk, telling one of his pilot colleagues he could understand why the engineers weren't all that impressed: 'The Avro was a cosmetic job only—the spars were made out of floorboard trimmed to size and I made sure I flew low and slow in case it fell apart.'

***

Many of the cabin crew antics are well documented by former flight service director Colin Burgess. Burgess's accounts bring to life a Qantas of a different age and one before the advent of mass transportation by 400-seat Boeing 747s saw the influence of characters as individuals fade into history.

Burgess's account of chief steward Max Collins's method of serving breakfast to first-class 707 passengers in the early morning over the South Pacific has pride of place in Burgess's memoirs.

Collins would position the meal tray behind the curtain into First Class then, as the in-cabin lights were switched on, would stand on the back of the trolley and push himself forward, plunking out a tune on his ukulele as he rolled into the cabin, singing as he went: 'How do you wake 'em? You Kellogg's Corn Flake 'em.'

Collins once talked a small member of the cabin crew into sitting on top of the food trolley while Collins covered him with parsley and garnishes and rolled him into the first-class compartment at meal time. Once there, to the astonishment of the passengers, Collins proceeded to carve the prime rump.

Mind you, there is still the odd echo of such behaviour, as former cabin crew member Peter McLaughlan can attest. On one 747 flight out of Honolulu some years ago a female passenger complained loudly about the fact that the seafood meal on the menu had run out by the time the meal trolley reached her. It so happened one of the cabin crew had purchased a scuba diving kit during his Hawaiian lay-over. After a few minutes had passed a wetsuit-attired cabin crew member, equipped with mask, snorkel and flippers, paraded down the aisle carrying a tray above his head and asking at the top of his voice: 'Who ordered the fish?'

Such echoes of the past might be more difficult to sustain in the cabin crew world of today where the four hundred plus passengers carried on aircraft like the 747 or A-380 are well beyond the more intimate numbers aboard the Constellations and 707s of the past. As one former flight service director put it: 'You might try your best but you're really taking care of what can be the equivalent of a small country town.'

13
POSTINGS . . . NOT ALL MILK AND HONEY

It can all sound so exotic. You're working for this great international airline and your boss has just come on the phone and told you you're in line for a posting. London and Buckingham Palace immediately cross your mind—or perhaps a house with a view overlooking San Francisco's Golden Gate Bridge.

While for a few of the Qantas staff of yesteryear, the romance of an overseas posting certainly lived up to expectations, there were many occasions when the freedom of being a long way from head office came with its fair share of primitive living conditions and, at times, all manner of risk. Even if you had second thoughts about a posting close to a war zone or some desolate island in the middle of the Pacific, refusing such an assignment didn't sit well on your company record as far as future promotion might be concerned and extreme family disruption was often par for the course.

Many of the tales of primitive living conditions come from those posted to the tropics or Pacific islands, which in the 1940s or 1950s didn't quite match the image portrayed by today's tourist brochures.

During the UK's H-bomb tests in the Pacific in the 1950s, Bob Weekes spent months living in a tent on Kiritimati, a raised coral atoll and part of the Line Island group, 300 kilometres south of Hawaii, while chartered Qantas Constellations ran shuttle services between Kiritimati and Honolulu in support of the tests. The tents served as officers' quarters and while there were only two or three flights a week during the peak times there wasn't much to do beyond that.

'It was real pioneering stuff,' says Weekes, who had to have security clearances from ASIO, MI5 and the FBI before he could board the Royal Air Force freighter to take him there in the first place. For some reason, those at Qantas head office had the idea that if you lived in the tropics you had no need of hot water or other creature comforts. 'That was all right for adults who could survive but families with children needed hot water,' explains Weekes.

One of Weekes's colleagues of those days, Hartley Shannon, remembered a Qantas engineer in Papua New Guinea who used his initiative to build his own hot water system, only to receive a stern rebuke when head office in Sydney found out about it. Papua New Guinea, according to Weekes and others with him at the time, rated about as unpopular as a posting to Darwin in those days, where the accommodation for staff was less than ideal.

'We'd taken over Darwin's former Berrimah hospital for transiting passengers and staff accommodation and I reckon the termites had eaten much of the hospital wood. Fortunately the paint continued to hold the building up.'

Lae in Papua New Guinea was no paradise either when it came to living quarters. 'We used to wonder whether Qantas designed the buildings for winters in Tasmania,' says Weekes.

Charles Wade, posted there as a traffic officer for two years in the 1950s, later described the early accommodation in Lae as Quonset huts with tin roofs and sisal craft walls on the edge of the airstrip. 'In the early morning you had to pull a sheet over your head, otherwise you would be covered in dust and gravel as the aircraft turned around to take off.'

Neither did it take Wade long to realise some of his work-mates worked hard and played hard. On his first night, at a party to farewell a captain who was 'going finish', the local vernacular for someone returning permanently to Australia, he witnessed the Qantas area manager knocked unconscious by an uppercut from an engineer. Later the same night as the party progressed Wade watched as a captain was ceremoniously dunked in a 44-gallon drum of water. Unfortunately, the captain, who was short of stature and very drunk at the time, got stuck in the drum and when someone realised he was in trouble they pushed the drum over.

The party pranksters would probably have been hard pressed to find somewhere larger than the drum for a dunking: one of the ironies about life on a tropical island was the inability to find anywhere to swim. Although the ocean lapped Lae's shores, croco-diles and sharks were an ever-present danger and even those who braved wading in the shallows risked standing on the dreaded stonefish, a precursor to excruciating pain and even a requirement for skin grafts.

Pilots mostly served for around two years but not even they received much special treatment when it came to a posting to Papua New Guinea. Shortly after Gordon Power joined Qantas from Canadian Pacific Airlines in 1957, he was summoned to the office of manager of operations, Phil Howson, and told he was being sent to New Guinea for two years. When Power gave the impression he wasn't all that impressed with the idea, Howson suggested he go home and think about it, commenting: 'You'll be going in two weeks, anyway.' As it turned out, in later years, Power would readily acknowledge the value of the flying experience gained there.

Out in the workplace, it was a case of 'expect the unexpected'.

Sitting behind Weekes in a Qantas de Havilland Beaver flying from the Highlands into Lae one afternoon were a New Guinea policeman and his prisoner, a convicted murderer on his way to Lae gaol. When the Beaver began to bounce around in the turbulence, the policeman asked Weekes for a sick bag. A few seconds later Weekes turned to see the policeman being violently ill while the prisoner held his rifle for him.

Papua New Guinea was an early posting for George Howling, who would eventually become one of the airline's most senior marketing executives. Howling, who had served in the Royal Navy during the war, joined Qantas in London in May 1948 and was transferred to Sydney two years later. He has two vivid memories of his arrival—it rained continuously for days and his 'induction' at his workplace on day one went something like this.

'Who are you?' he was asked by the chap he had been told to report to.

'Nice to meet you,' was the response when Howling explained he'd just arrived from London.

'What do I do now?'

'I don't know,' was the reply.

At first Howling was assigned to the cargo department but then was told that he would be sent to the traffic office at Mascot airport while a colleague, Ron Pascoe, was posted to Lae. But when the time came for Pascoe's departure, he was issued with six second-hand shirts as part of his PNG uniform. Disgusted, Pascoe refused to accept them. 'There was a helluva furore and even the then commercial director Bill Neilsen got involved but Ron still refused to take them. Eventually the shirt saga was resolved, Ron went to New Guinea and I went to Mascot.'

Howling's Mascot duties included spending time at the traffic office at Rose Bay flying boat base. 'It was wonderful. We'd all sit around fishing waiting for the flying boat to come in. There was extra pay for being on shift and even an extra week's vacation.'

After another stint back in head office working with Neilsen, Howling found himself still keen on a posting, so he raised it with his boss. Two days later he was running the traffic office in Port Moresby. Up at 6 a.m. every morning to dispatch the Catalina flying boat service out of Moresby's Fairfax Harbour, he then spent the rest of the day in the Qantas office, strategically located above the bar at the Port Moresby hotel. 'The office had a wooden floor and, since most of the staff spent a lot of the time in the bar below, if a customer came into the office to see someone, I'd thump a few times on the floor with my foot and they'd come up.'

But there were times when, Howling admits, he earned his pay. He awoke on his birthday in January 1951 to find himself covered in white dust. It was Sunday morning and since throwing soap powder over anyone celebrating a birthday was part of a local ritual, Howling was still dusting himself off when he heard one of the senior pilots, Fred Fox, shouting that they had to get a Catalina away as quickly as they could. Mount Lamington, on the other side of the mainland near Popondetta, had blown up. Until it happened, no one even knew Lamington was a volcano but its eruption killed more than 3000 people and devastated the country for kilometres around. Once the Catalina had gone, Howling spent the better part of the day kicking relief supplies out the open door of a Qantas DC-3 over what was left of the jungle.

Two months later Howling was posted back to the sales department at Sydney, given a briefcase, no instructions and told to go out and take care of the airline's travel agent contacts. He'd been at that for twelve months and late one Friday afternoon was told to go see Russell Tapp, one of the airline's original pilots and now line manager for the Far East.

'What are you doing tomorrow, George?' asked Tapp.

Since 'tomorrow' was a Saturday, Howling replied: 'Nothing.'

'You're going to Hong Kong. You won't be up there long as we're going to pull out of the place as it isn't making any money,' explained Tapp.

Howling stood waiting for more information but as nothing more was forthcoming he turned to leave.

'Oh, one thing, George. There's a place up there called Lane Crawford. They sell ice buckets shaped like an apple. Could you get one for me and send it back with one of our captains?'

That was the sum total of Howling's pre-posting briefing.

Ian Burns-Woods's first pre-posting experience later in the 1950s followed a similar pattern. He had started with Qantas in Melbourne as a traffic officer and was told he was one of two from his section who would be transferred to Port Moresby. After a series of farewell parties, Burns-Woods arrived in Sydney on the due date to receive his pre-posting briefing from the personnel department and collect six tropical uniforms. He had been told he would be leaving the same night for Port Moresby.

'What do you want?' asked the personnel officer when Burns-Woods arrived at his desk.

'I'm here to pick up my tropical uniform,' Burns-Wood stammered, now not quite knowing what to expect next.

'Where do you think you're going?' was the next question.

'I'm booked on the service to Port Moresby tonight at nine o'clock.' He passed over his ticket to confirm his credentials.

'We don't send anyone to New Guinea anymore,' came the smug comment.

It was only then that he found out they'd failed to tell him his posting had been cancelled a week previously.

But relief was at hand when he was directed to the office of the airline's traffic manager, who offered a solution. 'How about three months in Darwin to be followed by a possible two-year posting to Fiji?'

Burns-Woods couldn't agree quickly enough, as by now anything was preferable to the embarrassment of going back to Melbourne after all those farewell parties.

When they suggested he should get to the airport quickly to catch the Darwin flight, he had to explain he still hadn't collected his uniforms so all agreed he should leave it until the next day.

Burns-Woods arrived in a Darwin that had changed little in the fifteen years since the war and like Bob Weekes, he found the place somewhat less than exotic, even though its strategic location as the entry and exit point for all flights travelling along the Kangaroo Route to London and to Asia and the Orient ranked it as Qantas's second-busiest port after Sydney.

But at least it had improved slightly since Hartley Shannon had been posted there at the end of the war to re-establish it as a critical entry and departure point for all international traffic operating to Australia. Shannon had not only to contend with a war-shattered town but had to call for additional manpower from Sydney when the North Australian Workers Union threatened to pull out all the Qantas staff. One of the Sydney relief staff remembers arriving in Shannon's office to find him sitting with a loaded .38 revolver on his desk. Shannon resolved the strike but not before he was involved in a fist fight with the union's leader in Darwin's main street.

Although Burns-Woods and Bob Weekes served there some years apart, both have vivid memories of the frontier town. Weekes remembers a swimming pool and hot showers had been installed at the old Berrimah hospital for passengers, but staff had few luxuries. They were permitted to use the swimming pool when there were no passengers in residence, but, as with normal Qantas 'tropical policy', the hot showers were strictly off limits.

The single men's quarters comprised several large rooms, each divided into four by three-quarter height partitioning, which meant that each occupant shared a quarter of the benefits of a sole ceiling fan placed strategically in the middle. Anyone completing a night shift sweltered while trying to sleep during the day as the concrete floor heated up. 'The partitioning itself was so thin we used to say you could hear someone changing his mind,' quips Weekes.

Things were slightly better by the time of Burns-Woods's posting but, somewhat ironically, fourteen years later he would once again serve Qantas in Darwin—just in time to experience Cyclone Tracy.

While Darwin's staff facilities certainly left much to be desired, a posting to the Middle East could mean a whole different set of challenges, some involving considerable danger. Charles Wade was appointed Qantas's first representative in Cairo in 1956 and arrived several months before Egyptian President Gamal Abdel Nasser nationalised the Suez Canal, the precursor to all-out war. With tensions rising by the day, Wade soon discovered that not only was his mail being regularly opened by security services but everywhere he drove he was being followed by a black Citroën car. Eventually he decided to confront his 'shadow' and walked over to the car and told the driver that he needn't bother following him as he only intended going to the Australian embassy. Embarrassed, the driver tried to make out he didn't know him—but the black Citroën followed him to the embassy and home anyway.

With the political situation deteriorating, the British and French governments decided to evacuate the families of their nationals and Wade watched with disgust as the evacuees, among them women and children boarding Qantas flights at Cairo airport, were repeatedly harassed and humiliated by Egyptian customs officials. 'They would pick up each passenger's suitcase, tip it on the floor and then go through it with their boots.' He saw one dignified old English veterinary surgeon who had spent 40 years practising in Egypt have his thick spectacles torn from him and crushed under a customs officer's boot.

Things gradually worsened as animosity towards expatriates, particularly ones with British Commonwealth connections, led to little or no service in shops. Press censorship meant the only news available was that brought in by Qantas's London-based crews. Wade realised it was only a matter of time before he too would have to go and had agreed with his London boss Russell Tapp to send a coded signal should it become too dangerous to remain. The signal would be sent via cable and would simple be a request for 'permission to sell the company Ford'. Ultimately, however, London made the decision for him and, after an announcement that there would be a national strike in Cairo, Tapp ordered him to make his way to Iran before it became impossible for foreigners to leave.

As Wade drove to the airport he spotted an airport security guard he knew running by the side of the road. The guard explained that he had missed his bus and Wade's offer of a ride was gratefully accepted. When they reached the airport car park, the guard thanked him and saluted before going on his way.

Minutes later, as he himself entered the terminal, Wade had a tommy gun stuck in his ribs and someone demanding to see his airport pass. He turned to see it was the same guard.

After a long struggle to obtain a clearance number, something required by all expats who needed to travel into and out of Egypt frequently, Wade finally boarded an Arab Airlines flight and left Egypt behind him.

On 29 October 1956, Israel invaded the Sinai, the UK and France subsequently joined in and the canal was blockaded. The invasion, denied any political support from the United States, subsequently led to the resignation of UK Prime Minister Anthony Eden. In a remarkably swift reaction to the crisis and one that subsequently received high praise from the Australian government, Qantas re-routed its flights through Teheran, Turkey and Greece to avoid Cairo.

A decade later, one of Wade's colleagues, Peter Picken, arrived in the Middle East in time for another war. Picken had been sent to open Qantas's representation in Beirut and had been there for three years when, in 1967, tensions again began rising, this time between Israel and Egypt. Concerned that Qantas services operating through Bahrain might be affected, Picken began to quietly reserve accommodation in Tehran, the airline's alternative stopover point in the region.

It was as well he did. While Picken was watching his telex messages arrive one morning, the telex machine suddenly went dead. It didn't take him long to learn why. What was to become known as the Six Day War had broken out and Picken suddenly found himself with a London-bound Qantas Boeing 707 full of passengers about to arrive in Bahrain and liable to be stranded there unless they could get it out quickly to Tehran.

The complicated politics of the Middle East left Picken few options. Most of the normal destinations in the region were now closing to airlines, either because they were regarded as war zones or because the politics of the Israeli–Arab conflict wouldn't permit Qantas to land at them anyway. Unfortunately Bahrain was in the latter category and it soon became obvious that relations between Bahrain and Iran would never allow a direct flight between Bahrain and Tehran.

The only way out was to 'inaugurate' the first flight ever by Qantas between Bahrain and Doha in Qatar. The Bahrain–Doha flight, barely more than half an hour, would turn out to be one of the shortest Qantas international flights in the airline's history.

Immediately the aircraft landed in Doha, its two port engines were briefly shut down so that the door could be opened, allowing Picken to pass the required paperwork to Doha Customs who stamped it; the engines were started again and the 707 was on its way to Tehran within minutes. Within hours, all airspace closed because of the war and other airlines, including BOAC, which had the misfortune to have aircraft in Bahrain at the time, remained stuck there for days.

Picken's long Qantas career included postings to London, Hong Kong, Port Moresby, San Francisco and New York but, ironically, it would be Belgrade that would bring him some of his worst memories. Coincidentally, the man he would replace in the Yugoslav capital would be his namesake, John Picken, who, although no relation, had opened the station for Qantas several years earlier.

Belgrade was not a destination Qantas energetically sought out to serve, but when pressure started from the Yugoslav airline JAT to open services to tap the large Yugoslav diaspora in Australia, Qantas knew they had to match it.

Qantas's lack of enthusiasm for opening a service to Yugoslavia was driven by the fact that it could see very little value in the service. They expected JAT, as the country's own national flag carrier, would enjoy not only a preference among Yugoslavs but could be expected to dramatically cut fares on the route to levels Qantas would have difficulty matching economically.

In his pre-posting briefing Qantas's director of airline operations, Keith Hamilton, told John Picken a Qantas refusal would also run the risk of the government giving the route to Australia's domestic airline Ansett, thus finally opening the gates for Ansett to compete internationally with Qantas.

Hamilton obviously believed the service had doubtful long-term value for either airline! His instructions to Picken were blunt: 'Get over there and do what you can to stop it, and if you can't, stay there and run it for a couple of years.'

John Picken's arrival with his family in Belgrade turned out to be an omen for what was to come. Despite adequate notification of his arrival, no one was there to meet him and neither were there any messages for him. With no phone numbers to call, he waited impatiently for an hour or so until, with all the buses to the city gone, he looked around for alternative transport.

Handicapped by an inability to speak the language, he finally located a small hire car facility that offered him the only car they had, a tiny Fiat that would hardly have carried their bags let alone his wife, two children and himself. When he protested, they came up with a dirt-covered Peugeot. With no maps and realising he would have to drive on the right-hand side of the road, he asked a nearby policeman for directions into Belgrade, only to find out twenty minutes later that he'd been sent in the opposite direction.

Neither did Picken have any idea where the Hotel Slavia was, his intended destination, but by sheer chance as they crossed over the highest part of a bridge arch, one of his children caught sight of the hotel's sign. Finally, about to go to sleep after a hectic day, the family suddenly became aware of a vibration shaking the hotel and looking out onto the street below saw a line of Russian T54 tanks rumbling down the middle of the boulevard. Expecting next morning to find the nearby square full of military vehicles and soldiers, they soon discovered it had been a rehearsal for celebrations marking victory over the Nazis in World War II.

In the weeks that followed, while he struggled to assemble his office, John Picken found Yugoslavs, with few exceptions, generally hostile, with a default position to say 'no' to everything. By the time his namesake Peter Picken came to replace him he at least had been able to find suitable housing accommodation after months of living in the hotel.

So while Peter Picken and wife Joan might have been lucky in one sense, they found other aspects of the posting far from satisfactory when, eighteen months into their two-year posting, Joan was confronted by a man brandishing an AK-47 trying to break into their house. With Joan screaming hysterically over the phone for assistance, the man was in the process of shattering the front-door glass when help finally arrived.

Police later revealed he'd been discharged from prison that morning but the Pickens never found out what his original crime was, why he was trying to smash their door down, or, for that matter, what later became of him. Picken first suggested that a still-distraught Joan come back to Sydney while he served out his two-year term but the company decided otherwise. They both returned to Sydney only to find there was no job there for him. He left the company soon afterwards.

14
SPIES, BOMBS AND BICYCLES

If he thought opening an office in Yugoslavia was a difficult proposition, John Picken was fated to get a glimpse of the world's other brand
of communism with his posting to Hong Kong in 1969. It was the
time of China's Cultural Revolution when Mao's Red Guards were
rampant. He remembers sitting in a restaurant one lunchtime when,
just as the soup had been served, an enormous explosion on the street
below blew out the windows at the far end of the dining room.

'Someone at our table, presumably startled by the blast, dropped
his spoon on his plate with a clang which could be heard over the
bang and tinkling of falling glass.

'The Englishman sitting next to me had not spilled a drop of
soup and had shown no response at all to the blast, but at the sound
of the spoon falling had leaned across to one of his equally unfazed
colleagues and said condescendingly of the spoon-dropper: "Must
be an American."'

Charles Wade too experienced the worst of the Red Guard
period in Hong Kong. At the height of the crisis, security guards

and police were employed to protect passenger and crew buses to Kai Tak airport. On one occasion the security alert was so high Qantas was forced to take passengers by launch to the end of Kai Tak's runway where they were transferred to the terminal.

'One day they would be attacking buses and letting off bombs in Happy Valley, the next day it would be the same thing in Kowloon,' Wade recalls.

A favourite tactic of the Red Guards was to cut a hole in the floor of a small car, then, when stationary in traffic, drop an airline bag with a bomb inside onto the roadway and drive off. On one occasion Wade was travelling along Nathan Road when his driver, Lau, spotted what appeared to be a bomb in the middle of the road. Shouting for Wade to open the windows and lie on the floor he swerved and avoided the mystery package.

Such road obstructions certainly were not to be messed with. One Saturday afternoon an off-duty Hong Kong policeman spotted a bag on the tramline and when he tried to remove it the bomb exploded, killing him instantly.

Across the border from Hong Kong, in the 'other' China, memories of the Red Guards and the Cultural Revolution were still raw when Paul Miller arrived to open Qantas's Beijing office in the early 1980s. Just married, Miller and wife Judy lived for eight months in a hotel room while Miller and his small expatriate team established the ground handling, operational and sales requirements for a once-weekly Qantas service.

Qantas made no secret of the fact that, looked at in airline terms, the commercial viability of air services between Australia and China would be marginal to say the least, but an approach to the Australian delegation by their Chinese counterparts at an International Civil Aviation Organisation meeting in Montreal in

1983 set the political hares running, with Foreign Affairs pointing to 'strengthening ties and stimulating activities in various aspects of the bilateral relationship'—the euphemism normally applied when commercial realities need to be 'adjusted' to match government interests.

With only a six-month course in Mandarin before leaving Australia, Miller readily accepted the suggestion by his Chinese hosts to employ a translator, a local taxi driver, and when they finally moved into an apartment, a domestic aide as well. Miller initially assumed the trio were there to learn from the foreigners but it soon became clear they were actually there to keep an eye on the Millers!

'Once we became used to being spied upon, you could use it to your advantage as I could stand under the main light fitting in the office and complain loudly about some small matters the locals weren't able to fix,' Miller recalls.

'That often helped.'

Miller soon discovered the household domestic had never used a vacuum cleaner, washing machine or even a steam iron. 'The poor soul would ring the interpreter and say the washing machine and iron were broken because when you opened the lid or stood the iron on end, they ceased working.'

Transport, in a country where there were few cars, presented an early problem. It took several months to acquire a new Toyota Crown station wagon for the office and a Toyota van for the airport that, in a Chinese capital with thousands of bicycles, presented its own hazards. The purchase of the Toyota Crown came with the requirement for Miller to get a driving licence and, despite the bicycle onslaught and the fact that Chinese drove on the right-hand side of the road, Miller was confident he could handle it. But the 'skill' test for the licence proved to be totally unexpected.

Directed to attend Beijing's General Hospital on a Thursday morning, designated as 'foreigners' day', Miller soon realised what was required for a licence was not a test of one's driving ability, but a medical test instead. After sitting in the waiting room surrounded by around a dozen others waiting for the call, Miller was finally ushered into the side room. A doctor appeared and told him to strip down to his underpants.

'Problem was the room had no door and I was soon surrounded by the dozen or so Chinese who had obviously never seen white skin with hair on the chest and other than black hair on the head,' he says. Hooked up to blood pressure machines on both arms and acutely embarrassed as his new-found Chinese 'friends' explored every part of his torso and face, Miller found that his blood pressure went through the roof. He was told to return the following week.

Determined to avoid a repetition of his first outing, Miller sought out the only Western doctor in Beijing, a GP from western Queensland attached to the Australian embassy who prescribed a relaxant to assist him through the next week's ordeal. 'Unfortunately I took more than the recommended dose and I vaguely remember almost sliding under the front door of the hospital and impersonating a rag doll during the examination.' But Miller passed and was now given the good news: not only did he receive his licence but he was now also allowed to swim in a public pool!

As Miller expected, driving was not to be for the faint-hearted. 'Many of them had never seen a metal car with four wheels and seemed to assume it was a mirage. They'd ride their bicycles into it!'

But at times, that 'something new' had an unexpected effect on a people who had experienced little contact with the West. Asked by the Australian embassy if he could provide the Australian expatriate children with a special treat for Christmas, Miller had the company's two-metre koala suit flown in from head office, planning to wear it while handing out the presents. Padded out in the right places and with a large head, the suit was a popular attraction among children at Qantas functions in Australia but when Miller decided to give it a trial run in his office before Christmas, it had an unpredictable effect. As he sidled up and put his arm around Mr Leong, their humourless interpreter, the fellow froze on the spot, never having seen a koala, let alone one so large. Things only got worse when Miller, thinking he could calm him down, talked quietly to him from inside the suit. 'That sent him into a frenzy as he'd never encountered a talking bear before!'

Miller still remembers with affection such moments, which demonstrated how China's remoteness from the rest of the world brought such simple reactions from its citizens.

Miller's driver, Mr Wu, became a valuable member of the team and essential in getting around a city with no street signs in English and few Western-style shopfronts, meaning finding the right address was a constant challenge. When one of Miller's staff returned from a trip to Australia with a copy of the George Formby classic—'Oh Mr Woo, what can I do . . .'—and presented the tape to the driver, the Chinese Mr Wu naturally assumed the song had been written in his honour!

Mr Woo would also become something of a 'Mr Fix-it'.

When the first Qantas flight touched down at Beijing in late 1984, it brought with it the traditional first flight covers, which had been stamped by the post office in Sydney and were to be stamped by its Beijing counterpart, an important aspect of every inaugural flight. Despite the best efforts to ensure security, the box containing the covers went missing, finally traced three months later to the back corner of a cargo shed.

Now came the task of finding a 'friendly' Beijing post office willing to wind back their post stamp and complete the cycle. It was Mr Wu who, armed with a 'reasonable payment', finally found an amenable postal official and the task was completed.

Entertainment in China also carried its own risk, primarily the requirement to consume a clear 80–120 proof sorghum-based spirit known as Baijiu. With a Chinese tradition of requiring any guest to toast with three glasses, it could present a lethal combination. 'You could think of it as mix of cigarette lighter fluid, aviation fuel—pure dynamite.'

Miller served eighteen months in China before going on to a posting in Singapore but the two men who replaced him, Rod Plaister and Ron Willard, found themselves in Beijing at one of the most significant moments of the twentieth century—the Tiananmen Square student riots in June 1989.

When Plaister arrived in Beijing to take over from Willard, student unrest had been apparent for some weeks but it seemed, to Willard at least, that things were settling down. Then, one evening, while they were driving a young Chinese couple home from an airline party, one of the pair quietly remarked: 'We think something is going to happen.' It was to be a prescient comment.

The following day, a Saturday, around lunchtime, Plaister and Willard were heading home from a function when they heard several 'popping' sounds in the distance. A little further on, passing Tiananmen Square, they were turned back by a soldier. Not overly concerned, Willard, who was due to return home in a day or so, set off to do some last-minute shopping, only to return to the residents' compound to be told that convoys of trucks had been positioned close into the centre of the city.

Soon after that rumours reached them that tanks were also positioning and suddenly they were glued to CNN on their television screens. In the following hours the drama that would become known as the 'June Fourth Incident' unfolded in flickering images as tanks and thousands of armed troops cracked down on protesters in the vicinity of Tiananmen Square.

But as far as both men could judge, the remainder of the city remained unaffected and, while emphasising he never at any stage felt threatened, Willard recalls a feeling of 'deserting' his comrades as he made his scheduled departure on that day's Qantas service. Within days, Plaister too would be out, along with other expatriates, on a special Qantas flight organised by the Australian embassy to lift them to safety.

Plaister recalls returning to Beijing several weeks later where it appeared as if nothing had happened and the rest of his stay there was without incident. Both would later ponder at the ability of the China to absorb such a traumatic event in which, according to some reports, thousands had been killed.

***

Of course not all posting hazards were politically related. Sometimes the weather played a part.

Peter Snelling had been posted to New York and hadn't long moved from temporary hotel accommodation and into a rented house in early February 1969 when the worst snowstorm in New York's history dumped 38 centimetres of snow on the city, bringing it to a standstill. It would be the only snowstorm ever to close John F. Kennedy airport. Fourteen people died on the first day alone and many more were to follow on subsequent days, several at the airport itself when they sought refuge in their cars, turned on their car heaters and were asphyxiated.

The regular Qantas 707 transiting New York for London early in the morning had managed to land and, although authorities tried to keep the runways open with snowploughs, the snow kept falling as the airport closed. Despite difficulty differentiating the roadway from the sidewalk, Snelling finally reached the airport to find himself with a Boeing-load of stranded passengers and nowhere to accommodate them. His only alternative was to have the Boeing towed to a hangar and that's where they stayed for the next 24 hours. They were not alone and by mid-morning 6000 people were stranded at Kennedy as passengers and airport workers waited out the storm.

With catering and toilet facilities stretched to the limit, Snelling spent the time overseeing passenger comfort in the primitive hangar facility, with BOAC providing the catering for breakfast, lunch and dinner while snowploughs continued their battle to open the airport.

It wouldn't be the last weather-related incident that would give Peter Snelling cause for concern during his time at Qantas. Like Ian Burns-Woods, he would also be in Darwin when Cyclone Tracy arrived in December 1974.

Beyond the occasional dangers presented by war and weather, accommodation, as in those earlier years at places like Darwin and Papua New Guinea, was often far from ideal. While residing in a hotel in some exotic part of the globe might sound a romantic existence, crowded into the same room for months with your whole family while you searched for an appropriate house to rent tended to diminish its attractiveness, to say the least. Some were fortunate enough to be able to move into their predecessor's residence, a factor that would have some bearing on how they remembered such a posting in later years.

The lengths of the postings themselves were often irregular and occasionally arbitrary. Two years was common but changed company requirements often intervened, creating the requirement for unforseen and, at times costly, cross-postings or a return to a Sydney assignment.

Pilot John Fulton was told he was to be based in London for two years as a first officer. He'd enjoyed nine months there and had purchased an MG 1100 as personal transport when his boss, Torchy Uren, ordered him home for promotion to captain on DC-4s. When Fulton tried to convince Sydney they should pay to bring his MG home, he was confronted by a typical catch-22 situation. 'They told me I had to be there for two years for that,' he says.

There were, however, some exceptions when it came to the length of postings and few in Qantas could match Ward Washington's record as the airline's longest-serving overseas manager. Indeed, Washington's 40 years away from Sydney created something of a legend in Qantas and became a regular talking point among head office colleagues whenever postings were discussed, often eliciting humorous asides like: 'Does Ward Washington really exist?'

Some postings would provide moments of high drama for the Washingtons. Shan Washington sensed something was wrong when she arrived at Manila airport on the morning of Sunday, 21 August 1983. Crowds packed the airport and it wasn't until she was in the terminal that she was told Benigno Aquino had just arrived aboard a flight from Taipei. The former Senator Aquino, an outspoken opponent of the authoritarian rule of long-serving President Ferdinand Marcos, was returning home after three years in exile in the United States.

Then shots rang out. One of the airport staff quickly ushered Shan through the terminal as chaotic scenes broke out among Aquino supporters who had gathered to welcome his return. Aquino was dead, shot by soldiers as they escorted him off the aircraft.

Shan Washington's and Joan Picken's experiences in Manila and Belgrade respectively highlight the circumstances that could confront a Qantas wife on postings and there's little doubt they would both sympathise with the Murdoch family when Jeff Murdoch arrived in Port Moresby as country manager in 1989.

By now Papua New Guinea was no longer the benign environment that had existed in the years when Qantas operated there in the 1950s. Local criminals, termed raskol gangs, roamed the streets of Port Moresby and other main centres to the point where the country was on its way to ultimately be listed as one of the most dangerous in the world. The Murdochs had been there less than a month when, returning from a shopping trip to the suburb of Boroko, Robyn Murdoch drove straight into a riot as Papua New Guinean soldiers took their pay grievances onto the streets. One minute she had stopped in the traffic wondering how to avoid the disturbance; the next minute, she had armed soldiers stomping up onto the car's bonnet and over its roof.

One afternoon in September the same year, with four-year-old Sarah in the rear seat of the Mazda, Robyn stopped outside the Murray International School to collect their elder daughter Amy, when one of several raskols tore open the car door, jammed a knife at her throat and reefed her out of the car. Amy, already in the front seat, had the presence of mind to run into the school shouting as she went, as teachers began to arrive on the scene.

But by then the raskols were driving off amid the screams of Sarah, still in the back seat. They had gone only a few hundred metres when a distraught Robyn saw the vehicle slow down as Sarah was thrown onto the roadway. Fortunately the child was uninjured but Murdoch believes the assailants had been unaware of their back-seat occupant when they first drove away.

Several weeks later police found the vehicle trashed at a village behind Port Moresby airport but by then the Murdochs had done some family soul-searching as to whether Papua New Guinea was really the place for them.

'In the end we thought we had probably hit the "low" and it was all "up" from here,' says Murdoch. He turned out to be right. 'We stayed there three years and despite curfews and the like we made some great friends.'

There were, however, other posting 'hazards' who may not have been presented by carjackers, crazed escapees brandishing AK-47s or roadside bombs, but could be just as lethal in terms of career prospects.

One of the more critical assignments for Qantas station managers around the world was to meet and greet company board members, their families, and often their friends. Such people had to be given due deference and time often had to be spent ensuring they took away with them a good impression of their visit.

Beyond the chairman of the airline, each individual board member had equal status, but their demands often varied. Some asked for little help beyond perhaps a 'meet and greet' at the airport on arrival and a cursory check to see whether they needed anything during their stay. But human nature being what it is, others had an elevated view of their status as board members of Australia's national carrier and often a great deal of a manager's time was spent making sure their every whim was indulged.

Premium seats at sporting events, personal tours and access to the best table at signature restaurants were all part of the job for posted staff and even the most minor criticism of a station manager by a board member on his or her return home could have severe promotional implications and, in several cases at least, a quick return home from the posting.

Jim Bradfield, as manager in Greece, remembers greeting a lady friend of one Qantas chairman from a late-night arrival into Athens. She insisted on seeing the dawn rise over the Acropolis. Once that was achieved, she suggested another tour or two and a little shopping as well. Bradfield, by now showing the strain of having been up all night and with an important meeting to attend that day with Greek aviation officials, had to call on his wife to take over. 'She was a lovely lady but she set a cracking pace,' he recalls years later.

Even though some board members were undemanding, all station managers realised it was essential to keep a wary eye on their movements while they were visiting their area, often quietly smoothing the path behind the scenes when necessary. 'And you made sure you were in attendance at the airport when they left, just to make sure if the flight was delayed you were on hand to calm the waters,' says Bradfield.

Not to do so could be fatal for job prospects as Rick Granger was to find out on a posting to New York. Granger experienced two postings to the Americas region in the 1970s and 1980s and had the misfortune to have an important meeting with the company's US lawyers clash with the arrival of the wife of a board director.

First clearing his dilemma with his boss in San Francisco, Granger delegated one of his senior female staff to do the job, only to have Murphy's Law take over when she was unable to find the new arrival and returned to the office empty handed.

To make matters worse the board director's wife had arrived with little money and was forced to use what she had to hire a taxi. When the director himself arrived two days later, Granger's profuse apology appeared to be accepted but several months later he learnt that complaints had been lodged with management and his future prospects would be severely limited. Granger returned to Sydney on leave, found another job and resigned, going on to run a successful travel agency.

But despite the occasional traumas, most remember their postings with a high degree of fondness, benefiting from the experience and often creating friendships that last a lifetime. And those exotic locations such as London, Paris, San Francisco and Honolulu did exist for those fortunate enough to be posted there.

Some, of course, were more exotic than others. When Qantas opened its Fiesta Route through Tahiti and the Caribbean to London in the 1960s, Les Cassar was posted to Acapulco, a destination guaranteed to please any Qantas manager. Cassar also had the advantage of living across Acapulco Bay from the city and, to add to his good fortune, the Qantas station engineer who lived nearby had access to a speedboat.

Three or four days a week Cassar and the engineer took it in turns to water-ski across the bay to the Qantas office close to the opposite beach. Cassar then showered and changed into his work attire at the nearby Las Hamacas hotel before wandering in to work at his office, next door to the hotel.

But the days of postings to many of the more exotic ports are long gone, often avoiding the likelihood of staff ending up in a war zone. These ports have been sacrificed to the economic imperative of employing longer range aircraft capable of flying nonstop from Australia to destinations half way across the world. And while cities like London or San Francisco may still have their charms on the postings circuit, the days of water-skiing across Acapulco Bay are certainly over.

15
PENNY PINCHING AND CLASHING PERSONALITIES

Those who worked close to the top of the airline in its post-war years often have two primary recollections of those days. One is the emphasis on keeping tight budgets, which often led to extraordinary financial oversight by head office. The other is an almost total lack of rapport between its founder and chairman Hudson Fysh and Cedric Oban Turner, the man responsible for managing the airline.

The airline's first chairman, Fergus McMaster, a western Queensland grazier of Scottish ancestry, had enough faith in the dreams of Hudson Fysh and Paul McGinness to establish the airline in 1920 and while McGinness's role in the company was relatively short, Fysh guided it through the years of war. He eventually succeeded McMaster in 1951, serving first in the joint roles of chairman and managing director and later as chairman until his own retirement in 1960.

A man of unquestionable morals and integrity, Fysh's public persona was the outwardly austere, old-world image of a safe, reliable, dependable airline man. In his two decades at the top, he saw the company emerge from a few hundred staff who all knew each other to a globe-circling enterprise at the forefront of the world's airlines.

In those early years of his chairmanship, Fysh never lost touch with the basic financial requirement for running an airline and Peter Picken's assertion that 'Fysh knew how much the second pencil the airline ever bought had cost,' is probably not that far from the truth.

Even those of senior rank posted overseas had to be careful what they spent money on. Finding a suitable dwelling to live after arriving in London in the 1950s was not an easy task due to housing shortages but country manager Lou Ambrose had done better than most. He had found a flat in the exclusive Hyde Park Gate area, a stone's throw from the residence of a Greek shipping magnate and the Australian high commissioner. Ambrose thought it an ideal location until he heard Fysh was scheduled to come to London for talks with BOAC. Concerned at what Fysh might think of his up-market 'digs', Ambrose temporarily moved in with another Qantas family until Fysh had left for home again.

Fysh's influence obviously filtered down through the ranks of the finance department in those days. Within a week of arriving at his posting to Cairo, Charles Wade remembers a head office accounts clerk asking him the whereabouts of the Cairo petty cash float of five Egyptian pounds. When Wade cabled he had 'no idea', a return memo informed him his reply 'simply wasn't good enough'.

During his time in Cairo, Wade would find there were times when Fysh's strong wartime experiences fighting the Germans cost the company in other ways. When he set out to buy a company car, Wade found the most practical and inexpensive would be a

Mercedes Benz, but word came back that there would never be approval for a German vehicle. Wade had to make do with a British model, even though it was more expensive.

During the critical years of Qantas expansion it was Fysh's management style that led to direct confrontation with those who had come to believe that such a style was now a thing of the past. Fysh, as chairman and justifiably proud of his founder's role, found it hard to contend with a new brand of executive who possessed a different vision for the airline's future. The new order first came with the arrival of Cedric Oban Turner as general manager and developed into a situation at the very top of the airline that was little short of poisonous, on occasions splitting the airline into two camps: those who respected Fysh for his years of contribution and those who were convinced his time had passed. Eventually the relationship of the two men at the top plumbed such depths that Qantas old hands looking back still wonder how the airline even managed to function.

Turner and a later successor, Keith Hamilton, were the two men most credited with bringing the airline into the modern era, although Turner himself paid a price, never achieving the role he coveted: that of chairman. Born in Dubbo, New South Wales, he had spent several years with financial firms in Europe before gaining airline experience with Imperial Airways. An imposing character, good-looking and over six feet tall, he was recommended to Qantas by Imperial, but not before earning a reputation for abrasiveness, a trait that his former British colleagues later complained about in their dealings with him.

Despite this British perception, there was no doubting Turner's consummate analytical skills as he rose through the airline's administrative ranks. Working and travelling copious hours, Turner made his vision for Qantas his life, uncompromising to the point where he and Fysh disagreed on everything from international policy and government relations to industrial relationships with key groups within the Qantas camp, particularly its pilots.

Those who watched the relationship deteriorate could often see it from both sides. Assistant general manager 'Scottie' Allan, who had been with Qantas since its earliest days, had worked closely with both men and acknowledged Fysh's brand of loyalty and integrity had made Qantas what it was, but felt that Fysh was now unable to come to grips with the technical aspects of the modern era. Like several others he later described Fysh as a 'nice' person whose days had now passed.

Allan, who admired Turner for his ability, once describing him as the 'central strength of Qantas', also regarded him as 'remarkably selfish' with an ability to be 'nasty' to people behind their back.

Captain R.J. (Bert) Ritchie, technical director in the late 1950s and who himself later became the airline's chief executive, describes Turner as 'a man of great dominance, and coupled with that dominance, dictatorial and pretty sweeping in everything.

'There was a great deal of animosity, in fact enmity, between Turner and Fysh. Turner regarded Fysh as a fool. I regarded Fysh as a sincere, well-meaning, highly ethical man, but a simple man. Not able to match it with scheming people like Turner—and I don't mean that in a derogatory way. Turner was a general, seeing his way ahead.'

Fysh himself was under no illusion about the relationship: 'In the case of C.O. Turner and myself,' he wrote, 'there existed an association of two key people . . . who were as poles apart in their outlook on many vital human feelings, yet obliged to work together for the common good of Q.E.A.'

While some of their colleagues wondered how it all worked, in terms of essential communications between the chairman and the general manager, it didn't. But what did work was Turner's vision, supported by a small, loyal team around him who created the template for the future expansion of the airline into Asia, Europe and the Middle East in those post-war years, where most of the countries Qantas flew to were not yet interested in reciprocal rights to Australia. It would be on his 'watch' too that critical aircraft decisions were made, such as the choice of the 707 over pressure from the UK to buy the Comet.

But Turner's brilliance came with an Achilles heel and one that was to further deepen the rift between him and his chairman. He had developed a drinking problem that, along with being anathema to his puritan chairman, would at times make him something of a figure of ridicule to staff. While any who remember him will first acknowledge his unparalleled place in Qantas management history, their stories of his battle with Queen Anne Scotch would become the stuff of legend throughout the company, still recounted whenever his name is mentioned today.

Scottie Allan attests that Turner never drank during the workday but often succumbed the moment he boarded an aircraft, leading Allan to speculate it was not so much a fear of flying, as some suspected, but more a question of having nothing to do. Sadly this circumstance exposed his frailty to staff throughout the network.

At times, it appears, he didn't even know where he was. The story may be apocryphal, but Brian Wild tells of Turner on his way to Vienna to open a new Qantas office when his 707 stopped at Bangkok to refuel. Thinking he had already arrived at his destination, Turner is alleged to have walked to the front door of the Boeing and declared the Vienna office 'open' from the top of the airline steps!

One of the more bizarre episodes is recalled by Ian Burns-Woods from the time he was a young traffic officer at Melbourne airport in 1959. Along with five of his colleagues, Burns-Woods had gathered in the tiny fibro shack that served as the Qantas traffic office to be informed by their boss of the impending visit by C.O. Turner aboard a Constellation.

'His arrival would be at around 1500 hours the following day and we needed to ensure we were squeaky clean in crisp white uniform shirts and sharply creased blue trousers, all atop with our white peaked caps.

'And don't forget to polish your shoes, we were told. This man is astute and misses nothing.'

Since the Super Constellations were notorious for engine problems, Burns-Woods's team was not surprised when told that Turner's aircraft had been delayed and would not now arrive until early evening. Six hours late, they stood in nervous anticipation at the foot of the aircraft steps as the door of the aircraft opened and a succession of passengers disembarked. Once the passengers had gone, Burns-Woods watched as a flight steward emerged gripping something with both hands.

'With the aid of another crew member he slowly descended the steps carrying our long-awaited visitor on a stretcher!' Stunned, and feeling like mourners at a funeral, they soon gathered that the occupant of the stretcher was not dead but was mumbling, while one arm hung limply over the side.

Their aircraft duties completed, Burns-Woods's team once again formed a line at the foot of the steps, farewelling the passengers as they embarked on the last leg of their journey to Sydney. 'Then the stretcher reappeared and we resumed our silence while the cortege passed before us, back onto the aircraft. By now our illustrious leader was out cold, his arms folded across his chest like a revered dictator lying in state.

'As the plane taxied away we were told that he drank heavily on aircraft because he hated flying. In this instance, because of the engine delay, I guess he got an early start.'

Travelling with Turner while he negotiated with other airlines and aviation authorities worldwide could bring demands above and beyond the call of duty. Tom Roff, who negotiated Qantas's dealings with other airlines, greatly admired Turner, but admits to having put his boss to bed overseas on several occasions. But others who travelled with him needed to be wary of what they said when Turner was 'under the weather' or even when he appeared to have fallen asleep. Jack Dawson, another of his loyal colleagues, can recall examples of members of Turner's negotiating party making indiscreet comments about him while he was passed out after a drinking session. 'Their careers often came to an abrupt halt once they realised he had not missed a thing,' says Dawson.

Turner's behavioural indiscretions weren't restricted to aeroplanes. George Howling, then serving in Hong Kong, remembers being invited to a dinner party at the Qantas Japan manager's residence while C.O. Turner was in town. Howling and other guests, including UK poet Dame Edith Sitwell and several leading businessmen, were enjoying summer evening drinks overlooking the home's spacious garden when 'C.O.', as he was known to all in Qantas, stood up and walked a few paces onto the lawn to relieve himself.

'I thought Dame Edith was going to slide under the table,' records Howling.

Howling also confirms what many others would describe as the Jekyll-and-Hyde nature of Turner's personality. 'On the aircraft and with Qantas people around him he would drink and be unpleasant but on his own he could be charming. Often he would come to Hong Kong and spend a week there and wouldn't get drunk. We would invite him to dinner parties with friends of ours who had nothing to do with airlines and he would be absolutely delightful company,' says Howling.

As time went by, those close to Turner became increasingly concerned his excessive drinking would destroy any chance he had to succeed Fysh as chairman. When speculation about Fysh's successor arose in the press in the mid-1960s, one of his closest confidants, the airline press relations manager John Ulm, in a brutally frank personal note, left Turner in no doubt what was at stake.

Ulm's memo directly tackled the drinking problem, claiming it was leading to despair within his close-knit team in addition to affecting his image outside the company.

But it was to no avail. In a decision made by Prime Minister Menzies and Treasurer Harold Holt—reportedly taken without consultation with their Minister for Civil Aviation Senator Henty—the secretary of the Treasury, Sir Roland Wilson, already a member of the board, was appointed to take over as chairman from June 1966.

Wilson's pre-eminent role as Australia's most influential financial practitioner led to inevitable tensions with Turner who, as with his relationship with Fysh, found it difficult to accept any constraints.

Neither did Turner curb his drinking. Within twelve months of Fysh's leaving Turner too would be gone, forced to retire at the age of 60 on 30 June 1967. Both harboured bitterness at their treatment: Fysh on the grounds that the company he founded had left him financially disadvantaged in his retirement; Turner feeling the pinnacle of his ambition had been denied him.

16
FLAWS AMONG THE BRILLIANCE

'Who needs imperial honours when you have the Qantas board?' Often attributed to former senator and Labor government minister Gareth Evans, these words sum up respective Australian governments' use of Qantas appointments as political capital.

When it comes to airlines there's been a tendency to look at the most significant eras of their history through the prism of aeroplane development. Qantas is no exception, largely because, as the oldest airline in the English speaking world, its progress has been sharply defined from the wood, wire and fabric days of the DH-86 biplanes that operated its first overseas service in 1935, to the Constellations that circled the world in the 1950s, the Boeing 707 jets that slashed the Constellation flight times in half and into the mass travel era of the Boeing 747. But what's often missing from that examination are the people who made it all happen, not only those who monitored technological developments, and assessed and recommended their value, but also those who took the enormously expensive decisions to invest in aircraft, infrastructure and support equipment.

As with any human endeavour involving intelligent, highly motivated people, they have brought their own mix of personality and talent into a high-profile industry with constant political, technical and economic challenges. In the case of Qantas, through and beyond the days of McMaster, Fysh and Turner, those who have occupied positions at the very top of the airline's structure—as chairmen, board directors or chief executives—often have been strong-willed people whose beliefs and ideas, not to mention egos, have had a marked impact on the airline during their time in office.

Some enjoyed being the public face of the airline, pushing back against what they have seen as unwarranted government interference or pushing forward against commercial threats from other airlines and organisations, relishing the public exposure Qantas brings in the Australian context. Others, several of whom probably had the most significant impact on the airline's future or its very survival, remain virtually unknown to anyone outside the airline itself.

In the case of the airline's chairmen and its board, at least until the privatisation of the airline in the mid-1990s, it is rarely possible to separate the influence of government from the way such appointments were made. In terms of chairmen, there were exceptions of course.

Wilson's appointment as his successor must have been difficult for Fysh to accept, particularly as, during the time Wilson had served on the board, the pair had clashed dramatically over gossip surrounding Wilson's personal relationship with a member of the airline's staff, Joyce Chivers. Chivers, who appears to have been a polarising character within the company, had been appointed without Fysh's knowledge to the New York office in the 1950s, leading Fysh to suspect her appointment had been made behind his back by Wilson and Turner. Fysh subsequently ordered the airline's security chief

Gordon Fraser to check on the rumours about the nature of their relationship and the impact it was having on the company.

Chivers, whom Ulm describes as 'physically attractive but without much talent' worked in Ulm's public relations team, and became widely disliked throughout the company.

Whatever the truth of her relationship with Wilson, any Qantas manager appointed to New York soon learnt to tread warily when it came to Chivers, who even knew before they did when board member Wilson was due in town, a situation that could lead to difficult moments for the manager. Peter Picken recalls on one occasion going to the airport with his company car and driver to meet Wilson only to find Chivers already there. Picken's driver had parked the car on the kerb and, as Picken stepped forward to open the door, Wilson turned and asked for the car keys.

Handed the keys, Wilson drove off with Chivers, leaving Picken and his driver to find their own way back to the office.

When Chivers's posting to the Americas region came to an end, other staff organised a party to coincide with her departure for Australia, gathering at a venue at San Francisco's Fisherman's Wharf, where John Fordham remembers holding up an open phone line through which the Qantas airport manager described her aircraft taxiing for take-off. Loud cheers went up as he confirmed its wheels had left the ground.

Wilson doubtless brought financial rigidity to the airline and his extensive network, established over so many years at the top of the public service, certainly helped the airline in its relationship with Canberra. Rare though they may have been in Wilson's case, even he would contribute to one of the airline's lighter moments.

Wilson lived in a pleasant, single-storey home in Forrest, one of the national capital's better suburbs, in a house that he used as a hobby, having done much of the improvement work himself. Set some distance back from the road behind a high hedge, one of its features a metre or so inside the front gate was a metre-deep fish pond built from native rocks and decorated with water plants.

During his time as Canberra manager, John Picken had the responsibility for ensuring that Wilson's Qantas board papers, flown from Sydney a few days before the board meeting, were delivered promptly to its chairman. These were not the type of documents one trusted to a courier and needed to be personally delivered.

Picken remembers it was the middle of winter and Canberra was being lashed with driving rain when he dispatched one of his staff, Alan Penton, on the delivery assignment. It was pitch dark by the time Penton arrived at the Wilson home and, in the icy conditions, Picken believes Penton decided to take a short cut to the front door rather than take the path around the pool. The result was probably inevitable.

The first Picken heard was a phone call from Lady Wilson to explain she didn't know whether to laugh or cry when she answered the door to the bedraggled figure of Penton standing there, soaking wet, mud from head to foot, but holding aloft the still-dry satchel containing the board papers.

'She invited him in to dry off but he'd replied the rain would wash the mud off anyway and retreated into the night.'

When Picken broached the subject with Penton next morning and asked him what he thought of the front garden, Penton replied it had been 'too dark to see much'.

'He obviously didn't want to talk about it,' says Picken.

The tale was another to enter the Qantas legend, albeit one of the few snippets of humour ever associated with stories about Wilson, although a select few can recall one visit to New York where his former role as secretary of the Treasury helped him out of a tight spot. Wilson needed money, so a New York staffer was directed to accompany him to a nearby bank where he could cash his traveller's cheques. But when he signed the cheques and the teller asked for identification Wilson discovered he had left his passport back at the Qantas office. There followed moments of embarrassment as the bank teller repeatedly declined to accept the staffer's assurance as to the identity of his chairman, until Wilson asked to be shown an Australian bank note. When a note was produced Wilson jabbed his finger at the signature on the note: 'That's me, secretary of the Australian Treasury.'

The signatures matched and the bank cashed the cheques.

After the death of the first Lady Wilson in a motor accident in Mexico in 1972, Joyce Chivers became the second Lady Wilson in 1975.

At least Wilson's successor, in 1973, Donald George Anderson, as a former director of the Department of Civil Aviation (DCA), had aviation experience.

'DG', as he was known by those who worked with him, arrived at Qantas after sixteen years leading the DCA and at a time when the Whitlam government and its transport minister, Charles Jones, were anxious to merge the DCA and the shipping and ground transport arms into one mega-department. Jones's problem therefore was how to move the highly regarded Anderson out of the way without creating unnecessary problems for himself throughout the industry. Legend has it that when Whitlam asked Jones what they would need to offer Anderson to smooth the way, Jones suggested the chairmanship of Qantas, knowing Anderson would be quick to accept.

Jones may also have been aware of what others close to Anderson had known for some time—that the years of arguing with a succession of ministers and struggling against the relentless political influence of tough airline chiefs like Eddie Connellan and his supporters within Jack McEwen's Country Party and Sir Reginald Ansett's Liberal Party connections had taken their toll on Anderson.

Late in 1973, with Wilson's term about to end, Jones summoned Anderson to his Parliament House office and the pair went to see Whitlam. They were back in Jones's office 30 minutes later and Anderson broke the news to two of his close advisers that he had accepted the Qantas chairmanship: 'I'm just tired of feeding pearls to swine.'

It was a comment somewhat out of character for Anderson, but an indication of his weariness and frustration with the political system he had operated under for so many years. His health was already deteriorating when he joined Qantas. He served only two years as chairman, resigning shortly before his death at 58 in December 1975.

Anderson's successor, Cyrus Lenox Simson Hewitt, already a member of the board, would turn out to be one of the more controversial appointments. Often cited as a protégé of Sir Roland Wilson, Hewitt fought an at times courageous battle, often in international forums, against the onslaught of the low-cost fares offered by charter operators that full-service airlines like Qantas, with their higher cost structures, would struggle to match. At the same time he immersed himself in the minutest detail of Qantas's operations, such as persistent questioning of the airline's catering.

No chairman before, or probably since, has taken such an intense interest in on-board catering. While it was an ever-present concern for staff, there is little doubt that Hewitt's concentration on aircraft catering lifted the standard, quality and presentation of the airline's in-flight service. He was interested in everything from in-flight service to the standard of the marmalade and yoghurt served to passengers.

Always well briefed, Hewitt developed a fearsome reputation, particularly among those serving on outstations, quizzing them on all matters relating to their responsibilities. Along with their head office colleagues, they quickly learnt that an honest 'I don't know but I shall find out' answer was acceptable to any question. An off-the-top-of-the-head response that proved incorrect could be fatal.

An inveterate traveller, Hewitt spent much time in the air, often to the relief of head office personnel who had developed their own in-house codes with their outstation colleagues. As he boarded a Qantas aircraft in Sydney a five-word telex—'Our gain is your loss' would flash around the world.

While George Howling, who had the major responsibility for the areas that attracted Hewitt's attention, spent much of his time running down the solutions, he also saw another side of Hewitt rarely visible to other staff. Howling remembers him and his wife Nan being invited by Hewitt to spend a few extra days together after a conference they'd attended in Europe.

'It was absolutely delightful. He was a wonderful dinner companion, never mentioned Qantas once and was charming the whole time. Mind you, once we'd returned to Sydney things returned to "normal,"' remembers Howling ruefully.

Despite such traits, there was no doubting Hewitt's ability to grasp important issues.

In his difficult early days setting up a service to Belgrade, John Picken was surprised to find himself standing behind Hewitt as he checked in at the hotel for his room key. Since neither had known the other was in the country, Hewitt explained he'd been in Europe and decided to make an informal and unofficial visit to Belgrade.

'He said he'd therefore like to have breakfast with me next morning, listed a number of topics, said goodnight and walked off.'

Nervous about what was to come, on reaching his room, Picken poured himself a stiff whisky and prepared some notes for the breakfast encounter. 'I must admit I was deeply impressed, despite not expecting to see anyone from Qantas he had concisely listed everything of importance that we need to address, a list of subjects already in a logical sequence for discussion.'

In *A Certain Grandeur*, his bestselling book on the Whitlam years, Graham Freudenberg describes Hewitt thus:

> In Hewitt, [Rex] Connor felt he had a kindred spirit, both were strong nationalists, both loners, both impatient of the windy orthodoxies of established channels, both saw themselves as tough minded negotiators, both authoritarians, both more easily able to inspire fear than affection, yet both had great charm in private, both were extremely confident in the ability of their applied intelligence to master any problem.

With his five-year term coming to an end, Hewitt fought a determined battle with the Fraser government to be re-appointed for a further five years. When the government offered him only a one-year extension, he fought even harder, claiming a less-than-five-year appointment was 'unprecedented' for a Qantas chairman. In the end he lost, bringing to an end the appointment of public servants into the top job.

Most in Qantas thought it was about time. Even Bert Ritchie, in his last months as chief executive, and not long after Hewitt had been appointed chairman, had compiled a critical summary of the government appointments to the board, and particularly that of chairman.

In a confidential brief to the minister, Peter Nixon, Ritchie highlighted the policy of using the chairman's appointment as a 'gift of government', at the expense of the airline's commercial or competitive requirements. 'This has not always been best for Qantas as a company and the many thousands of dedicated employees who are not public servants and have made Qantas their career,' Ritchie wrote.

Hewitt's successor as chairman, James Bolton Leslie, was a striking contrast. A decorated war hero and one of Australia's leading businessmen, Leslie brought a totally different approach to the chairmanship.

Leslie appears to have been a reluctant candidate. Cruising on the Nile when Malcolm Fraser offered him the job, it took a while for his appointment to be confirmed, not least because of some indecision on his part. Having only recently retired as managing director of Mobil Oil Australia, the first Australian to be appointed to the role by the US parent company, he had been looking forward to a much quieter life.

In contrast to the publicity that surrounded the appointment of several of his predecessors, when Leslie finally arrived back in Sydney, he had already cleared immigration and customs before any Qantas staff in the arrivals area recognised their new chairman. Short in stature, with a dry, often self-deprecating sense of humour, he brought a more relaxed atmosphere to the chairman's role, but also formidable business experience and contacts.

While his predecessor had a testy relationship with the media, Leslie was generous with his time for journalists, willing to give a Qantas view often contrary to the government's own concept of how the airline should be run. Close to Prime Minister Fraser, he showed little hesitation in taking on the government if he felt the airline was not being treated fairly, even at the expense of offending the responsible minister.

Contrary to many, Leslie believed that even a government-owned enterprise could match others in the commercial environment provided it was well managed, offered salary levels to match other comparative organisations and received government support in similar fashion to major competitors, like Singapore Airlines. Particularly sensitive to the government making political decisions that affected the commercial wellbeing of the airline, he was adamant that, if Qantas was expected to operate efficiently and profitably, and in Australia's interests, it should be the airline board's responsibility to make decisions to allow it to do so, not 'meddling' in its affairs by government.

And when it came to Canberra, Leslie was seen by some to have another advantage over his predecessor. While Hewitt had an unsurpassed knowledge of how to handle the public service, Leslie's appointment by a Liberal government could be expected to improve the airline's relationships with Canberra. But it didn't take him long to demonstrate there were clear distinctions between the airline's owners and its board, at one stage taking the unprecedented step of leading the entire board to Canberra to confront the minister, Ralph Hunt, with proof that government policies aimed at allowing domestic airlines Ansett and TAA onto profitable international routes were 'setting Qantas up for failure'. Bluntly listing nine steps that he believed would 'reduce Qantas to a shell, ready to be taken over at a bargain price', he told Hunt the government had already taken five of them.

Leslie and Bert Ritchie's successor, Keith Hamilton, could be regarded as a near-perfect combination to lead Qantas. While his chairman had no hesitation in fighting the battles against the political influence of the Murdoch and Abeles–led Ansett, Hamilton set out to restore a balance sheet hampered by a perilous debt-to-equity ratio, at the same time setting Qantas on a course for a future he was convinced would be in the Asia-Pacific region. It was a region he knew intimately and had been an integral part of his own rise to the top of the airline.

Hamilton's appointment as general manager in 1976 immediately brought a much sharper planning and marketing emphasis to the airline, and a management style very much in contrast to that of his former pilot predecessor. His youthful features masked an impressive knowledge of the industry and the ability to encapsulate complex issues into the most simple, erudite terms. Marge Strang, as his personal assistant, was in awe of his ability to dictate board papers in one 'take', off the top of his head. A heavy smoker, known for compulsively rattling his cigarettes and lighter in his jacket pocket while talking, he enjoyed a gamble but, like Turner, appears to have had little personal life outside the airline. Strang says in the ten years she worked for him he never once mentioned anything relating to his personal life and could remember him only making one reference to a domestic issue.

'He broke into his dictation one day and asked me whether I knew anything about combination fridge-freezers. When I recovered from the initial shock and admitted I couldn't help him much, that was the end of it.'

While Hamilton attracted great loyalty from those close to him, most would learn to be wary of becoming too close. His Machiavellian traits tended to keep even those closest in a constant state of nervousness and, although he was renowned for his ability to identify those with the talent to reach high positions in the airline, an equal number would fall by the wayside.

'He would not hesitate to give tough assignments to those younger executives he judged might have future leadership roles in the airline, but at times you could liken it to throwing a batch of them into a vat of hot oil. Those who managed to climb out made it, others slid back from whence they had come, often never to surface again,' explains one of his closest associates.

Like his mentor Cedric Turner, Hamilton was a chief executive for his time, transforming the airline from its heavy traditional emphasis on flying operations. Although he insisted on being fully briefed when necessary, he left engineering and operations to those he considered most qualified, while he concentrated on marketing, financing and route structure, areas he considered more relevant to the times. In his final year at the helm the airline recorded a record profit of $58 million.

Hamilton's successor was the airline's deputy chief executive and chief operating officer Ron Yates, the only CEO in the history of the airline to have been an engineer. One of Australia's most respected engineers, Yates brought to the job an intimate knowledge of the airline, from the days of its post-war Lancastrians and Constellations through to his close association with the choice of both the Boeing 707 and the 747. Unlike Hamilton, he showed a readiness to present a more public face of the airline, often highlighting its heritage and world standing in speeches to technical forums and through other public appearances. But, like his predecessor, Yates appeared to enjoy the 24-hour-a-day commitment to the job, although occasionally taking it to extremes, once suggesting to technicians installing a new phone system that they include a handset in his office toilet. Once Jim Leslie heard of it, he reportedly talked him out of it.

Yates's successor, John Menadue, attracted wide popularity among his staff, although he later confessed he found difficulty working with Jim Leslie and the board, a situation that, although the company was recording profits, would lead to a dramatic falling out in 1989. The termination of his contract became a very public dispute, played out in the media spotlight in a situation where there could be no winners.

There was also the vexed case, at least as far as the airline was concerned, of other board appointments. Long regarded as 'jobs for the boys' and described by one former Qantas executive as 'political thank-yous', Qantas staff, and even the media, often had cause to wonder what some of the appointments brought to the airline, despite the heavy emphasis on their 'wealth of union experience' or 'business acumen' as individuals.

While some doubtless did make a contribution, many did little beyond utilising the prestige such an appointment brought with it, not to mention the free travel. Staff would often look with disdain at board members' use of the perks their position offered and how they interpreted them, occasional examples flickering widely throughout the Qantas rumour mill. One director's wife gained notoriety for arriving for a holiday in Fiji to discover she'd left her bathing cap at home. Obviously finding the local products not to her taste, she had her own flown over.

Another director won dubious renown for compromising the company's long-standing trust arrangement that allowed in-company mail to be carried on flights without having it subject to customs requirements. Presumably to save the postal expense, he sent his tailored trousers back from Hong Kong, only to have authorities discover them on one of their rare intercepts. Heavy fines followed.

For Roland Wilson at least, one of the perks of office appears to have continued after his retirement as chairman. Not long after he took over as chairman, Jim Leslie is understood to have discovered a consultancy valued at $1 that enabled Wilson to access discounted staff travel. Leslie asked for the contract to be cancelled but whether it was or not is unknown.

It's hard to imagine Qantas board meetings being other than staid business affairs, although personalities being what they are, they had odd moments of relief.

It was customary for a chief executive to invite a newly appointed senior executive to a board lunch to meet members of the board, and when Hamilton appointed Doug Scott to the senior engineering role, it was Scott's turn to grace the table. Hamilton was only too aware of Scott's unflappable demeanour and his ability to call a spade a shovel, so, taking him aside beforehand, Hamilton advised him to play it safe and speak only when spoken to so as to avoid any of Scott's renowned 'one-liners'.

As it transpired one of the items on the board agenda that day concerned a proposal to sell one of the airline's Combi freight 747 aircraft to an African airline that would use it to transport heavy metals out of their country.

Scott had only just sat down to lunch when one of the board members, Mary Beasley, politely asked whether the Combi would be capable of handling such heavy loads, to which the confident Scott replied: 'You can take my word for it. It will go down the runway like a dog with worms.'

Hamilton's reaction is not recorded.

Occasionally a board member brought a refreshing change of

pace, although in the case of former union man Sir Jack Egerton, political correctness often took a backward step.

Egerton, a big, bluff, though popular Queenslander, was appointed to the board by Whitlam in 1973 and it's doubtful the board had seen anything like him before.

Tradition had it that when a new appointment attended his or her first board it was customary for them to initially take the seat next to the chairman at the top of the table. When businessman Tristan Antico arrived for his first board lunch, he had hardly settled into his 'privileged chair' when Egerton, sitting in his own assigned seat at the far end of the table, announced in a loud voice: 'Hey Trist, don't get too bloody comfortable up there. Queenslanders and wogs usually finish up down this end.'

But it would be while in the company of Aboriginal federal parliamentarian Neville Bonner that Egerton made one of his most notorious comments while a director of Qantas Airways.

When the British Concorde arrived in Australia to show its paces in the hope of a firm Qantas order for the supersonic jet airliner, Bonner and Egerton were among the elite group invited to ride the aircraft back as far as Singapore on its way home.

As the Concorde streaked across the sky at 40,000 feet over the middle of Australia, Egerton turned to Bonner and offered: 'Well, Nev, I guess this makes you the first supersonic boong.'

To his great credit, Bonner burst into laughter, probably evidence of Egerton's ability to easily cross the politically incorrect divide.

Despite his acceptance of an imperial honour creating some animosity among the Labor heartland, Egerton's party background would prove a valuable contribution to the board's deliberations.

UNUSUAL LOADS

17
GUM TREES FROM WHEEL WELLS

'You mean we're sending hundreds of Australian gum trees to Athens? You've got to be kidding me.' That was the reaction of one Qantas corporate executive late in 1986 when ordered to head to the New South Wales Forestry Commission's nursery in Sydney's north-west and take delivery of 600 examples of *Eucalyptus largiflorens*.

But had he been a Qantas cargo man, the strangeness of the request would have held no surprise, although even he would have had to acknowledge the origins of the requirement for such trees were a trifle unusual to say the least.

During the 1950s, Athens was a key transit point on the Qantas' Constellation whistlestop services to London. The Constellations had long gone by the 1970s when a crop of trees on a hillside in line with the airport runway had grown to such a height that they were now presenting Qantas with a problem in the take-off path of its Boeing 747s climbing out of Athens. It's not that there was a danger of crashing into them, simply that the normal climb-out requirements for Qantas tended to be much more rigid than those that applied to other airlines operating out of Athens, because the presence of the trees restricted the take-off weight Qantas wanted to use on its nonstop flights to Bangkok, particularly through the hot Athens months of July, August and September.

And since restricted take-off weight invariably meant off-loading freight and reduced the revenue the aircraft could earn, Qantas chief operating officer Ron Yates tossed the problem to the airline's manager for Greece, Jim Bradfield.

Bradfield, said Yates, needed to take a 'personal interest in the removal of the offending trees'.

'I'm prepared to loan you an axe or a chainsaw if that would expedite the project,' was one early Yates suggestion.

But when Bradfield broached the subject with Greek aviation authorities, he was in for a surprise, prompting a series of telex exchanges that still exist in Qantas files.

'You won't believe this but the offending trees are Australian eucalyptus trees. Source of entry into Greece believed to be from the tyre tread of Qantas aircraft,' a Bradfield telex to Yates explained.

Yates's reply was somewhat tongue in cheek: 'I'm briefing our operations people that their future propagation efforts should be restricted to small shrubs. Hopeful you will soon cable that relief has been granted.'

Several weeks later Bradfield was able to advise Yates the deed had been done: 'Native Australians cut down to size by the Greeks.'

Yates was so delighted with the revenue advantage gained he offered to donate 600 eucalypts to the Greek government as a token of his airline's appreciation, a gesture the Greeks accepted for planting on the barren slopes of Mount Parnes, about an hour's drive from the Greek capital.

Thus, in late October 1987 Bradfield, the Australian ambassador to Greece, Les Johnson and assorted Greek government officials gathered at Mount Parnes to complete the cycle of the Athens trees, only to be confronted by a vicious wind tearing across the hillside, prompting Bradfield to suggest the occasion be limited to a brief ceremony in the comfort of a tavern not far from the hillside.

'In fact the wind was so bad it was difficult to hold your footing on the site and we felt it would be unfair to expose the government officials and almost 200 members of the Greek–Australia Association to the elements,' Bradfield recalls. But the Greek contingent insisted that the job be done there and then, and each person chose a tree and set off to plant it on the hillside. 'Some even came back for more and insisted their children plant one as well.'

A later photograph sent by Bradfield to Yates shows Bradfield and Ambassador Johnson, hair ruffled and their jackets almost torn off by the wind as the ceremonial holes were dug.

'I can guarantee the series of toasts which followed at the taverna certainly made up for it,' he confessed.

What he would also finally confess 30 years later was the trees they planted on Mount Parnes's windswept hillside that windy afternoon weren't the 600 seedlings Ron Yates had sent from Sydney. They had been quarantined on arrival by Greek Customs and had to be destroyed. Bradfield had to find his own eucalypts in Athens to keep the promise!

Bradfield later served as the airline's director of freight, where he experienced firsthand the full range of oddities the business of air freight brings.

***

Being appointed to run the air-freight side of Qantas was not something that executives went out of their way to achieve. Up until more recent times, it was largely regarded as merely a 'top up' appendage to the main passenger carrying role of the airline, almost a case of if there was any space left over after passengers and baggage were loaded, extra freight would be tossed on. Often freight's low priority, particularly in the days of propeller-driven DC-4s and Constellations, created serious problems for Qantas station managers.

George Howling remembers being so unpopular with his most important commercial clients in Hong Kong that he committed a cardinal sin in the airline business—arranging the re-routing of a Qantas service without telling head office in Sydney he was doing it.

Howling's problem was that so much Sydney-bound freight had piled up in the airline's Hong Kong freight shed that he couldn't even go to lunch without being subjected to a harangue from the colony's top businessmen. It meant too that he was losing business to his main competition, Cathay.

Cathay's advantage rested on the fact that a regular flight crew was assigned to operate its service to Australia, while Qantas chopped and changed its crews, many of whom were reluctant to carry beyond the bare minimum of freight on such a long-haul route.

Howling's opportunity came when one of his old pilot mates, Phil Oakley, recognised his dilemma. Oakley suggested if his flight that night went via Manila then they could carry enough fuel for that short sector to enable them to throw on as much of the backlog as they could move. Then Oakley would simply refuel in Manila and continue on to Sydney.

So off went Oakley, informing Qantas Sydney after leaving Hong Kong that he needed to make an unscheduled 'technical stop' in the Philippines.

The freight problem solved, Howling was once again back in the good books with his valued clients but that hardly allayed his concerns that such a serious breach of company policy could get him in deep trouble. But the weeks went by and he heard nothing, until the customary note arrived on his desk advising of the coming summer schedules. He was delighted. The DC-4 would now call at Darwin on the way to Sydney, solving his freight problems.

The next day another note arrived, this one from his boss, Lew Ambrose, the airline's line manager for the Far East. 'Next time George, I suggest it would be better if you consult with head office before you do such things.'

'So I got out of it, although they'd known all along,' says Howling.

'I don't think many people in this airline ever re-routed an aircraft off their own bat.'

***

Aside from Howling's accumulated freight dilemma and Fred Fox safely dropping chooks out of his Catalina flying boat to a patrol station in Papua New Guinea in the 1960s by wrapping them in newspaper, there are endless tales of the challenges associated with the air cargo business, most of the more bizarre ones involving the carriage of animals, birds, reptiles, panthers and even whales.

Domestic pet stories abound. There's the one about the cat that arrived in at the Sydney cargo terminal for dispatch to the owner in New Zealand. When the cargo officer went to prepare the necessary paperwork for the shipment, to his horror he noticed the cat was dead. Thinking quickly he rounded up a similar tabby, one of the several that always frequented the cargo shed, and off it went to Auckland.

When the owner arrived at Qantas cargo in Auckland to collect it she shocked the cargo man with 'That's not my cat.'

'How do you know it's not your cat?' responded the cargo man, pointing to her name on the paperwork and hoping to retrieve something from what was looking like an embarrassing situation for the airline.

'My cat was dead. I was bringing it home to bury it.'

Dog stories dominate too, led by the Qantas traffic officer in Darwin who decided to give a half-dozen pedigree dogs some exercise during their stopover on the way to Singapore. It wasn't long after the war and the dogs were destined to replace some of the animals that had been lost during the Japanese occupation. Unfortunately for the traffic officer, the exceedingly grateful dogs disappeared through the airport fence never to be seen again. So, using similar initiative to his Sydney colleague's dead cat 'solution', the Darwin man and his mates rounded up every stray dog they could find and sent them on their way. What happened on their arrival in Singapore is not recorded but, as the story goes, this was the main reason most of the dogs in post-war Singapore weren't quite pedigree.

Sometimes it was the pet owners who had the Qantas cargo staff scratching their heads, although Bill Easton, who worked in Qantas cargo for many years, says they often provided some light-hearted relief.

Some cat owners were so attached to their animals they would ask if they could 'accompany them out to the aircraft just to say goodbye,' unfortunately having to be told such a farewell gesture was not permitted across a busy airport tarmac.

Easton remembers a woman ringing one evening to ask if she could speak to her dog, which was being held in quarantine. She called so many times with such insistence that the cargo officer, realising the dog was fairly small, finally brought it to the phone in its cage and propped the phone alongside it, while the woman made soothing noises to the animal.

Cargo staff occasionally took the opportunity to generate their own lighter moments and pranks were not unusual. When the

Port Moresby cargo staff tried to load a dog destined for Lae onto a single-engine Otter aircraft, they found the wooden box it was packed in wouldn't fit through the door into the Otter's cargo hold. Keen to make the most of such a unique opportunity, they dismantled the box, reassembled it in the hold, then placed the dog in the box and off went the Otter across the Owen Stanley Ranges to Lae where the cargo people in Lae found they couldn't get the box out no matter what they tried. Finally calling Port Moresby for help, they were met with peals of laughter over the phone.

Occasionally antics would backfire. Easton remembers when an extremely intelligent cockatoo with a very impressive repertoire was forced into an extended stay at Sydney cargo and the staff tired of its constant chattering. Every time it started they would tell it to '@#&% off'.

When the owner eventually collected his bird and had to limit its public appearances, Qantas was confronted with serious legal ramifications.

George Howling's bird experience was also embarrassing. Howling was working in Sydney cargo in his early days in Qantas when well-known zoological administrator and philanthropist Sir Edward Hallstrom sent along an exotic parrot for shipping to a zoo in London. Somehow or other the bird got out of the cage and headed towards the high ceiling in the cargo office. Despite frantic attempts by Howling and his offsider to retrieve it, the parrot finally flew out the office door and into Bridge Street.

When Howling broke the news to his boss, he was abruptly told the penalty. 'You ring and tell Sir Edward yourself.'

Hallstrom was far from pleased, leaving Howling to suspect that the missing bird might have been the reason he was sent to work at the airport soon after and his offsider was sent to New Guinea!

Certainly among Qantas people the most notorious cargo flights were the monkey charters to Australia from the Asian subcontinent during the manufacture of the Salk vaccine. The aeroplanes used were DC-4s and Lockheed Constellation freighters and those who flew them still shudder at the memory of hundreds of monkeys, often in cages containing six to ten each, stacked into the aircraft for the long haul to Australia.

Pilots and the animals' handlers were issued with special blue overalls for the flights and a trip to the toilet at the rear of the aircraft meant running the gauntlet down an aisle between screaming monkeys, throwing everything from food to faeces at the hapless crew. The loadmaster was the worst affected, as feeding them meant he received the onslaught from every direction. On arrival in Sydney the blue overalls would be burnt and the complete aircraft cleaned and fumigated.

Bruce Smith confesses that, as the last flight engineer ever employed by Qantas, his late recruitment and low seniority meant he was often the first chosen when it came to the dreaded monkey charters.

Smith did three trips, out of Kuala Lumpur, Singapore and Calcutta. 'The stench was horrific,' he recalls. On some in-cabin configurations, they loaded the monkeys in the rear half of the Constellation where they could be separated from the five-man crew up the front by a bulkhead.

'The smell was so bad we used to use rolls of masking tape to seal off the bulkhead. Anyone who removed it was under pain of death from the rest of us.'

Sadly, beyond a few photographs, little remains of the monkey charters in the Qantas archives, although the documents that are there support Bruce Smith's belief it was not for the faint-hearted. One is a hand-written recollection by flight traffic officer Bill Colbert of a DC-4 charter out of Dhaka in the 1950s, pointing out the discomfort of having more than a thousand monkeys on board an aircraft that not only lacked pressurisation but also had to fly no higher than 7000 feet to avoid the risk of the animals freezing to death.

The combination of turbulence at low altitude and the stench in the cabin after four or five hours hardly bears thinking about. Added to Colbert's woes were engine problems that forced them to divert to the Royal Air Force base at Butterworth in Malaya, where the RAF officer on duty denied his request to provide hangar space for the monkeys out of the intense heat, suggesting he place their cages under a row of newly planted metre-high trees at the edge of the airfield.

After a spare engine arrived from Singapore, they continued on to Darwin and Sydney, where Colbert learnt later that the aircraft's captain had been disciplined for his handling of the engine problem. Colbert was unimpressed, having taken pains to note the diligence of the crew in quickly loading the aircraft in Dhaka to avoid a curfew limitation that would have forced an overnight stop and therefore saving both Qantas and CSL additional costs.

'But I have learned, especially in the employ of Qantas, that somewhere along the line someone must be made the scapegoat,' says Colbert. Not all the monkey charters were to Australia. Graham Crowther, as a second officer on Constellations, remembers crewing one flight to London in the 1960s.

Crowther still expresses his amazement at the ability of the animal handlers to suffer the stench: 'even nonchalantly eating their sandwiches in this environment.' But at least the monkeys were small and in cages. For Crowther, an elephant he once carried was an entirely different matter.

Although special reinforced wooden cages were designed to keep the animal in check, Crowther says at one stage of the flight the elephant looked like breaking out of its box.

'He might have been a baby but he was still well grown and was lying on his side and pressing so hard against the side of his crate the wood was buckling.

'Although we carried stun guns, something of the weight of an elephant loose in the cabin would have had disastrous consequences for control of the aeroplane.'

Carrying horses to the United States and across the Tasman to New Zealand in the 707 days was big business for Qantas, although it too had its moments. In the event a distressed animal was considered a danger to the aircraft, crews were issued with what was known in company parlance as a 'humane killer', actually a .38 calibre pistol with a flared barrel.

'The idea was to allow you to despatch it by holding the horse by the head and doing the deed without shooting yourself or putting a hole through the fuselage,' explains Bill Easton. '"There's something wrong with this picture," we used to mutter to ourselves!'

Along with lucrative animal carriage, some other cargoes had a value all of their own—like gold, for instance. Crowther once operated a Constellation charter into Jakarta in the 1960s, without being told what their cargo was to be. After landing he was surprised to see trucks arrive with hundreds of bars of gold to be loaded aboard.

'All the seats had been removed and the cabin floor stressed for the task, and, once on board, they covered the entire floor of the aircraft.'

The whole operation was conducted amidst high security in the middle of the night and it was around 2 a.m. when they finally took off for Singapore and the final destination, London. As they climbed away into the night out of Jakarta, he still remembers the captain commenting: 'Okay, chaps, where do you think we should quietly set course for? Peking perhaps?'

Crowther later learnt that the uplift had been part of what became known as the Green Hilton Agreement, signed by President John Kennedy and Indonesia's Sukarno in November 1963, in which thousands of tonnes of gold imported from Asia to the West was to be used as backing for the US Department of Treasury. Kennedy was shot three days after the signing of the agreement and ownership of the gold is still the subject of legal actions and conspiracy theories, some even linking the gold to the death of the president.

George Howling also had a brush with security problems relating to gold while running the Hong Kong office in the 1950s.

Gold was a common item on Qantas DC-4s operating between Sydney and Hong Kong in those days, whole boxes of it destined for transhipping onto Catalina flying boats to Macau and into China. Its value made it a dangerous business and shortly before Howling had arrived to take up his Hong Kong posting, gunmen had attempted to hijack another airline's Catalina en route to Macau. When a gunfight broke out, the Catalina crashed, killing all on board.

Security was heavy on the gold's arrival at Kai Tak airport, where the American chief of the trading company, flanked by security guards arrived at the airport in his Rolls Royce to oversee the transhipment.

The gold flights had been operating for some weeks when Qantas head of security Gordon 'Flashlight' Fraser took Howling aside during a visit to Sydney and told him he was concerned about the security of the gold even while it was on its way to Hong Kong.

'What do they do with the DC-4 during the night stop at Labuan?' asked Fraser.

'They put an armed guard over it,' replied Howling.

'Is it near the ocean?'

'Yes,' answered Howling, who could now see where Fraser was coming from.

Borneo's Labuan in the 1950s was about as primitive an overnight stop as you could get. It had a wartime airstrip and one twenty-room hotel, so to cater for the 40 people on a DC-4 stopover they'd built a jungle-like structure of bamboo and rattan as an attachment, with camp beds and a canvas bucket beside each bed to wash in. 'The civilian passengers went into the hotel and the poor bloody soldiers going up to Korea ended up in the attachment, but when we had a full load of civilian passenger they went in there as well,' says Howling.

Fraser's problem though, wasn't the security of the passengers, but the gold. Fraser got even more nervous when Howling told him the load was not checked before the aircraft left for Hong Kong the next morning.

'I better come up there and have a look. Smart people in a boat could soon work this out,' said Fraser.

Several weeks later Howling joined Fraser in Labuan and the pair made a surprise visit to the airport early in the morning to check out the security, only to find the guard sound asleep against the DC-4's wheels, his .303 rifle lying beside him.

Quietly they pushed the steps up the aircraft and climbed into the cabin where they could access the hold by pulling up a section of the floor. Despite its weight, they managed to lift one of the boxes of gold into the cabin and slide it under a passenger seat, then left without waking the guard.

On arrival at Kai Tak next day pandemonium broke out when the American with the Rolls Royce discovered a box was missing, until Fraser explained what they had done and that they needed to do something about it.

Not long after, Constellations replaced the DC-4s, over-flying Labuan on their way to Hong Kong.

18
NOT YOUR NORMAL PASSENGER SERVICE

For thousands of European immigrants heading for a new life in Australia in the 1960s, be it from places like Ankara in Turkey, Madrid in Spain, Malta or a half-dozen other locations, the first identifiable image of their new home was a Qantas Boeing 707 waiting on the tarmac for them to board. Often, years later, it would be the same Boeing 707s that brought them back to their country of origin, this time on what would be known as 'Affinity Group', or 'Visiting Friends and Relatives' charters.

Some of the earliest charters that followed the signing of bilateral immigration agreements between Australia and other countries in the 1960s were pioneering affairs. Those out of Ankara, Turkey were a typical example.

The initial task fell to the staff of the Australian embassy in Ankara who spent months processing the first 2000 immigrants who would make up the quota for 1968–69, to be followed by a further 3000 the following year. Most flights would operate between February and November to avoid the Anatolian winter and, with few exceptions, would land in Sydney or Melbourne, from where the immigrants would be gradually processed out into the community.

Such charters were often quite different from normal passenger services, not least because most of those involved had never flown before and presented a range of new challenges for government and airline officials. Extensive pre-embarkation training and briefing sessions were used to overcome the problem, along with discouraging plans to take everything from kerosene stoves to massive steel trunks on board. Some had never used a Western-style toilet before and had to be discouraged from standing on it.

Phil Button spent two years attached to the Australian embassy in Turkey in the early 1970s and had the initial responsibility for selecting the immigrants involved from all parts of the country. Button remembers the flights arriving in around midnight, needing to be refuelled and having to be airborne again by around 2 a.m., an arrangement made all the more complicated thanks to a government-imposed curfew to combat a threat of terrorism.

'Martial law had been imposed to take care of "Grey Wolf" terrorist dissenters, so seeing the flight off around 2 o'clock and then waiting around the airport for four or five hours made it a very long and tiring night,' Button says, although he admits there were small compensations: 'I was able to hear some Aussie accents and get some Aussie newspapers from the crew.'

One of Button's locally engaged staff accompanied the charters to Australia, acting as a translator during the flight. Button says between 1968 and the end of the program in 1975, more than 14,000 Turkish immigrants arrived in Australia on Qantas charters. Many thousands more came from other areas of Europe.

Qantas's John McHarg oversaw ground arrangements for other immigrant charter flights out of Malta, a highly anticipated event locally. He estimates if the island's population was 400,000, then it seemed most of them were actually inside the terminal and overflowing into the car parks, but adds: 'The crowds were invariably happy and good-natured, although there were plenty of tears as goodbyes were said to families and friends.'

McHarg says the take-off of the fully loaded Boeing on hot nights from the short Malta runway was exciting to watch: 'I sometimes wondered whether the skipper, as the concrete was about to run out, simply retracted the undercarriage and left the whole process of flight in the aeroplane's hands.'

Other Qantas charter assignments over the years often took the form of actual rescue missions, as in the case of the Tiananmen Square massacre in June 1989 when the Australian government chartered a 747 to bring Australians out of Beijing and Shanghai. Bob Parker, who was on that flight, believes it broke the record for the most senior group of cabin crew ever sent on such a mission.

'Denis Liston's team was comprised almost entirely of flight service directors. Denis had around 30 years of service at that stage, I had 25 and when we added up the total years of service of the FSDs, the chief steward and Denis's wife who was also a cabin attendant, the total came to 309.

'In fact the chief steward just happened to arrive in the office when we getting ready for the flight and decided to come along as well.'

Parker remembers an eerie Beijing airport with hardly a human being in sight: 'It's a strange sensation to arrive at an airport with no people around.'

Reminiscent of the record uplift of the Qantas Boeing 747 out of Darwin after Tracy in 1974, Parker's aircraft was so loaded when it took off for Hong Kong some adults and children were sitting on the floor. Then it was on to Shanghai to repeat the process.

But when it came to charters, whether human or animal, those flying in Papua New Guinea in the 1950s and 1960s always managed to set the 'standards' few other subsequent Qantas efforts were able to match.

Carriage of native workers, known in those less politically correct days as 'boi' charters, was designed to meet the requirements primarily of Burns Philp, Streamships Trading and other major island companies with large plantation holdings through the Territory.

If labourers were needed, the companies simply placed an order for the number required with the Australian Administration's Native Commissioner and away went a Qantas DC-3 to a centre in the Highlands or a coastal town where workers had been gathered for carriage to Port Moresby, Rabaul on New Britain or Buka on Bougainville.

It was all pretty straightforward by the standards of the day although inevitably there would be the odd 'conscript.'

If 60 or so villagers were needed and the numbers were slim, some unsuspecting local who had merely come to the airport to see what all the fuss was about would find himself on his way to Rabaul for twelve months' work on a plantation. Five shillings a month and all the stick tobacco he could smoke added to the adventure.

But there were occasions when a native's return home must have fallen short of his expectations.

Captain Roger Wilson set out in his DC–3 to take a group of workers back to Wabag in the Western Highlands only to have the weather close Wabag, forcing him to land at Baiyer River, about 65 kilometres away.

Wilson quickly gathered the natives, explaining to them in pidgin: 'Yupela got savvy along dispel ples, name bilong Wabag?'

'Yes,' was the reply. So, pointing in the direction of Wabag, Wilson sent them on their way on what amounted to a walk of several days.

Gordon Power was once given the job of flying a thoroughbred racehorse from Port Moresby into a newly established horse stud at Baiyer River in the Highlands.

Everyone appeared quite excited about the Baiyer River stud concept and arrangements had been made to record the horse's arrival there as part of a documentary film on the new venture. Unfortunately Power's first attempt had to be abandoned when the animal became so unsettled while loading that it reared and damaged the interior of the DC-3.

When the next attempt was made a few days later the horse continued to act up but, with a combination of injections from the vet and a degree of 'physical encouragement', the horse, now almost comatose from the injections, was finally locked in its stall.

Midway through the flight, loud thumping noises coming from down the back alerted the crew that the horse had recovered, so the vet headed off into the cabin to deal with it. Soon the thumping stopped but when the vet arrived back in the cockpit, his face now ashen, he announced the animal was dead. By now they were approaching Baiyer River where they were joined by the Cessna and the film crew, cameras rolling, flying in alongside them to record their landing.

'After we had parked they managed to get some magnificent footage of the first breeding horse being delivered tail first out of the DC-3's door,' Power admits sadly.

19
GOUGH . . . AND OTHER 'ROYALS'

Carrying VIPs has come with the territory since the very early days of commercial flying. Not only was air travel a time saver for movie stars, entertainers or royalty on occasions but they were among the few who could afford the status achieved by arriving somewhere by air.

In Australia's case, at the other end of the world from the main artistic or cultural centres, transporting VIPs became commonplace for Qantas and early photographs show leading lights such as Charlie Chaplin and Noel Coward standing nonchalantly beside the fuselage of a DH-86 or coming ashore from a Hythe flying boat.

As the years went by the British royal family became regular passengers. The files of those days tell of an element of unspoken rivalry between the UK's own national carrier and its 'colonial' airline counterpart. Thus, if you were carrying the royal pennant, things had to go right and while weeks, and occasionally months, were spent developing procedures to cover every contingency, Murphy's Law could suddenly take over, which is what happened spectacularly when one of the Qantas Lockheed Constellations had the prestigious job of taking Queen Elizabeth, the queen mother, home to England in early 1958.

The queen mother had left England late in January 1958 on a marathon around the world journey via Montreal, Vancouver, Honolulu, New Zealand and finally to Australia, where she officially opened the British Empire Services League conference in Canberra. Such was her popularity that extra police had to be called on to control the crowds and in three weeks she managed to pack in visits to most major capital cities as well as Tasmania. By the time she left Sydney, on 5 March in the Qantas Super Constellation, Her Majesty was probably looking forward to a smooth, uneventful journey home, the only major duty on her way being to declare open Nairobi's new £2.5 million airport at Embakasi on 8 March. Embakasi and its 3000-metre runway apparently represented much more than just slabs of concrete and an impressive new terminal complex; in the expansive words of one British journalist sent to attend the opening, it was 'evidence of the country's stake, and firm belief, in civil aviation and the symbol of the dark days of an African rebellion.'

It was a reference to the Mau Mau terrorist insurrection and civil war that had cost more than 12,000 lives and, as our correspondent took pains to point out: 'the analogy of Embakasi airport rising from the ashes of rebellion comes to mind when it is realised that the runway was almost entirely hand-built by large squads of Mau Mau undergoing "corrective" labour.'

The queen mother left Australia amid lavish praise from the Australian press at the resounding success of her visit, although in hindsight, given the unpredictability of the Constellation's Curtis Wright engines, perhaps they should have held their enthusiasm until she had actually made it back to England.

The royal flight's itinerary took it from Sydney to Adelaide, Kalgoorlie, Perth, Cocos Islands, Mauritius, Entebbe, Nairobi, Malta and finally, London.

The feverish preparations going on in Nairobi were doubtless hardly in the minds of the Qantas crew when, halfway between the Cocos Islands and Mauritius, a cylinder shattered, causing one of the four engines to fail. It was then that Murphy's Law really took over. Although a fresh engine was quickly installed, there was no replacement for the damaged engine cowling available at Mauritius but one was immediately dispatched from Australia aboard another Constellation only to have the rescue Constellation suffer a fuel pump failure in Perth. They quickly replaced the fuel pump, only to have a cyclone alert cause a further delay.

By now the Mauritius stopover had crept into three days, during which HM was forced to spend the time at a British embassy largely unprepared for such an eventuality, while the disappointed Kenyans reverted to Plan B, forcing Kenya's governor, Sir Evelyn Baring, to step up to the dais and read a message from the marooned queen mother, declaring the new airport open in her absence.

Spare a thought for Qantas engineer George Dusting back in Mauritius, working to get the aircraft moving again. It must have been a frustrating time as, even after the replacement engine was installed and the new cowling fitted, the engine test run revealed that three other cylinders had to be changed.

Finally, after four days, the royal party was airborne for Entebbe, only to have another engine develop distributor problems and another delay. This time Uganda's local British diplomatic mission found itself the unexpected host to HM while Dusting and other engineers again were in action, at one point their labours resulting in a false start, when, after being told the aircraft was ready for departure, the queen mother arrived at the airport to find work still in progress. Still hoping for a departure she decided to rest aboard, only to finally give up around 1 a.m. and return to Government House.

Meanwhile, a BOAC Britannia aircraft had been strategically positioned at Nairobi, its crew anxiously waiting to come to her rescue. One of the cabin crew later recounted how excited they were at the prospect. But Qantas wasn't finished with its regal patron yet and after an eighteen-hour delay she was on her way again, only to have another mechanical problem develop at Malta.

By now, to her enduring credit, the queen mother had stuck with the Australians well beyond any normal expectations, but it seemed Malta was the last straw. The BOAC Britannia, already on its way—empty—to London, was diverted to collect her for the final leg home. Those on the Constellation reported through it all she had shown a remarkable degree of patience and understanding. Although the English press couldn't resist the odd barb at Qantas's expense, at one point wondering why Qantas could not have come to its own rescue by using a 'Constellation it had standing by at London,' the queen mother herself was gracious in her later comments, commending the efforts of the crew.

Fortunately for Qantas, most of the royal flights over subsequent years went off without a hitch and are remembered more for the more private, personal and at times humorous incidents that occurred. Carrying the Duke of Edinburgh was always an enjoyable experience for Qantas crews, although one anecdote among Qantas engineers from the Constellation days has him being roughly pushed away from a window during the start-up procedure by the flight engineer who was unable to check whether No. 2 engine had fired. Apparently the prince was blocking his view.

There's little doubt the dedicated Constellation or Boeing 707, configured with a special bedroom, lounge and other private facilities, encouraged a relaxed atmosphere, particularly for the duke, himself a pilot, who often spent a large amount of time on the flight deck with the crew. Qantas captains who had served in England during the war found they had much to talk about although sometimes they got a little more than they bargained for. Former Captain John Fulton tells of flying the duke back to Karachi after he had opened the Commonwealth Games in Perth in 1962. First officer Arthur Whitmarsh, who had won a Distinguished Flying Cross with No. 460 Lancaster Squadron during the war, had been reminiscing with the duke about flying, racehorses and a range of other subjects and thought he'd check with the duke on whether, on such flights, it would be polite to invite the queen into the cockpit.

'No,' came the reply. 'She's only interested in anything that eats hay and farts.'

Fulton reports that Whitmarsh, the aircraft's captain Neil Snodgrass and himself stared fixedly ahead for a few moments before any one spoke.

There would be other embarrassing moments carrying royals. Captains Bob Rosewarne and Geoff Jones had Princess Anne and Captain Mark Phillips on a flight from Bangkok to Melbourne and, as the second officer was handling the descent into Melbourne, Jones decided to tidy up the cockpit by clearing away the crockery. Unfortunately nobody had told him the royal couple were changing clothes in the upper-deck lounge. As Jones, coffee tray in hands, kicked open the cockpit door to place the cups and saucers in the galley he was confronted with the princess fastening her bra.

Rosewarne later dined out on the story, describing how there was a crash of crockery as Jones dropped the tray and scuttled back into the cockpit to the sound of Mark Phillips laughing uproariously, with Rosewarne quietly suggesting that Jones could expect twenty years in the Tower of London if he was lucky.

While the royals might have been in trusted hands on such flights, other captains discovered there was intense British activity behind the scenes. Before flying the queen from London to Singapore in a Qantas 747 in 1992, Roger Carmichael was given a detailed briefing by the Royal Air Force air commodore in charge of the royal flight.

'The RAF will be watching you, flying underneath you all the way, listening. Don't talk to them if you don't have to,' Carmichael was told. Once they reached east of India, an RAAF aircraft would take over the assignment.

On Carmichael's Boeing 747 all of first class had been converted into a bedroom with 28 members of the royal entourage and security officials the only others on board.

Carmichael remembers some interesting exchanges he was to have during the flight. They were due to arrive in Singapore at precisely midnight but as he began his descent he realised they had gained time on the flight and, since such royal arrivals had to be precise, advised Singapore air traffic control he would circle in a holding pattern for a few minutes.

'You can't do that,' came the reply.

'I suggest we can. We have the queen of England on board,' Carmichael explained.

'No, you haven't. She's not coming until later in the month.'

It was at this point Carmichael realised the air traffic controller had got his arrival confused with the date the queen was actually returning to Singapore from Australia. There was a silent interlude until his holding pattern was duly confirmed, presumably when a more senior air traffic controller intervened.

Protocol on landing dictated that Carmichael quickly get out of his seat, leaving the rest of the crew to shut the aircraft down while he went back to take possession of the traditional signed memento of the flight from Her Majesty.

Under strict instructions to speak only if spoken to, Carmichael stood by as the queen thanked him, then the duke appeared, looked at him and asked: 'Did you land at the right airport?'

Momentarily flabbergasted, Carmichael could only reply, 'Yes. I'm sure I wouldn't have my job if we didn't.'

Carmichael could never be sure but he believed the duke was referring to a mistake made in the early days of Boeing 707 royal flights when Singapore's two airports, Changi and Paya Lebar, were close together and had runways aligned in the same direction. Coming out of the overcast the 707 landed at Changi and when the captain realised his mistake he quickly taxied back to take off and land at Paya Lebar. Long retired but still puzzled twenty years later, Carmichael wrote and asked the duke whether in fact that was what he had been referring to that night in Singapore. HRH replied that it had been a long time ago but he felt sure that would have been the case.

Flying Pope John Paul back home after an Australian visit was another feather in Carmichael's cap, with his Boeing 747 Special Performance aircraft fitted with a huge four-poster bed on the upper deck. Qantas chairman Jim Leslie was on the flight, along with a phalanx of cardinals making up the entourage and an all-male cabin crew, since no women were permitted on board a papal flight. Once again Carmichael experienced some peculiar air traffic control exchanges.

Normal procedure was to have His Holiness send a message of goodwill to the prime minister or leader of any country over which they were flying. This could create some interesting radio exchanges as they flew over countries like Somalia where the air traffic controller's English was limited to the aviation terminology he was required to use as part of his job. Asking him to pass on the good wishes of His Holiness the Pope was well beyond his comprehension. After minutes of frustration trying to get the message across that a chap known as Il Papa was trying to communicate a blessing, Carmichael and his crew began to double up with laughter at their futile attempts, until co-pilot Stuart Fraser took over and translated the message into French.

'We think it finally got through, but I've never been sure,' says Carmichael.

***

Flying politicians in the days before RAAF VIP squadrons were equipped with aircraft capable of long-range international travel was another unique experience for Qantas crews and some of the stories of much admired former Qantas chief pilot, the late Alan Terrell, have moved into Qantas folklore, particularly while carrying former Prime Minister Gough Whitlam.

Terrell and Whitlam spent many hours in the air together, with Whitlam, who had served in the RAAF during the war, always managing to find time to sit in the jump seat behind the crew. They swapped stories and at times offered each other the odd snippet of advice—political or other—although there was one occasion, flying the PM from Samoa to Vancouver, when Terrell's advice didn't help the PM all that much.

Because the distance involved between Samoa and Vancouver was beyond the Boeing 707's range, Terrell needed to allow a brief stop in Honolulu early in the morning to refuel and had flight planned for a simple, quick turnaround so they could quickly be on their way again. But several hours out from Honolulu, still in the middle of the night, Terrell received a signal that the mayor of Honolulu wished to greet the Australian prime minister on arrival.

Realising no such meeting was on the schedule, Terrell had the crew wake the PM and a few minutes later an obviously less-than-keen Whitlam was in the cockpit expressing his surprise and asking Terrell what dress attire he should assume.

'Prime Minister, at 5 a.m in the morning in Honolulu they'll be in shorts, Hawaiian shirts and long socks,' was Terrell's confident prediction.

Whitlam retreated back to the PM's suite to change into something casual. As they approached the terminal after landing, Terrell was aghast to see a conga line of officials spread across the tarmac, all dressed in lounge suits and ties.

He hardly had time to think about what he would say to his VIP passenger when the cockpit door opened to reveal a Gough Whitlam dressed in a bright sports shirt and light slacks.

'Alan, please be assured that will be the last time I shall be seeking your sartorial advice,' offered the PM before descending down the aircraft steps to meet the greeters.

Punctuality, not appropriate attire, was the problem on another occasion when flying the PM from Colombo to an important meeting in Brussels. After a three-day stopover in Colombo, Terrell and his crew were ready for a 10 a.m. departure when time began to drag on. Soon the PM was an hour late and, by 11.30 a.m., word reached Terrell that he was still talking with Sri Lankan Prime Minister Sirimavo Bandaranaike.

Eventually Terrell was relieved to see a flurry of activity as officials strode quickly towards the aircraft, a quick farewell between the two prime ministers at the foot of the steps and Whitlam bounding aboard, straight into the cockpit.

'I'm sorry I'm late Alan, but it's important I get to Brussels on time.'

. Terrell, who had spent the waiting time making some flight recalculations, figured it could be done if they travelled low at about 20,000 feet to make up time: 'I'm pretty confident we can do it, Prime Minister, but it's going to cost the Australian taxpayer a lot of money in fuel.'

'I don't give a bugger about the Australian taxpayer right now, Alan. Just get me there on time.'

Years later Terrell remembers the sheer enjoyment of having Whitlam spend much of the time in the cockpit as they flew over the Middle East. 'He was with us for an hour or so and treated us to a wonderful travelogue as he pointed out the historical landmarks across Mesopotamia et al. The extent of his knowledge made it a fascinating experience.'

While VIP flights like Vancouver and Brussels were important assignments, they paled into insignificance when it came to the pre-planning required for Whitlam's journey to China in October 1973. Not only was Whitlam the first Australian prime minister to visit the country, but it was to come within eighteen months of US President Nixon's ground-breaking visit in February 1972.

The China of the 1970s was no easy place to get to. East–West relationships were still delicate and, although Whitlam's initiative was welcomed by the Chinese, flying into the Middle Kingdom was a whole new experience for a Western airline and required intricate planning.

The first step was to be a ground survey with Captains Phil Oakley and Terrell, who had flown together since Qantas's early

Papua New Guinea years, leading a twelve-man team to discuss the air and ground handling requirements.

Accommodated at a government guesthouse in Peking, they had allowed for at least four days of meetings at the headquarters of the Chinese Civil Aviation authority, which turned out to be a new experience for the Qantas team. First the leader of the Chinese delegation spoke for over an hour, then Oakley, as leader of the delegation had his turn, before introducing Terrell who addressed technical issues. They adjourned for lunch at 11.30, planning to reassemble at 4 p.m.; during the interim, the Chinese would interpret the contents of the discussions.

When 4 p.m. came, the Chinese leader briefly outlined the main points in the discussions and, to the surprise of the Australians, declared the discussions over.

'We spent the rest of the time eating extended Chinese banquets and touring the sights,' recalled a grateful Terrell.

The next step was the survey flight, which would be operated by a 707. Since the Chinese would not permit the use of still-British Hong Kong as an originating point, the survey flight would come out of Japan to Peking on the same routing as the eventual official flight. As the Chinese had only recently purchased a Boeing 707, Terrell was startled when a whole team of Chinese aircrew turned up to accompany them. At one stage he counted seven of them in the cramped Boeing cockpit at the same time.

After arrival, Oakley and Terrell were able to quickly resume their technical discussions with the Chinese, who soon made it clear that the VIP flight itself would require an unusual Qantas crew complement of seven, comprising three pilots, two engineers, a navigator and lastly, at the Chinese insistence, a radio operator as well. And the Chinese insisted on having their own navigator on board, presumably to ensure the aircraft didn't inadvertently stray over any of their military installations.

Beyond that, arrangements went quite smoothly, although the same could not be said for another member of the team, Food Services Manager Rolf Gschwind, whose assignment was to inspect the catering facilities for use on Whitlam's return flight from China at the conclusion of his visit. Gschwind became concerned when the first day passed with the Chinese explaining there was a delay with the catering inspection arrangements, but when the delay stretched into the second day he became even more concerned. When it looked like Day Three was heading the same way he pressed further, only to finally learn that no such catering facility existed! While he accepted it had been a case of the Chinese saving face, something had to be done, and quickly. Gschwind went to the Australian ambassador, Stephen Fitzgerald, who suggested they use the embassy kitchen, which was at least capable of handling large diplomatic dining arrangements. On inspection Gschwind found it could easily cover the task.

Now, with the catering elements in place, all appeared ready to provide the Australian prime minister with a smooth transition into China. Little did they know!

Since Whitlam would be paying an official visit to Japan on his way to China, Japan manager John Picken's staff had spent weeks working on arrangements for Whitlam's stay in Japan and also to ensure a smooth departure for China. At the outset, Picken got some idea of the complexity of the task when 30 organisations turned up for the Japanese government's briefing session on the Whitlam itinerary for Japan. Most arrived in either dark business suits, military or government uniforms or, in the case of the meeting's convenor, the Department of Protocol representatives, in formal morning suits of striped trousers and cutaway morning coats.

Security too, was high on the agenda as the Japanese terrorist organisation, the Seki Gun Ha, was reported to be training for an assault on Tokyo airport and the Japanese feared that any visiting head of government could be an attractive target.

In the days leading up to the visit, apart from a Japanese demand that the aircraft be positioned at Nagoya, 350 kilometres south, during the Japan stopover because of parking limitations at Tokyo, Picken and his team gradually sorted out the bureaucratic demands. By the time the official flight arrived, only a few issues were outstanding, several of which related to the actual flight into China itself. The first was the requirement for a flight plan, which had been based on flying through South Korean airspace to overhead Shanghai and then direct to Peking. Both the Japanese and the South Koreans had approved the flight plan but the People's Republic of China was now insisting that, since it was still technically at war with South Korea, over-flight of South Korea would not be possible. The extra distance involved meant a substantial change to the timing of the red carpet farewell from Japan and the comprehensive official arrival in Peking, so a new flight plan had to be obtained from British Airways, who had experience flying west of Tokyo.

While that was requested urgently from the British, another problem surfaced when it was revealed that the navigator assigned to the flight couldn't speak English, which resulted in an hour-long exchange Picken will never forget: 'Firstly the Chinese interpreter translated all the operational and navigational requirements, which she didn't understand, from Mandarin to Japanese. I translated from Japanese to English and then translated the replies and questions back to Japanese. The Chinese interpreter then translated from Japanese to Mandarin. And on it went. Our two pilots and the Chinese navigator were all rolling their eyes and taking notes—the only things they had in common.'

Travelling back to the Qantas Tokyo office after the meeting, Terrell remarked dryly: 'This won't look good for any of us if we finish up landing in the middle of the Gobi Desert.'

Picken couldn't have put it better himself.

For the next two days, along with keeping his own office moving, Picken repeatedly contacted the British Airways office in Hong Kong to chase up the flight plan to no avail until, with the prime minister scheduled to depart the following afternoon, BA Hong Kong telexed that the flight plan had been sent.

On the day of departure, while the pilots went to the British Airways operations office to obtain the flight plan and make the necessary adjustments, Picken went to his own office to clear up any outstanding paperwork. While there he was handed a pile of correspondence that he nonchalantly dumped into his in-tray.

By the time he returned to the airport everything seemed well under control and the Prime Minister of Japan and the Crown Prince were on their way to the airport.

Suddenly he was confronted by an anxious Terrell. The flight plan hadn't arrived and he had been forced to lodge a plan without any knowledge of high-altitude winds. The best he and Oakley could do was estimate they would probably be 15 minutes late on the blocks in Peking, not a good result when flying the Australian prime minister and an aircraft full of Australian press representatives on their first visit to China.

Even as Mr and Mrs Whitlam climbed aboard, Terrell poked his head out the cockpit window and gestured to Picken whether the plan had arrived. Picken signalled it hadn't but was at least thankful it would be an on-time departure.

With the aircraft gone, Picken returned to his office to await notification from Peking that the 707 had arrived, still concerned at the prospect of a traditional Chinese fanfare welcome for the Australian party being delayed. While he waited he began to flick through the papers he had tossed onto his desk that morning to discover the flight plan the third item in the pile. It had been mistakenly faxed to his office instead of BA flight operations!

Fortunately Oakley and Terrell's makeshift flight calculations had been reasonably accurate and the Qantas Boeing 707 landed at Peking 17 minutes late, although the late arrival was to have a sequel for Picken.

Four years later, the former prime minister recognised Picken, now Qantas manager for Queensland, at Brisbane airport. When the conversation touched briefly on that departure out of Tokyo, Whitlam explained that very strong headwinds had caused them 'to arrive a little late'. Doubtless Oakley and Terrell had found the 'excuse' they needed and Picken didn't have the heart to explain the real story.

In contrast to the anxiety and drama of the Tokyo departure, the welcoming ceremony at Peking, a colourful affair involving hundreds of costumed Chinese and rows of bandsmen, lining the tarmac had a humorous sidelight. Catering man Rolf Gschwind, who had arrived in Peking several days earlier, watched as the Boeing's engines were shut down and the assembled throng waited for Whitlam to appear at the aircraft doorway, the signal for the start of much dancing, flag waving and band music. As the seconds ticked by in silence, Gschwind noticed a catering lorry head for the rear of the aircraft, ready to load replenishments for the flight back to Tokyo. Suddenly Gschwind saw the rear door open unexpectedly and the figure of Qantas's executive chef Henri Leuzinger step into the doorway. Obviously mistaking him for Whitlam, the band launched into the Australian national anthem and flags began to wave, prompting Leuzinger to slink back inside the door, the music fading into a few jumbled notes as the band realised its mistake. A few moments later the Whitlams appeared at the correct forward door and the official welcome resumed.

Whitlam generally proved popular with those who flew him, as did John Gorton, a former fighter pilot himself in World War II. Although political shades rarely enter into the accounts of those who flew the aeroplanes, most acknowledge that prime ministers generally accepted the realities associated with weather-related delays and other issues beyond the pilots' control, although Roger Carmichael recalls dealing with a testy Bill McMahon while flying from Singapore to Bali.

In those 707 days, Bali had few navigation aids and no instrument landing system, which meant circling down from as high as 16,000 feet to remain well clear of the surrounding mountainous terrain. McMahon, who had been invited into the cockpit to watch the landing, began to show signs of impatience, appearing to believe it was all a waste of time, at one stage remarking: 'Whenever are we going to bloody well land?'

Carmichael took pains to explain they didn't want to hit a volcano by trying to get there too quickly!

***

While prime ministers and the like might be the top of the ladder, so to speak, when it comes to VIP airline travel, there are others who make the grade at various levels, ranging from the likes of Frank Sinatra and Judy Garland to high-flying businessmen, some requiring handling with kid gloves, others expecting little more than the comforts of first-class service they are paying for.

Contrasts, even on the same aeroplane were common, as in the case of one incident involving Australian businessman John Elliott, who carried his commendable 'Australianness' onto the aeroplane with him, down to the suggestion that Qantas first class meals should include the option of a Four'n Twenty pie.

Roger Carmichael remembers Elliott as a pleasant and most forgiving VIP passenger, particularly when the unexpected occurred. Some of the early Boeing 747s had a habit of gathering condensation in the ceiling above a row of seats on both sides in first class, with the result that, as the aircraft climbed steeply after take-off, a small quantity of water would drop onto any unfortunate passenger who happened to be sitting there. After his aircraft had reached cruise level on a flight out of Sydney to the United States, Carmichael was told by his cabin crew that there was a crisis in first class that needed his attention.

He arrived to find Elliott and another well-known Australian businessman who had been sitting in the same row on the opposite side of the aisle, wet from the condensation fault. Offering his apologies to both, Carmichael couldn't help remembering the contrast. While the businessman was railing at the shortcomings of Qantas engineering and its treatment of first-class passengers, Elliott was laughing his head off. 'I've had nothing but respect for him ever since,' was Carmichael's comment.

As for the availability of Four'n Twenty pies: in the late 1980s, Foster's was in the process of taking over Courage Breweries in the UK and, as Foster's boss, Elliott found himself flying Qantas between Australia and London every fortnight. A confessed 'pie tragic', he suggested to the airline his favourite pies should become part of the first-class service. The airline agreed.

After that he'd eat several pies on the first leg to Singapore and then another couple on the leg to Bahrain. But at times, thanks to the Qantas reaction to his request, Elliott got more than he bargained for: 'On one trip we were about to leave Bahrain for London when the chief steward told me they'd put 24 Four'n Twenty pies on board.

'Well by that time I didn't want any more pies and, when I said so, he asked what he should do with them. I suggested he put them on for breakfast in economy. It must have worked as he came back a little later and told me they'd all gone.'

Elliott's taste for iconic Australian food didn't stop with the humble pie. He later wrote a five-page letter suggesting some improvements the airline could make to its services, one of which was the addition of Vegemite in first class.

'They already had it in economy so why shouldn't we have it too,' he says.

Along with the Vegemite request were twelve suggestions as to how the airline could improve the food in first class. 'Three weeks later I got a five-page letter back and they had an excuse for not doing anything about most of them,' says Elliott, still sounding disappointed. But he did get his Vegemite in first class.

Much to the delight of cabin crew, some VIPs brought with them a rich sense of humour. Among the famous folks carried by flight attendant Liz Cook was Frank Sinatra, who just happened to be on the same flight as Paul Hogan and his colleague John Cornell.

'This was the pre-*Crocodile Dundee* days and they were just fabulous. Paul Hogan kept asking me: "Does Mr Sinatra realise that I'm on board?"'

Another of her most memorable passengers was former Beatle John Lennon. 'He got on in Singapore and was sitting in the front row of first class. He refused to eat any aircraft food and proceeded to eat some packaged Japanese food he'd bought in Singapore. It was the most ghastly smelling food and the smell went right through the cabin all the way to London,' says Cook.

***

Flying VIPs wasn't restricted to normal international flights. One of the most successful Qantas public relations moves was the airline's long-standing practice of naming its 707 and 747 aircraft after Australian cities and towns. Tradition dictated that, once aircraft had been named after the airline's two foundation towns of Longreach and Winton in Queensland and all capital cities were represented on the nose of a Qantas Boeing, regional cities and towns would be chosen through a well-defined process based on state representation and population.

It was a decision that was not only a source of pride to the centres concerned but resulted in valuable local media publicity, culminating in invitations to visit Seattle to christen the brand-new aircraft on its delivery to the airline. Usually the small party would comprise the member of parliament for that area, along with the mayor and local representatives of press, radio and television. It was an experience long remembered by many and, provided the weather in Seattle cooperated, a four-day visit included an inspection of the Boeing production line with a celebratory dinner at a Seattle restaurant and culminated in a christening ceremony to splash champagne over the aircraft before it set off on its delivery flight to Australia. Often the party would be the only passengers aboard the aircraft on its delivery flight to Australia, making it an even more memorable occasion.

Boeing was a gracious host and could be relied upon to handle the most sensitive moments with commendable diplomacy, even when the occasional decidedly left-leaning Australian politician made pointed remarks about the fact that Boeing was also the maker of military hardware.

The mayors from the largest regional centres to small country towns represented a welcome cross-section of Australians, and it was obvious their Boeing hosts particularly enjoyed their company. These were, the Boeing people would always tell Qantas, the 'real Aussies!' There were some memorable occasions. Lengthy descriptions of the current wheat harvest, the lack of rain for six months and the state of outback roads were often standard fare at the celebratory dinner, sat through with commendable interest and patience by their Boeing hosts, although there was one occasion where they were forced to sit up and take notice.

One mayor concluded his remarks about the attractions of his particular portion of Australia, announcing as he sat down he was now looking forward to comparing the fillet steak in front of him with the top-grade product he was accustomed to at home. All eyes in the room were upon him as he took the first bite and began to withdraw the fork from his mouth—only to see his top dental plate come out with it! His Boeing hosts handled it with their customary aplomb, turning quietly away towards their own meals, although one could imagine the incident was a highlight of discussions on their way home after the dinner.

But not all the VIPs handled by Australia's international airline were restricted to royals, prime ministers, mayors or movie stars. In 1990 Qantas found itself handling a group of men unique in terms of their age and worldly experience—the return to Gallipoli of those veterans who had gone ashore that fateful April in 1915.

20
THE RETURN OF THE GALLIPOLI VETERANS

The 100th anniversary of the Anzac landing in 2015 demonstrated the special meaning the Anzac legend has for Australians, as VIPs from royalty through to prime ministers spoke to the thousands gathered before them above the beach at Anzac Cove.

To a few of those watching in 2015, it would have brought to mind a similar, though less-elaborate ceremony on the 75th anniversary in 1990 on that same beach. On that morning in 1990, sitting in the front row as dawn broke on 25 April 1990, were 60 men who had forged that legend on the Gallipoli Peninsula.

All were in their nineties and for some it was the first time they had been out of Australia since they left its shores in 1914 to take part in 'the war to end all wars'. This time they made it to Turkey not aboard cramped troop ships but aboard a Qantas Boeing 747 renamed *Spirit of Anzac* and carrying its own special flight number, QF1915.

The decision by the Australian government to take a small group of Gallipoli veterans back to the peninsula in 1990 to mark the

75th anniversary not only presented a major logistical exercise for the Department of Veterans' Affairs, but a unique challenge for Qantas.

The veterans themselves would be the central characters on an aircraft specially configured for the task. With them would be a full load of legatees, government officials, military personnel and journalists who would attend a range of commemorative services spanning the length of the Gallipoli Peninsula, from Anzac Cove to Suvla Bay and Cape Hellas, where other contingents of the Allied forces had landed.

It was an exercise months in the planning, beginning with the careful selection of 60 of the 150 veterans still alive in 1990 and considered capable of making the trip, given their age and the long distances involved. All would be subject to close medical assessment before departure, the primary aim to ensure they returned home from the scene of their wartime landing safe and well for the second time.

Eight war widows were among them, several of whom would be seeing their husband's grave for the first time. There was no shortage of volunteers to look after them and Veterans' Affairs was deluged with offers from doctors and nurses to make the trip, along with individual carers to cater for the every need of their aged guests.

While administration matters relating to the veterans themselves were being put in place, other aspects of what was to become a substantial military support operation were taking shape. Royal Australian Navy frigates were positioning to form a seaborne backdrop for the dawn service at Anzac, while HMAS *Tobruk* would be carrying everything from medical supplies, helicopters, vehicles and even Portaloos as part of the ground logistical support.

The 26 doctors and nurses allocated for the journey spent the weeks beforehand visiting their charges, getting to know them, shopping with them and helping with other chores, all designed to help them feel comfortable about taking on the trip. Not that many of the veterans had any qualms about it. Most regarded it as an unprecedented opportunity and one that would make them the last of a generation to ever make the journey to a place they would never forget.

The Anzacs lost 7400 from two divisions, the British 22,000 from eight and the French 10,000 from one. Turkish estimates were around 80,000 casualties and, despite the marked difference in life expectancy in comparison to the Australians, Turkish authorities had managed to find one soldier who had been above the beach that day.

The dawn service was to be a traditional one at Anzac Cove, followed by a wreath-laying ceremony at Lone Pine. Soon after, Australian Prime Minister Bob Hawke and British Prime Minister Margaret Thatcher would attend the international service at Cape Hellas, at the far end of the peninsula.

As the departure date drew nearer, Qantas began preparing the *Spirit of Anzac* Boeing 747 for the flight, converting the aircraft's first-class section into a fully equipped aeromedical intensive care area, with a curtained stretcher, oxygen cylinders and appropriate medical equipment. Additional stretchers were in place towards the rear of the aircraft.

The crew were to be volunteers, among them Captain Les Hayward, whose father had taken part in the first day of the campaign, and flight service director Sigmund 'Ziggy' Jablowski, a Vietnam veteran in charge of the cabin. Two of the Anzac veterans returning on QF1915 were Ernie Guest and Jack Hazlett, both former Qantas engineers.

To make the departure easier for the veterans, Qantas had arranged for the aircraft to be boarded in a hangar at the Qantas Jet Base at Mascot using scissor-lift equipment to avoid the veterans having to climb the aircraft stairs.

There was a short ceremony at Mascot as a large gathering of VIPs farewelled the aircraft towards its first stopover at Singapore for a two-night stay, which included a visit to the World War II memorial at the former Changi prison. From there it was to be nonstop to Istanbul.

It soon became evident that this hardy band of men had not lost their sense of humour or their taste for a drop of refreshment. Nor had they lost the odd larrikin streak—one spotted pinching the backside of his female carer as she took him on an exercise walk down the aircraft's aisle!

Pomp and ceremony prevailed on arrival at Singapore before the group was taken direct to their hotel to rest up before their first official engagement that evening, a pre-dinner drinks affair in a relaxed hotel atmosphere.

But there would be anxious moments when the group gathered for drinks and a head count revealed one of them was missing. The alarm was raised, and concern escalated when repeated calls to the old digger's room and knocks on his door failed to get any response. Hotel management was quickly summoned with a master key and the worst was feared as the door opened. But to everyone's relief there was our missing veteran, stretched out, fully clothed, flat on his back on the bed. Open nearby was the room's mini bar, emptied of its contents. All the free liquor therein had obviously been too tempting to resist.

Neither was the Singapore departure without its dramas for the military contingent on the aircraft, when one of the soldiers failed to turn up for the bus ride to the airport and was left behind. Worse still, the treasured Gallipoli 1st Battalion flag had also gone missing during the transit and QF1915 was forced to leave without it. Fortunately, soon after the veterans departed, the flag was found, rushed overnight on another flight to Athens, then on to Istanbul, finally reaching the tour leader, retired army major Bill Hall, on the day before the dawn service.

Emotions ran high among the veterans as the aircraft taxied to a stop at Istanbul and, as the television crews and news photographers jostled to record the arrival, one of those memorable moments occurred which could never have been scripted. One of the veterans, short, wiry Jack Ryan, descended onto Turkish soil for the first time in three-quarters of a century and stepped forward to be introduced to a Turkish veteran of the campaign standing at the foot of the steps. Immediately clasping his former enemy's hand, and using a vernacular long lost with his era, Ryan exclaimed: 'It's great to be back—as a cobber.'

Few who attended the dawn service at Gallipoli that April morning could be unmoved by the solemnity of the occasion, although one Turkish protocol officer was heard to wonder out loud 'why Australians would spend so much effort remembering a defeat.' One of the Australian journalists in the party tried to explain it, but soon gave up and turned back to his notebook.

Prime Minister Hawke delivered an emotional speech during the service at Lone Pine later that morning and, when the ceremony was over and the guard marched off to the strains of 'Lili Marlene', there was hardly a dry eye to seen.

A few days later the diggers were winging their way home, obviously flushed with pride that they had survived it all again. The only casualty turned out to be one veteran who slipped on the Istanbul hotel staircase as they were leaving for the airport, boarding the flight with his head heavily bandaged.

Asked by a crew member how he was feeling, he replied: 'I'm okay. I had a bandage around my head the last time I left here too.'

21
HOW TO SMUGGLE
A FUTURE PRINCESS

The story broke in the *Sydney Morning Herald* on 1 March 1981. It told how, with rumours rife that a royal engagement was in the offing, the world's media was searching everywhere from the UK to Africa, for the future Princess Diana. In fact, she had been helping cut burrs on a family property, Bloomfield, near Yass in New South Wales.

When the media swarm finally descended on the Yass property, Diana's mother, Mrs Frances Shand Kydd, repeatedly denied her daughter was there. In fact Mrs Shand Kydd may not have been totally telling fibs. Diana had also spent time at the beach on the New South Wales south coast.

The media finally gave up and things at Bloomfield returned to normal. By that time however, unknown to all but a handful of people, the future princess had been spirited out of Yass and onto a Qantas aircraft to London, virtually under the noses of the press.

What must rank as one of the Australian carrier's most bizarre undercover operations, with its own secret codes, a clandestine roadside rendezvous in the middle of Sydney and hushed conversations in private rooms, began with a phone call to the airline's then manager for New South Wales, Brian Wild, on an afternoon in early January 1981. Managing director Keith Hamilton wanted to see him urgently. Hamilton and Wild were close colleagues, both having worked together on the development of the airline's international aviation policies in the 1960s and 1970s.

'I've got a special job I want you to do. It involves getting someone out of the country quietly,' said Hamilton even before Wild had closed the door behind him.

Handing Wild a handwritten note, Hamilton offered: 'I don't know much about it myself. Ring this government fellow in Canberra and he'll brief you, then come back and see me.'

'That was it,' Wild remembered decades later. 'He wouldn't even tell me who the person was we had to get out.'

Wild's call to Canberra didn't fill in many details either, beyond 'I can't tell you the name at this stage but we have to get this person into the Sydney international terminal undiscovered and onto your flight to London.'

'When?' asked Wild. The question was particularly pertinent as Wild had another problem. The airline was in the middle of one of the most severe strikes in its history, after Australian unions had banned Qantas aircrew in support of cabin crew industrial claims.

Not only was the strike crippling the airline but Mascot's airport terminal was being besieged on a daily basis by television crews and other media looking for the latest news on the strike. Getting a VIP out of the country undetected under these circumstances wouldn't be easy, to say the least. 'Probably in the next week,' came the answer Wild didn't really want to hear.

'I'll leave it to you as to how you get someone into the government lounge at the terminal,' was the Canberra offering.

Canberra suggested Wild liaise with the airport's manager, Reg Crampton, 'who also knows something is going to happen.' That heartened Wild a little as he and Crampton had been neighbours for years.

A phone call to Crampton confirmed that the airport manager hadn't been told who they were dealing with either, but the two men agreed to meet at a hotel near the airport to talk. Crampton arrived with maps of the airport marking the gate they could use to enter away from public gaze, showing the access path to underneath the airport concourse and a lift that would take them directly into the lounge.

Back with Hamilton several days later, Wild now learnt that he was dealing with something that would be known as 'The Reid file,' the subject of which, a 'Miss Reid', would need to be on QF1 to London on the afternoon of 17 January. (Wild would never find out the reason for the 'Reid' title but surmised that John Reid, a prominent board member of the day, had been involved in the matter.)

Hamilton had more bad news as far as the media was concerned. That day's QF1 might just be the first flight out with an all-volunteer staff crew, a burning issue with the striking workers and one guaranteed to attract a larger-than-normal media scrum to the airport.

Several more days were to pass until the man from Canberra let Wild in on the secret. The passenger would be Diana Spencer and further details of the operation would follow, he was told. Now, at least, Wild was able to piece a few facts of his own together, having read reports of the press trying to trace her from one end of the planet to the other. Later he learnt that Diana had quietly arrived in Australia to talk to her parents before the announcement of her engagement to Prince Charles.

What followed in the 24 hours in the lead-up to the QF flight to London had enough ingredients to merge a James Bond drama with a Mack Sennett comedy.

Wild was told to wear clothing that could easily be recognised and that he would need to be standing on the intersection of O'Riordon Street and Gardiners Road at 2.30 p.m. on 17 January to await the approach of a light-coloured Toyota Corona.

Wild duly arrived at the corner with plenty of time to spare and, right on time, a Toyota emerged out of the traffic. 'There's the driver and another fellow in the front seat and I hop in beside Diana and her mother in the back seat. A Corona's not that big a car and I can tell you it was a bit of a squeeze but everyone was having a chuckle about it all.'

Frances Shand Kydd delighted in telling how they had avoided the press at Yass the previous day. Apparently, to distract a hovering helicopter, she had run outside, brandishing a broom towards the aircraft and the pilot had taken the hint and moved away, while Diana was smuggled into a car and out the back gate of the property. She had then spent the previous night at an apartment in Earl Street, Randwick.

The relaxed laughter and stories continued until the rendezvous with the Crampton vehicle at the airport gate and, as they approached the terminal from the airside, Wild suggested they should say their goodbyes before he and Diana left to enter the terminal building. 'There were kisses and hugs, more laughter, and we were into the lift and up to the government lounge.' There the two remained chatting, until the departure of QF1, slightly delayed due to the strike.

Once the aircraft departed, Wild was on the phone to the airline's regional director in Singapore, John Ward, who was to meet the aircraft there. Ward had already taken the precaution of booking a seat for Diana on a British Airways flight in case Qantas cabin crew, who were still operating aircraft between Singapore to London, suddenly decided not to do so.

With volunteer staff acting as cabin crew on the first sector of the future princess's flight to Singapore, things were anything but normal. In-cabin service for Diana and other passengers was in the hands of 'flight attendants' ranging from accountants to ticket sales managers who had been given a rudimentary run-through on the safety procedures and how to operate the food and drink trolleys. Busy with their own problems, it took most of them some time to realise who the slim, attractive passenger in first class was.

Dave Rubie, whose weekday job was sitting behind a desk in the airline's corporate planning department, now found himself in the role of air chef. He had just managed to heat the meals to begin preparation for the meal service when the captain announced over the public address system that they were preparing to land in Port Moresby. '"Why Port Moresby?" I thought to myself. We're supposed to be going to Singapore,' Rubie later recalled. He hadn't been told that, because the aircraft refuellers at Sydney were also on strike in support of the cabin crew, a stop was needed in Port Moresby to top up on fuel.

'I had to put all the meals back in the oven.'

Then, on arrival at Port Moresby, Rubie was given the job of looking after Diana in the Port Moresby terminal while the aircraft was refuelled. 'I should point out that it was a rare experience to have to walk around making small talk with a future princess for 45 minutes in what could only be described as a wretched terminal building.'

Once back on board Rubie resumed his air chef duties, which he admits were hardly up to the traditional Qantas standard. That soon became obvious, when he wheeled the meal trolley into first class and started to carve the beef.

'One of the passengers immediately got up and suggested I might need a hand and started to carve the beef for me. Then another came over and dished out the vegetables.

'They were great blokes and we proceeded to work as a trio serving all the first-class passengers,' recalls Rubie, after all these years still unsure whether they recognised the hash he was making while carving the beef or they just wanted to help.

John Ward had smoothed the way for Diana's transit of Singapore and she was soon on her way towards London's Heathrow, where regional director UK and Europe, Julian Hercus, had been briefed to slip her unseen into the country. Hercus was only too aware of the risks at his end. Heathrow, a labyrinth of corridors and narrow passageways, was notorious for its 'spotters'—airport workers who, for a small fee, were quick to alert the press of any VIP trying to avoid exposure on arrival. To avoid detection, he planned to have one of his key airport staffers, Peter Izard, meet the aircraft at the terminal gate and go on board as soon as the door opened.

'Peter had long experience with the airport's handling procedures and if anyone could get her through unnoticed, he could,' Hercus recalls.

Izard went straight to the passenger in the front row of first class.

'Good morning Miss Reid,' he announced, at which Diana, looked up, a surprised smile on her face: 'Oh, are we still doing that?'

Once into the terminal the pair headed for the VIP suite where Hercus was waiting.

'Fortunately she had only hand luggage, so, while Peter remained to handle the paperwork, we headed towards our car,' says Hercus, later estimating that they were driving out through the airport security gate within 15 minutes of QF1 docking at the terminal.

'It must have been one of the fastest arrivals ever at Heathrow,' he boasts.

During the 45-minute drive through London's early morning traffic to an address in Earl's Court, Diana spent part of the time leaning forward on the back of the front seat, giggling occasionally as she recounted her journey from Bloomfield to London. 'She also said she was extremely happy to be home and peppered me with questions about what had been happening in England while she had been away. She was a delightful person and told us how much she appreciated our efforts.'

The saga might have been over for Diana on delivery to Earl's Court but it wasn't to be for Hercus. Within hours, officialdom at Heathrow had caught up on the lack of a customs declaration, a serious offence for an international airline, and a terse 'please explain' had arrived at the office of Qantas's security chief, Reg Brothers. It also pointed out that Heathrow's Alcock and Brown lounge 'had also apparently been used for someone other than a head of state.'

Peter Izard eventually smoothed the ruffled Heathrow administrative feathers and Wild was able to tell Keith Hamilton that 'Operation Reid' had been a success. Frances Shand Kydd arrived in London with the remainder of her daughter's luggage and the following month Prince Charles and Diana announced their engagement.

That July, after the wedding of the Prince of Wales and Diana Spencer at St Paul's Cathedral, Brian Wild received a letter of appreciation from Buckingham Palace, an autographed photograph of the couple and a slice of their wedding cake. The letter and photograph take pride of place in the Wild's Sydney home, although he admits the cake has long since passed its use-by date.

A CHALLENGING BUSINESS

22
STRIKES AND FUEL . . .
A LETHAL COMBINATION

It wasn't a new aircraft, just a shorter, faster and higher flying version of other Boeing 747s in the Qantas fleet, but its introduction into Qantas service in January 1981 would lead to one of the most bitter and divisive episodes in Qantas's long history of industrial troubles.

Purchased to operate into the short Wellington runway and meet the threat of a Pan American nonstop service across the Pacific to San Francisco, the 747SP (Special Performance) became the lightning rod for a strike that would bring to the surface a litany of grievances stretching back decades and pit the industrial muscle of the union movement against the Flying Kangaroo.

It started innocently enough, over a cabin crew claim for allowances for increased workload and the number of their members required to man the SP. But, in the often-complicated world of industrial relations, it raised other crewing anomalies that had origins in the respective roles of male and female flight attendants. More significantly, it brought to the surface another issue that for years had been anathema to the union movement—Qantas's use of staff labour in industrial disputes.

The gender cabin crew anomaly had a relatively straightforward historical context. The early days of the Empire flying boats on the Australia–UK route had been an all-male steward affair. It was a physical role that involved tangling with heavy mooring lines in bouncing seas at places like Singapore, Batavia and Darwin, and transporting passengers to and from the aircraft in boats.

Not until Lockheed Constellations began flying on the route in 1948 were 'hostesses' introduced, largely at the suggestion of Mrs Fysh, the wife of the airline's founder Hudson Fysh, who would subsequently take a personal role in the selection of the first successful candidates. Their addition was more about glamour than much else, requiring them 'to be immaculately groomed and corseted at all times,' a situation that continued to exist into the very early days of the Boeing 707s.

But by the arrival of the 747s, the female flight attendants believed their role had changed. They might comprise only three of the fifteen crew on board, but they nonetheless considered themselves an integral part of the crew and had formed their own association, with close links to the pilot union. The fact that they were not members of the cabin crew union would have a significant bearing on the start of the industrial action that followed the introduction of the 747SP.

As the SP's introduction approached, the manning of the aircraft became a critical issue, with the company claiming the number of crew required to operate the smaller version of the aircraft should be reduced from fifteen to twelve. Weeks of negotiations followed, culminating in a company threat to stand down any cabin crew member who refused duty and the cabin crew union accusing the company of 'industrial blackmail'.

By the end of January, with no progress being made in negotiations, the company began training the first of the staff volunteers it intended to use—a decision that triggered a serious escalation of the dispute.

Watching closely from the wings was the Australian Council of Trade Unions (ACTU), which represented more than 5000 Qantas employees in Australia.

The ACTU and Qantas had locked horns for years over the company's use of staff labour as a strike-breaking instrument. From a union viewpoint at least, the method had been notoriously effective in keeping the airline flying, union representatives watching angrily as executives and management staff were quickly rostered out to airports to carry out a variety of tasks normally undertaken by union members, from preparing food in the catering centre to cleaning aircraft.

On 5 February, the stewards placed bans on the operation of the SP, causing the cancellation of its first commercial service from Brisbane to Wellington. But the service operated the following day, crewed by twelve flight hostess association members, whose overseas branch did not consider themselves part of the dispute.

The dispute escalated on 11 February when the ACTU imposed a ban on the SP for the use of staff labour, a ban mainly directed at pilots and flight engineers whom the unions claimed had carried out additional duties on board the aircraft.

To avoid cancellation of the following day's flight out of Brisbane for Wellington, the company had gathered twelve pilots and two flight engineers who would carry out the necessary emergency procedures, but Brisbane ground staff refused to push the SP back from its terminal parking bay, presenting the company with another dilemma.

Unlike its predecessor the Boeing 707, the 747 ran the risk of serious engine damage if its reverse thrust was used to roll it back, but its captain, David Shrubb, managed to gain just enough rearward movement to turn the aircraft around. Passengers on the Wellington flight that day received no in-cabin service but at least they reached their destination.

Over following days, when an attempt by Qantas to have the ACTU lift the bans failed, signs began to appear that the original crewing claim by the flight stewards that had led to the dispute was now secondary to the airline's use of staff labour. The ACTU had bigger fish to fry.

Then, in a provocative move in the early hours of 14 February, Qantas ordered union staff at Mascot to clean aircraft in accordance with health and quarantine requirements. When they refused, they were stood down and a mass walkout of staff of seventeen unions followed. At the same time Transport Workers Union members cut fuel supplies to all Qantas aircraft, a move that could be expected to ground the airline.

The critical decision to escalate the dispute through a demand to clean the aircraft had originated from what would later become known as the 'war room', on the sixth floor of Qantas head office in Jamison Street, where the airline's director of marketing, Trevor Haynes, and personnel director, Ken Appleton, had drawn together a team of seventeen executives from key areas of the company who met twice a day and often into the night.

Haynes became known as the 'man in the black hat' for his determination to take the fight to the unions, repeatedly ordering airport managers to stand down any staff who refused to work. Appleton, more conservative and capable of compromise, oversaw the tactics involved in negotiations in the Arbitration Commission.

By now, staff training of volunteers had begun in earnest, as the union bans gradually led to more and more Qantas jumbos grounded at Sydney and Melbourne. Staff training for this dispute presented a unique set of circumstances from other earlier disputes, which had largely involved strike-breaking activities on the ground at the airline's catering centre, and for cleaning aircraft and unloading baggage.

Replacing cabin crew on the aircraft themselves involved taking on far more serious operational tasks strictly related to civil aviation legislative requirements such as safety instruction, passenger evacuation and other procedures necessary in case of an emergency on board an aircraft.

As those in the 'war room' dictated the day-to-day efforts to keep the unions off balance, calls went out to all corporate branches to immediately release volunteers for training in emergency procedures. One of Appleton's personnel staff, John Picken, began organising sessions for the volunteers to undertake at the airline's Emergency Training Centre at Mascot. Much to Picken's relief, there was no shortage of volunteers, each of them directed to arrive at the airport equipped with 'passport, togs and towels', the latter because their emergency training was likely to see them immersed in the training sector's pool!

Customer relations director, Jim Bradfield, who oversaw much of the training itself, later admitted it was hardly sophisticated.

'We would get them in overnight after they finished work and it was basically safety training as we didn't worry too much about the way they served the meals. We had a meal galley cart to show them how it opened and shut and fortunately the food had been trimmed down anyway, to box lunches in some cases.

'To meet the DCA [Department of Civil Aviation] requirements we concentrated on the safety briefing and the life jacket drill, along with ditching in the company's emergency training pool.'

Volunteers were then issued with a Qantas cap and a badge that said 'I'm your cabin crew' and were sent off on their rostered flights. As it turned out, staff labour experiences in the cabin crew role provided some of the dispute's rare moments of levity—Dave Rubie's two first-class passengers feeling obliged to help him carve the beef in first class on the future Princess Diana's London flight being one example. On another flight, the company's chief financial officer, Larry Olsen, forgot to lock the wheels on his bar service trolley, only to see it career off down the aisle when the aircraft climbed suddenly.

The dispute itself soon became notable for several of its more bizarre elements, the first of which became known as the 'spitting incident'. It effectively drove an irreversible wedge between the company pilots and flight engineers, and the striking cabin crew. Reacting to suggestions of 'tampering' with food on board, pilots insisted on specially prepared meals, particularly after one cabin crew member supposedly threatened to feed them 'pan-wiped steak,' the identity of the 'pan' leaving little to the imagination.

Two weeks into the strike, and aware that an SP aircraft carrying a crew of the strike-breaking female flight attendants was returning from Fiji, word went out that a group of cabin crew was gathering at the airport to meet it.

In an effort to avoid any confrontation between the female flight attendants and the striking cabin crew as the women exited the terminal through the arrivals hall, the company had arranged transport to meet the aircraft at its terminal gate. Meanwhile, Qantas Captain Les Hayward acted as a decoy, positioning himself conspicuously in the arrivals hall as if to meet the in-bound crew.

When the cabin crew team realised they had been duped, they turned on Hayward and a scuffle ensued. Hayward later told the Arbitration Commission he was spat upon, and 'roughed up a bit'.

Television news footage of part of the incident was presented at the Commission. Two cabin crew were be sacked by the company, although their dismissal would later be commuted to suspensions while their case was heard by the Commission. Only one would be re-employed by the company.

Probably one of the unusual aspects of the dispute was the decision of the several hundred cabin crew operating overseas at the time of the strike to continue flying. Their decision, which would be a key factor in keeping the airline in the air, was based on the realisation that once they arrived back into Australia they would be asked by the company to continue working and, on their refusal, would be stood down.

Another reason was a financial one and had its origins in an earlier, and equally bitter, dispute in 1966 between the company and its pilots. When negotiations for a new pilots' award broke down and pilots walked off aircraft around the world, the company immediately withdrew any financial support for accommodation and travel, leaving most of them to find their way home at their own expense. Cabin crew members working overseas had no intention of suffering a similar fate. Thus they continued to crew aircraft back and forth along the Kangaroo Route between the UK, Europe and Singapore, between Honolulu and mainland USA and other last ports of call before Australia.

Their decision was something of a lifesaver for the company, leaving its main challenge one of providing volunteer staff to man aircraft only to these first ports of call outside Australia. Had the overseas crews decided to join the strike, there is little doubt the airline's whole fleet would have been grounded.

But the company was struggling, with only a thin strand of its normal worldwide service still operating and fuel bans imposed by ACTU member unions forcing aircraft to make technical stops at close destinations like Port Moresby, Noumea, Fiji and Jakarta to load as much fuel on board to enable them to reach Australia and get out again. At one point the fuel situation became so critical that the company made arrangements for a tanker to transport 23,000 litres of fuel from Singapore to Noumea to relive the pressure.

By late February, with more than 100,000 passengers affected and despite a Fraser government directive employing the RAAF and the RNZAF to relieve some of the pressure by using Hercules transports to carry stranded passengers across the Tasman, Qantas was reaching crisis point. With the company bleeding revenue, the board warned the government there was a possibility it may have to stop operations for six months and require a cash injection of more than $250 million to recover from the strike.

But moves were taking place behind the scenes. Unknown even to those running the dispute in the sixth-floor 'war room', chief executive Keith Hamilton—who had left Haynes and his team to run the dispute but was now seriously concerned at the price the airline was paying—had made direct contact with the ACTU's president Cliff Dolan. Reports also later emerged that Hamilton had discussions with Bob Hawke, but this was never confirmed.

The first those in the 'war room' knew of change in the air was when Hamilton appeared one morning and himself took the chair at the regular briefing of the Haynes committee.

Insisting the dispute needed to be quickly resolved, in one brutal manoeuvre he axed Trevor Haynes from the committee and announced he would lead the team to the Commission hearing that day. Hamilton's appearance before the Commission would be one of his rare public appearances during his time as the airline's chief executive, but it sent a strong message that daily confrontations were to be curtailed and an agreement reached to solve the dispute.

By 13 March, after a total of 37 days, the strike was over. Compromises by both sides marked the 1981 strike as the beginning of the end of the use of staff labour by Qantas. But the bitterness generated by the dispute remained for some years, particularly between some male members of the cabin crew and the female flight attendants, the latter lodging complaints of continuing harassment, citing repeated phone calls to their rooms in the middle of the night, rude notes left under their hotel doors, even instances of honey being smeared on aircraft phone handsets.

The company itself also came under fire from the female flight attendants, who accused it of discriminatory practices in relation to a lack of promotional opportunities within the cabin crew structure, denying them the ability to reach the rank of chief steward or flight service director. In a paper outlining their case twelve months later, their overseas branch president, Lesley Squires, also claimed that the 1981 dispute had itself promoted attitudes of bullying and harassment by a small minority of male cabin crew.

Squires accused male cabin crew members of compiling a 'hit list of girls who flew' that had been distributed to certain male flight service directors with a suggestion 'to make life miserable' for the hostesses named on the list.

While Squires acknowledged the large majority of male cabin crew were 'thoughtful sensitive and friendly colleagues,' she claimed it was a company responsibility to resolve the issue. Eventually, 'the girls' as they would be referred to, won the right to their own promotional structure and seniority as full members of the airline's cabin crew. The 1981 strike was the last major staff labour battleground between the company and the union movement before the dramatic grounding of the whole of the Qantas fleet worldwide under a new management in 2011.

When Qantas's results for the 1980–81 year were tabled in parliament in October the company announced a loss of $19 million, adding the comment: 'Had it not been for the serious industrial dispute in February–March 1981, the company would have achieved a near break-even result.'

There were other casualties. Trevor Haynes soon left the company for a senior executive role with another transport group, only to die in a helicopter accident off the Queensland coast. Those who manned the 'war room' were also saddened by the untimely death of Haynes's second in command, Ken Appleton, who succumbed to cancer several years later.

Colin Geeves, the airline's industrial relations director, who had played a major role in formulating the company's role in the dispute, was also a victim of the dispute, finally retiring several years later after being shifted aside by the company. The company's treatment of Geeves further convinced many who worked with him that industrial relations in Qantas was a 'poisoned chalice' that would be sacrificed on the altar of union demands when the company saw fit.

As for the 'spitting' incident: Les Hayward and those involved, now all retired, still meet occasionally at reunions. 'We're the best of mates,' says Hayward with a smile.

Though the manpower aspects of the strike would be settled and an atmosphere of relative industrial peace would prevail, the dispute once again highlighted the vulnerability of the airline to the lifeblood of its operations—fuel supply.

In fact, the fuel bans introduced during the cabin crew strike marked the twelfth time in twelve months the airline had been denied fuel supplies, most occasions as a result of oil industry industrial problems that had nothing to do with the airline.

But fuel was no longer simply an industrial problem. By the 1970s it had reached the stage where its price was now ranked alongside wages and salaries as one of the airlines' major cost impediments, a far cry from the days of the 1960s where every new annual fuel contract signed by the company was at a lower price than the previous one.

The main change came with the formation of the Organisation of Petroleum Exporting Countries (OPEC) in the 1970s that, along with wars in the Middle East, sent the airline's annual fuel bill from $17.5 million in 1972 to a whopping $208 million in 1980.

Fuel costs now had a bearing on a whole range of decisions by the company: from how it set its fares to the engines it purchased to power its fleet, with whole task forces established to study every possible avenue to save fuel. Many savings would come with the arrival of the Boeing 747, with aircraft engine manufacturers being pressed for significant improvements in fuel efficiency. When Rolls Royce guaranteed a 5 to 6 per cent fuel improvement over the Pratt & Whitney engines on the early 747 aircraft, it wasn't long before the Qantas fleet was being re-equipped.

Technology too was now allowing individual engines to be closely monitored during flight for fuel burn. Even the aircraft's fuselage was subject to aerodynamic study, with the slightest leak in door seals being quickly attended to.

Nothing on the aircraft escaped scrutiny. Older, heavier seats and catering equipment were replaced by lighter versions and materials used for blankets, curtains and carpets became part of the weight-reduction equation.

Despite achieving the most energy-efficient aircraft possible, the cost of fuel itself would continue to be one of the airline's major challenges up to the present day, with Qantas announcing a record-high fuel bill of $4.5 billion for 2014. It's probably fortunate for their peace of mind that there's no one in Qantas today who can remember filling a Boeing 707 for 12 cents a gallon—or just over two-and-a-half cents per litre!

23
WHEN THE WHEELS FELL OFF THE TRICYCLE AND OTHER POLITICAL PROBLEMS

There's no escaping politics for a government-owned airline: they are just something accepted as coming with the territory.

In Qantas's case, its iconic status combined with its high profile guaranteed that even the most minor of political eddies was capable of distracting it from its core business for a few days or a week, only to be swept away as quickly as it had come. In the company itself, many such cases became known as 'cheap shots', often contrived around a politician knowing that even an off-the-cuff criticism of the airline would guarantee him or her a good 'run' in the media for a day or so until it was either found to be justified or sank without trace when proven otherwise.

One Liberal government senator is remembered for stepping from his first-class seat, presumably at the taxpayer's expense, and rounding on the company for serving 'Canadian' bacon for breakfast when an Australian airline should be required to support its local product. Whether he didn't know or hadn't bothered to check that Canadian bacon is a generic term for the product didn't really matter too much. His criticism made the newspapers and radio for 48 hours but received little coverage when the true story was explained.

When a radio shock-jock lambasted the airline on his top-rated network for not having a particular brand of wine available in first class, he didn't bother to explain that the wines for first class were selected by a team of Australia's premier wine experts, led by such industry luminaries as Len Evans, and his particular label just hadn't made the 'cut' for the current three-month on-board wine listing. Neither did he reveal his commercial relationship with the winery. It was a decade or two later before the term 'cash for comment' enforced radio commentators to declare their interests.

Such examples, while they might generate questions in parliament and gain media exposure, were merely irritants when compared to the main game of politics in the airline business, where millions of dollars and the political and financial interests of industry giants were at stake.

So, no one in Qantas was in any doubt that a radical plan to revolutionise the Australasian airline industry would see the airline confronted by the combined might of the joint owners of Ansett—Sir Peter Abeles and Rupert Murdoch—and their powerful influence on the Labor government.

The plan would be known as 'The Tricycle'—a proposal to merge Qantas, Australian Airlines and Air New Zealand into one entity and was designed as a solution to a whole range of developments that were confronting Qantas and the aviation industry worldwide.

It was mid-1987 and Qantas had been watching with concern the impact of privatisation and mergers that was occurring overseas. In the UK, British Airways had been privatised and airline mergers in the United States were creating mega-carriers with both international and domestic arms. Their sheer size and economic muscle threatened to swamp the market places of smaller players like Qantas and Air New Zealand. At the same time, Qantas had been pressing the Australian government for an equity injection of several hundred million into the airline within the next four years to keep the airline's debt to equity ratio within reasonable bounds. While some considered privatising the airline might overcome the problem, the very idea was anathema to sections of the Labor Party.

Meanwhile, across the Tasman, the New Zealand government had made no secret of its desire to sell off a large part of Air New Zealand, if necessary to a foreign buyer, a prospect that might result in one of the mega-carriers controlling a carrier on Qantas's doorstep.

The merger plan gradually gained momentum with Qantas itself, although those involved were only too aware that any proposal to merge Qantas, Air New Zealand and Australian Airlines would require substantial compensatory benefits for Abeles. Thus, in its early consideration, the plan incorporated giving Ansett access to the lucrative trans-Tasman route, an offer that would bring an expectation of between $30–60 million in increased profits to the Australian domestic carrier.

In mid-March 1988 chairman Jim Leslie flew to Canberra to meet with Minister for Transport and Communications Gareth Evans, carrying the still top-secret proposal in his briefcase. Leslie, his chief executive John Menadue and Menadue's deputy, John Ward, had every reason to keep the issue secret as long as possible. Only too well aware of the close relationship Abeles enjoyed with Prime Minister Hawke and his government, they didn't want to risk the whole proposal being derailed before they had the chance to fully explain its wide-ranging advantages.

Leslie's later notes of the meeting revealed a hint of his surprise as Evans, along with his departmental secretary Peter Wilenski, welcomed the proposal. There is little doubt that one of the key factors in the proposal—the prospect of selling off sufficient shares in the venture—was the one that most appealed to them. This one action would solve Qantas's equity problem without recourse to the government's budget, provide an added boost to the Closer Economic Relations (CER) agreement with New Zealand and presumably meet the New Zealand government's aim to privatise its state-owned enterprises.

Over dinner that evening Evans and Leslie agreed they should seek a meeting with Hawke as soon as practicable. Leslie also stressed that both he and Evans should then immediately meet with New Zealand Prime Minister David Lange. Leslie considered this essential before Ansett got to the New Zealand prime minister first.

But even before Evans had set up a meeting with Hawke, the cat was out of the bag and Tricycle was no longer a secret. Abeles was on the telephone from London, warning if it went ahead he would immediately cancel any arrangements Ansett had with Qantas, enter into arrangements with other foreign airlines and make it as 'difficult as possible' for Qantas. Evans later admitted to Leslie it was likely that Abeles had also telephoned Hawke.

Whether Abeles was fully aware at this stage of the tantalising profits he was being offered on the Tasman route is not known but later developments indicated that, even if he had, they wouldn't have been enough.

Two days after his initial meeting with Evans, Leslie was back in Canberra for a meeting with Hawke, who quizzed him on whether

Ansett should be given access to other international routes, a long-held Ansett ambition. Leslie made it clear that would be against Australia's national interests as there were now only four other countries in the world—the United States, Canada, France and Japan—that had two international airlines.

Evans and Leslie left the meeting, taking with them a Hawke request that the issue remain confidential until he had had the opportunity to talk to Abeles on the latter's return from overseas. Within days, Abeles made it clear in a telephone call to Leslie that the merger would not proceed unless Murdoch and he agreed to it, but signs also began to appear that it was Murdoch who was really driving the Ansett argument, with Evans admitting that he was receiving pressure from other senior government ministers and the union leadership.

Alarm bells were soon to grow louder when, at a meeting between Evans, Abeles and Murdoch, Ansett made it clear they wanted half the capacity on the Tasman route and a restriction on any use of Qantas Boeing 747s on domestic routes in Australia, at least until 2000. They later extended this demand to banning the use of Boeing 767 aircraft.

Gradually, with Ansett demands increasing, along with the prospect that if the matter went to cabinet, it would suffer a defeat due to old allegiances between the Hawke government, the union movement and the domestic carrier, the merger concept was heading for life support. Added to that, by late April 1988, a decision by the New Zealand government to look further at the sale of their national carrier, the merger proposal began to unravel and 'wheels' began to fall off 'The Tricycle'.

Many in the industry still speculate how the future Australian aviation industry might have looked had the 'Tricycle' gone ahead, although the coming decade would still see massive changes in the Australian aviation industry.

Qantas would acquire a share in a privatised Air New Zealand by other means, Australia's domestic aviation industry would be deregulated, and Ansett would achieve its ambitions as an international carrier, only to be eventually taken over by Air New Zealand and subsequently collapse in 2001. British Airways would take a stake in a merged Qantas and Australian Airlines before Qantas too was privatised.

The Tricycle may have been a bold plan but there were too many political rocks in its path.

WHEN DIPLOMACY COLLIDES WITH 'CHINESE WALLS'

Negotiating air service agreements between countries is a complex business that can bring into play not only the aims of the respective airlines but also the national interests of the governments involved, and circumstances can differ depending on the ownerships of the airline itself.

For decades, particularly in post-war years, privately owned Pan American was readily identified as an instrument of US foreign policy, its services often acting as the vanguard for developing relationships into areas considered of strategic or trade importance to the United States itself. But government-owned flag carriers like Qantas occasionally needed to walk a thin line between their own commercial aims and the diplomatic minefield presented by existing international relationships. There is perhaps no better example of the dilemma confronting Qantas than when the airline proposed opening a service to Taiwan. With already well-established services to Beijing and Shanghai, there was little doubt how authorities there would view any parallel flights into a territory they considered should still be part of mainland China.

Negotiations for Taiwan services began in the late 1980s under the watchful eye of the Department of Foreign Affairs who, although supporting the venture, was anxious not to create too much concern with 'big brother' across the Taiwan Straits. While it was obvious mainland China was aware of the talks, great care was to be taken to ensure any offence would be limited.

The first problem to be overcome related to the formation of the company that would operate the service, leading to the creation of an entity to be known as Australia Asia Airlines. That done, there was then the task of repainting the Qantas 747s that would fly to Taipei with a new colour scheme, with the Australia Asia logo replacing the normal Qantas one, and a special tail design representing a Taiwanese dancer with long streamers. Initially, crews to fly the service were to be issued with uniforms of a different colour from their normal Qantas attire but gradually this was reduced to a requirement for different badges and caps specially manufactured with Australia Asia motifs.

Finally, with the contract signed, the critical moment arrived for the Chinese to be 'officially' informed that the deal had been done, leaving Australia Asia's general manager Alan Terrell wondering how the Chinese would receive the news. Predictably the letter of response from the Chinese to Foreign Affairs took Australia to task for even considering services to their unpopular neighbour, citing their displeasure at the exercise and describing it as a 'disgraceful state of affairs'.

When Terrell asked Foreign Affairs how they would proceed in the face of such a response, he was told the letter was merely a Chinese 'draft' and the Chinese would be sent back Australia's own 'draft' apologising for what had been done. 'Then the official versions of the letter would be exchanged and that would be the end of it!'

Australia Asia Airlines began flights to Taipei in 1990, operating until the service became commercially unviable and was withdrawn in 1996. By that time Qantas was no longer a government-owned airline making any requirement for a 'Chinese wall' unnecessary.

24
RED TAILS AND BLUE TAILS . . . THE STORY OF A REVERSE TAKEOVER

Airline mergers and takeovers are extremely complicated affairs, not merely because of the necessity to rationalise management and staff, route structures and commercial aims, but also to safeguard cultures.

When Prime Minister Paul Keating announced in 1992 that his government had approved the sale of Australian Airlines to Qantas, it was part of a series of steps that would change the face of Australia's airline industry, leading to the sale of 25 per cent of Qantas to British Airways and the eventual privatisation of the Australian international carrier. To the outside world it probably appeared a fairly normal series of transactions. Qantas agreed to part with $400 million for Australian, while British Airways added $665 million to the government coffers for the privilege of bringing two long-time partners and occasionally fierce competitors together. But achieving synergies amid cultural differences is never an easy task, particularly with airlines, where the staff might wear similar uniforms and do similar jobs but have a deep, individual sense of pride in the emblems painted on their aircraft tails.

Over its history, Qantas had some experience in the business of moulding cultures together, where backgrounds, egos and ambition have had difficulty merging for the common good. Indeed there have been occasions where, particularly at the top, one could wonder whether Qantas was two separate airlines in one, illustrating perhaps that it doesn't need a merger factor to expose the natural conflicts, particularly between strong personalities who have their own views on where the airline should be heading. Such divisions went all the way back to those early days of clashes of ideas between Qantas founder Hudson Fysh and his general manager Cedric Turner.

Both sides might have brought their own particular vision and values to important aspects of the airline but appeared rarely in agreement as to the priorities for implementing them. Somehow it worked, but both could probably be thankful a faithful staff got on with doing a job when, as they say in the industry, the rubber finally hit the runway.

To prove mergers can be fraught with problems an example can be found in the mid-1950s when Qantas and British Commonwealth Pacific Airlines (BCPA) got together. Inevitably in such situations, one side of the equation preferred to refer to the marriage as a 'merger', while to the other it was nothing short of a 'takeover'.

BCPA came into being after the war as an agreement between the governments of Australia, Britain and New Zealand to match the services of Pan American across the Pacific. Looked at in retrospect, at least from a Qantas viewpoint, it was a strange decision, given that Australia already had an international airline flying through Asia and the Middle East to London, with its own ambitions for the Pacific, leaving every likelihood that a

Qantas wholly owned by the Australian government would be competing against a BCPA in which the same government had a 50 per cent shareholding.

The government finally resolved the issue in 1954, agreeing to a Qantas takeover of BCPA and that same year Qantas began its own services across the Pacific to San Francisco and Vancouver. In many respects it was not a happy merger, as the former BCPA staff were spread through Qantas management and network. While the majority of them simply got on with the job, much of the Qantas in-house memory of that time is based around BCPA's former general manager, Alec Barlow, who was placed in charge of the Pacific route and headquartered in the United States. There is some evidence that Fysh and Barlow didn't see eye to eye, which might explain why the latter ended up so far from head office so early.

There's little doubt that several of the long-serving Qantas management executives didn't get on with Barlow either, but who was at fault in that is a moot point. Certainly Lew Ambrose, one of the Qantas 'originals' from the days of the first DH-86 flights from Australia to Singapore in the 1930s, doesn't seem to have disguised his personal feelings.

Qantas veteran Norm Leek remembers hearing the story of Ambrose returning from a stay in the United States and being asked what he thought it was like working there under Barlow. 'Like Belsen with food,' was his curt reply. The fact that Ambrose didn't restrict such caustic references to Barlow probably best illustrates the animosities that existed anyway and didn't require a merger situation for exposure.

George Howling, then serving in Hong Kong, remembers receiving letters from Ambrose dripping with sarcastic comments about his own peer group in Sydney. When Ambrose heard

Howling was returning to Sydney at the end of his posting and would be working for another of Ambrose's pilot colleagues, Bill Crowther, a person highly respected both inside and outside the airline, Ambrose offered: 'George, if I was hanging from a cliff by my fingernails he would step on them.'

Howling said when his Hong Kong secretary asked if he wanted to take the offensive letters back to Sydney with him he declined, ordering her to destroy them. There is no record of a reciprocal attitude by Crowther, although Howling speculated that Ambrose's attitude might have had something to do with Crowther's senior rank during the war years.

Not that Crowther was the sole target when it came to Ambrose's feelings about his former colleagues. Ambrose appears to have taken his acerbic sense of humour and personal feelings with him when the time came for him to leave the airline. When a colleague inquired as to what he intended to do in retirement Ambrose replied, in his customarily slow, measured tone: 'Aah, I will return to my little memsahib in our home in Northbridge. My first project will be to build in my backyard a large strong cage. In it I will house all the savage beasts and birds of prey, together with all the poisonous snakes and spiders I can find, just to remind me of my days on the executive floor of Qantas House.'

While the passing years and a series of chief executives doubtless brought their own tribal power struggles, the airline marching towards privatisation via a takeover of Australian Airlines was a far cry from the days of BCPA. But there would be a few shocks in store. When it was all over one of the questions asked by many was 'Who has taken over whom'?

To suggest the decision to sell Australian Airlines to Qantas was unpopular with Australian's staff would be something of an understatement. Trans-Australia Airlines, formed in 1946, had a history deeply identified with the development of post-war Australian aviation and had been instrumental in overcoming that 'tyranny of distance' that separated far-flung centres of population. Always prepared to lead the way in aircraft development, it was the first to operate pressurised aircraft in Australian with its Convair 240s in the late 1940s; its Vickers Viscounts were the first turbine-powered airliners to fly here in 1954; and it entered the jet age with the Boeing 727 in 1964.

In between, with Ansett Transport Industries, it would become half of the airline 'twins' that, under the government's 'Two Airline Policy', dominated Australia's domestic skies for many of the years to follow, until deregulation of the domestic airline industry appeared on the horizon in the 1980s.

It was around this time that one of the main players in the eventual shape of Qantas–Australian Airlines would appear on the scene.

James Strong had been executive director of the Australian Mining Industry Council, a lobby and research organisation based in Canberra when he was appointed TAA's general manager in 1985 to replace Frank Ball, who had joined the airline as a pilot after the war. As in the case of Qantas and Captain Bert Ritchie's replacement by Keith Hamilton, Strong's arrival also heralded a changing of the guard from leadership grounded in operational experience to more emphasis on finance and marketing. A lawyer by profession and with no background in aviation, Strong dramatically transformed the airline's customer focus, culture and image. Within twelve months the company emerged under a new name, Australian Airlines, with new corporate colours.

The first serious moves towards privatisation came in the late 1980s as the Hawke government struggled to bring the left wing of its party along with the concept, at first floating the idea of a merger between Qantas and Australian. There followed a series of false starts, including a plan to privatise 100 per cent of Australian but excluding an investment by Qantas, and the sale of 49 per cent of the latter. But the problem lay not only internally within Labor Party ranks. There was also the quid pro quo to be considered for the other major player in the game: Ansett Transport Industries, now controlled by Sir Peter Abeles and News Limited, both with significant influence with the Hawke government.

The major breakthrough came with the arrival of Paul Keating as prime minister and the decision to sell 100 per cent of both airlines. Now the question was more about how to structure the sales to generate the most return to the government and whether selling them separately or together would be in the best interests of all concerned.

By now there was new leadership at Qantas, with former chairman of Ford Australia, Bill Dix, following Jim Leslie into the Qantas chair and twenty-year Qantas veteran John Ward taking over from John Menadue as chief executive. Dix and Ward believed the two airlines were worth less separately than privatised together, but both were aware that much was going on behind the scene as other suitors gathered.

British Airways, Air New Zealand and Singapore Airlines were showing an interest in Australian but it was clear British Airways' real aim was a future with Qantas and, while Singapore Airlines was known to be lobbying the Keating government, there is no evidence it put a final bid on the table.

In April 1992 Qantas made a formal offer of $150 million for Australian Airlines, a figure that must have been a mild shock to the government, given that speculation had figures as high as $1 billion bandied about.

When Dix and Ward flew to Canberra late in May 1992 to discuss the offer with the government's task force on asset sales, it soon became obvious that, while the $150 million was well short of the government's expectations, there were clear indications that Qantas was the preferred buyer. It was simply a question of how much. Now with renewed confidence, when a figure of $400 million was suggested, Dix and Ward conferred briefly in private, then indicated their interest. Anxious to move quickly, they spent most of the flight back to Sydney drafting a paper for the board's approval. Ward later confessed they had been prepared to offer more. 'I believed $500 million would not have been out of the question as that was what we thought we could borrow to fund 100 per cent of the transaction,' Ward recalls.

On 2 June, in what he described as 'a little bit of history', Keating announced the government had approved the sale of Australian Airlines to Qantas and what would subsequently lead to the sale to British Airways of 25 per cent of the new entity and its eventual privatisation in 1995.

Now the first of the real challenges began, challenges that were influenced by several significant recent events. The first was the domestic pilots' strike in 1989 that presented the Australian aviation industry with the worst crisis in its history. Originating out of a 29 per cent pay claim by the Australian Federation of Air Pilots (AFAP), protracted negotiations failed to solve the dispute, leading to the mass resignation of more than 1600 pilots in August 1989. The AFAP's resignation tactic proved a fatal mistake. Fearful of a wage break-out, the government stepped in to support the airlines, directing the Royal Australian Air Force to carry stranded passengers while the two domestic airlines began recruiting in Australia and from overseas, employing new pilots on individual contracts and therefore outside the periphery of the AFAP.

Qantas pilots, who had earlier broken away from the AFAP to form their own international body, continued to fly but refused to carry domestic passengers.

While he led Australian Airlines during the early days of the pilots' dispute, James Strong didn't see out the strike, resigning eighteen months before the end of his five-year contract to join one of Australia's prominent legal firms. Former senior Qantas executive John Schaap took over at Australian and was there to see the strike settled. But Strong was not away from the industry for long and, by the time of Keating's 'little bit of history' announcement, he had been appointed to the Qantas board.

With the merger deal done, Ward and Schaap worked to establish a template to bring the two airlines together. It was not easy. Many in both airlines, but particularly at Australian, held legitimate concerns about future job security; morale in some areas of Australian was affected by the perception of a 'big brother' takeover; and still others harboured bitterness and feared recriminations.

It's an unspoken belief that low morale in any airline is a dangerous business and Ward initiated a comprehensive staff communications program aimed at alleviating concerns, quickly arranging to talk to Australian's staff at their main ports around the country. The first meeting was to take place in Melbourne, the location of Australian's head office and its major engineering and maintenance base. Held in a conference centre not far from Tullamarine airport before a gathering of several hundred of the airline's staff, it was not a comfortable meeting. Some staff made no secret of their unhappiness with frequent interruptions from the floor during their new chief executive's presentation. The atmosphere improved slightly at venues in Adelaide and Perth but the message was clear: many of them felt that when it came to preference for similar jobs, theirs would be the first to go.

In many respects their concerns were understandable. Qantas staff numbers now stood at 23,000, Australian's at 9300, making it obvious which was the dominant partner. With both domestic deregulation and privatisation on the horizon, each airline had already retrenched around 3000 staff in recent times. With further staff reductions the obvious way to obtain cost synergies in the merger, more would have to go. Ultimately a further 1500 left.

Ward recalls not all the concerns came from staff. Several members of the Qantas board, including Strong, saw the prospect of low morale among the former Australian staff providing Ansett with a unique opportunity to increase its market share at Qantas's expense. Ward wasn't too concerned. 'We accepted that might happen initially but by the end of our exercise we would have a substantially lower cost structure which would enable us to margin-ally price our operations to get it back.'

But both Ward and Schaap recognised the main issue to overcome had to do with culture. 'I can't remember the number of times I heard someone tell me 'This is not a merger, it's a takeover,' says Schaap. 'It was very much "them and us"—Red Tail versus Blue Tail.'

'And when you had two people doing the same job you had to pit them against each other to select the best, but when you do that you actually establish a "war front" in the eyes of some people.'

Schaap says morale also tended to breed a defeatist attitude in some, which the rumour mill encouraged. 'Some obviously had a feeling of "why should I bother as I've heard someone else is going to get the job anyway" which had to be overcome and, while you did your best to convince people nothing was predetermined, you had to be honest and say that whoever is the better will get the job and the other will be offered a redundancy. It was a tough call.'

Schaap says such issues were further complicated by a type of 'fifth column' that was being created by a few who had opted to accept redundancy without contesting their jobs in the belief they wouldn't get them anyway. 'I'm sure some of them were pretty bitter when they left and, while they might have taken their own decision to leave, they didn't hesitate to spread gossip which tended to unsettle others.'

'The fact was,' admits Schaap, 'no one from Australian felt particularly loved, but in the end a merger is a merger no matter how you put it and there will always be some untidy ends.'

As the weeks went by, Schaap also found even his own location in Australian's former headquarters in Melbourne was working to his disadvantage, giving his own people the impression he was cut off from Sydney where they believed all the decisions were being made. When he pointed this out to Ward, he was given an office in Sydney next day.

Gradually the two companies began to come together, with the engineering and maintenance work remaining largely the same for each airline. Engineering support areas such as spares procurement and planning were rationalised, as were backroom functions like yield management, an area critical to maintaining economic fare structures. Since most of Australia's capital cities had both international and domestic terminals, staffing duplication had to be resolved, although there were other surprising outcomes. One was the staffing of overseas offices, which most in Australian Airlines might have thought beyond their reach, but with a domestic airline arm now an important addition to the international structure, a degree of cross-fertilisation by the infusion of people familiar with domestic pricing and packaging was essential. Choosing the people was not the only hurdle. A further complication were the airlines' respective domestic and international computer systems that didn't 'talk' to each other, requiring a great deal of the initial merging to be manually structured.

Integration of the two pilot bodies of the airlines too had its problems, although these had more to do with sensitivities related to the lingering bitterness created by the 1989 domestic airline pilots' dispute. While the Qantas pilots had not been part of the 1989 dispute, many of them regarded the small group of Australian Airlines senior management pilots who had continued to keep the airline flying during the dispute as little more than 'strike breakers', and the pilots subsequently recruited by Australian Airlines as 'below standard'.

From their viewpoint, Australian's management pilots maintained they weren't 'strike breakers', claiming, as the AFAP's pilots had resigned, there was no strike to break. The differences had a direct bearing on two extremely sensitive issues among pilots— seniority and a proprietary belief in their respective training regimes.

It's probably reasonable to suggest that, when it comes to the place they occupy in an airline's structure, pilots have a fairly well-developed sense of their importance in the scheme of things, not only because without them an airline cannot fly, but also because airline flying is a very professional business that is unforgiving of mistakes. Training standards are high and monitoring of those standards tough and persistent throughout the whole of a pilot's career. It's also probably safe to say that, generally speaking, Qantas pilots considered themselves without peer in the Australian industry, a belief that was naturally reflected in any negotiations in the merging of the two groups.

As for seniority: it's a very hard-won promotional right that relates to both the type of aircraft and the roster pattern a pilot will fly. In this respect the bulk of the Australian Airlines pilots were at a distinct disadvantage, their seniority only dating from their hiring during the pilots' strike in 1989, therefore creating a vast seniority gap between the two groups.

Even from a distance of more than a quarter of a century, it is difficult to appreciate the intense animosity that existed as a result of the strike, perhaps partly illustrated by a comment from one senior Qantas captain in the earliest days of the merger that 'no Australian Airlines pilot will ever sit in the left-hand [captain's] seat of a Qantas aircraft.'

Early feelings were raw. At one stage, when it was decided to move an Australian Airlines management pilot to Sydney, several members of the Qantas pilots' union refused to fly with him, prompting Qantas's senior management pilot, Ray Heiniger, to call a meeting of several hundred of his crews at the Cooks River Rowers Club where he told them it was a management decision and nothing to do with them or their union. Subsequently one pilot did refuse to fly with the transferee but, after that, the problem went away. Other decisions had positive effects, particularly when Qantas deputy chief pilot Ian Lucas volunteered to move to Melbourne and join the ranks of the domestic pilots.

Like many of his colleagues Lucas had concerns that his move wouldn't work but considered it essential that such steps be taken as soon as possible. Lucas set out to assure his domestic colleagues he 'was not there to change the world'.

'My idea was to encourage the young fellows. I kept insisting that in twenty years time no one will remember who was red and who was blue,' he says. Lucas credits James Strong with giving him maximum support during his twelve months flying domestic routes, although the flying itself was totally different in some respects. 'Changing from flying a 747-400 on long international sectors to short hops in a 737 took a little getting used to initially. It was like jumping from a marathon to a sprint!'

The Australian Airlines management pilots responsible for the overseas recruiting during the strike still reject any suggestion from their Qantas counterparts that their pilots were 'substandard'. Former captain Ray Baker, Australian Airlines' manager flight standards at the time of the strike, was responsible for much of the recruiting that took place in the UK, the United States, Japan and South Africa. Baker says the standards demanded were so high that out of a total of more than 200 on the interview list for the UK alone, Australian chose fifteen. From the United States the airline took only twelve of those on offer and among the total batch hired were chief pilots and check and training captains from world-class airlines, including South Africa Airways. 'Even though they already held Boeing 727 and 737 endorsements, had done simulator checks and were the pilots we wanted, they still had to go through our ground school on their particular aircraft type,' says Baker.

Such were the difficulties faced when Qantas Boeing 767 fleet manager Wayne Kearns began to bring the two groups together into an eventual structure that basically resulted in the two pilot streams flying their respective fleets on domestic and international operations.

Fortunately, the vexed question of seniority and which pilots would be chosen to fly any new aircraft introduced to the Qantas fleet didn't have to be faced until the introduction of the Airbus A330-200 over a decade later but nonetheless a residual bitterness between the two groups continued to linger for years to come.

By mid-1993, with the merger well under way, two other significant factors had a marked impact on the process. The first was the influence of British Airways as a 25 per cent shareholder; the second was Bill Dix's replacement as chairman by highly regarded Australian businessman Gary Pemberton.

It was no secret that, for the Dix–Ward team, British Airways had not been the preferred choice. Both believed Singapore Airlines offered Qantas better strategic options, with larger long-term cost and network synergies and valuable future regional alliance prospects, but the $665 million on offer was too good for the Australian government to resist.

One of the two British Airways executives to take up a board seat was Sir Colin Marshall, that airline's chief executive. Although not widely circulated at the time, the fact was that their 25 per cent ownership also provided British Airways with right of refusal when it came to the appointment of a Qantas chairman. Marshall played a key role in what was to come, particularly when it came to the final 'name-branding' of the merged airline.

With Pemberton now in the chairman's role, extensive surveys had been done on brand identification and all had come up with the recommendation that, when it came to the airline's name, it should remain Qantas. But, when the day came for the board decision, it became obvious that not all board members were necessarily in agreement. James Strong, for one, is reported to have argued that Australian and Qantas were both 'very strong brands in their own right', intimating whether the 'Qantas' conclusion had been reached with 'undue haste'.

Importantly, it was the first meeting to involve the towering presence of Marshall, who left no doubt it was Qantas that the world recognised as the Australian airline, while Australian was, as Marshall rather bluntly put it, 'a relatively recent re-branding of an entity formerly known as Trans-Australia Airlines.'

'Whether James seriously wanted another name or not, Marshall effectively squashed anything which might have followed,' was how one board member summed up the discussion.

It was not an easy time for Qantas chief executive Ward, particularly when rumours began to circulate that his replacement was being sought by the board, rumours that eventually forced him to broach the subject with Pemberton who confirmed that a search was on for someone else to take the airline towards privatisation. By now several names, including Strong's, were the subject of press speculation but, as it turned out, he would not be the first choice with rumours circulating that another Australian with exemplary airline credentials, Rod Eddington, then running Cathay Pacific, had been the preferred candidate but had declined to accept the job. Initially too, when Strong's name was put forward it was not a welcome choice by some sections of the Labor government, forcing Pemberton to stand firm, insisting the appointment was not a government but a board decision.

So began a process that many in Qantas itself saw as 're-balancing' the red tail-versus-blue tail scenario, with Strong going on to use his not inconsiderable presentational skills to take the airline towards privatisation in 1995.

By then most of the original Qantas senior executive level had been swept away, many replaced by former Australian Airlines personnel. Some outside commentators noted that it appeared to be a 'takeover in reverse', with the blue tails achieving ascendancy over the red tails in many parts of the airline.

Although only at the top of the airline for a brief period, and lacking the public persona and presentational skills of his successor,

Ward would nevertheless be remembered for an unparalleled knowledge of the industry and for having inherited the running of the airline during one of its most difficult periods. In an address to staff in the early days of the merger, he drew on the timing of his own appointment and encouraged them to look to the future.

'We have to make this merger work. We have to bring it off as creatively, intelligently and as sensibly as we can.

'Some have suggested I was unlucky enough to get the job of running Qantas during just about its most difficult period. I drew the trifecta: a pilots' strike, the Gulf War and the recession.'

But he saw it as a challenge, urging them to do the same with the merger.

The circumstances of Ward's departure and Strong's succession received wide media comment, with one travel trade newspaper running adjoining cartoons—one depicting Ward going out a door saying, 'Now the company is merged and profitable, it's time to go', alongside another with the image of Strong entering the doorway with, 'Now the company is merged and profitable, it's time for someone to take the credit.'

There were other examples of how things would quickly change. Ward's annual salary when he left the company in 1993 was around $320,000. Within three years International Air Transport Association documents would list James Strong's remuneration at around $1.3 million, although it is not known whether that included bonuses. Still other aspects rankled with some of those in Ward's former team in the airline, particularly early criticism by their successors that the airline had too many new aircraft in its fleet that weren't achieving an adequate return on assets. Within months, as privatisation approached, they watched with irony as a new team took the airline to the market—highlighting the fact that it was offering shareholders 'the youngest fleet in the world'. It would be years before the company needed to buy new aircraft, certainly making a privatised Qantas a very attractive proposition.

Privatisation brought with it a new direction for the airline, one certainly free of government financial and policy oversight but where a marketplace of virtual 'open skies' brought new challenges. Further expansion took place with the introduction of a low-cost carrier, Jetstar, which would not only supplement the airline's domestic services but gradually encroach onto the regional overseas routes for so long the preserve of the Qantas Australia once knew.

25
REFLECTIONS

While there remains an obvious temptation to compare the Qantas of today to the Qantas we once knew, such comparisons have limited validity. The industry has changed so much as to render any benchmarks almost meaningless.

Society too has changed. Today it's hard to imagine management tolerance with characters like Ross Biddulph. Even turning the camel train around in Cairo would probably have won him a place on Twitter or Facebook and a serious reprimand, not to mention the company's reaction to his crews' impersonation of a 'study group' to gain entry to a religious museum in Italy.

Likewise it's hard to perceive the ramifications for Hugh Birch and Mick Mather had they delayed a Boeing rather than a Sandringham flying boat when Mather jammed the oversize billiard ball in his mouth in Noumea.

And imagine the furore that would follow when Qantas public relations man John Fordham was asked by his boss John Rowe to find some way to ensure his colleagues weren't dozing off during the post-lunch sessions of their marketing conference in San Francisco in the 1970s. Rowe was as surprised as the rest of the attendees when the auditorium's entrance door burst open and a naked female sprinted down the aisle and out a side exit.

The Qantas presented to us through the media today is an airline struggling through a series of 'near-death' financial crises, reports of the uncertainty of the future of its full-service international arm, union confrontations leading to the grounding of the fleet and the stranding of thousands of passengers worldwide and a constant struggle to remain profitable. Several of the traditional problems remain unchanged. While in the past the competitive battles revolved around protecting the airline's existence by holding back the giant US carriers from 'dumping' their excess seats onto the Pacific or calls for 'open skies' from Asian airlines, those open skies have arrived with a vengeance, largely led by airlines from the Middle East, China and other parts of Asia that didn't even exist in those days.

Also largely gone is a time when Qantas reputation for safety was a significant factor in the reason for purchasing a ticket on the Australian airline, an incentive long lost in an era where hundreds of dollars can be saved buying a seat on an alternative carrier.

Despite its enviable safety reputation and its exemplary performance in time of war and other emergencies, there can be no guarantees that even an airline such as Qantas will survive and one only has to look back to 2006–07, when a private equity takeover appeared likely. It would hardly have had time to establish itself when the global financial crisis hit in 2008. Just what impact the GFC would have had on the privately owned Qantas we know today will be the subject of speculation for years to come.

It could also be said it was an airline that was by no means perfect, and one that at times could demonstrate an arrogance and superiority—along with a belief it was always right—which detracted from its many virtues. But Qantas still retains a special place in the loyalties and collective memories of those who worked for it in past years whenever they gather to reminisce, inevitably however, with one oft-stated proviso: 'We're glad we saw the good years.'

ACKNOWLEDGEMENTS

So many of my former colleagues from Qantas have contributed to this work that it is near impossible to acknowledge them all. Without exception, they showed an instant willingness to mine their memories during long sessions with my tape recorder or spent countless hours putting their thoughts down on paper to bring to life eras that have passed. In most cases their retention of detail was little short of remarkable, particularly when it came to describing events that occurred decades before. What came through above all was a sense of pride in the years they spent in Qantas service, years they have never really 'left behind'.

Many of my old colleagues either contributed directly or steered me towards others in the Qantas family who could help.

To those I have inadvertently overlooked I tender my sincere apologies but there have been so many involved that oversights are inevitable. I hope they will recognise their contribution as my personal thanks.

I am especially indebted to Alan Terrell, Norm Field, Roger Carmichael and Gordon Power, whose commendable patience helped to show me what their world looked like through the narrow cockpit windows of Qantas aircraft, even when it wasn't all smooth flying. Sadly, Alan Terrell left us before publication but I hope his breadth of knowledge, integrity and sense of humour come through in his contributions. I was also fortunate to have the encouragement and advice of Captain Richard de Crespigny, who himself takes great pride in Qantas's history and who, after reading the manuscript, kindly offered to write a foreword.

I am deeply indebted to David Crotty, curator of the Qantas Heritage Collection, who once again performed miracles to provide me with photographs and files from his archives, many of which have been painstakingly gathered over recent years by a volunteer band of Qantas retirees.

Once again I have benefited from the encouragement and enthusiasm of Allen & Unwin's editorial director, Rebecca Kaiser, who fortunately believed the human side of an exciting industry worth telling, and editors, Belinda Lee and Susan Keogh, who managed somehow to improve the structure of an old journo's English along with tackling the split infinitives. I owe them much gratitude.

And last but not least my family, wife Jose who once again tolerated the frustrations of living with someone whose mind was frequently elsewhere, yet continued to contribute constructive suggestions, son Steven and daughters Suzanne and Frances, all three never short of encouragement and support.

And finally, our grandson Benjamin who on reading this one day, may appreciate what exceptional times they were.